Discarded Daughter

Arcangela Tarabotti: The Rebel Nun of Baroque Venice

Marsha Fazio

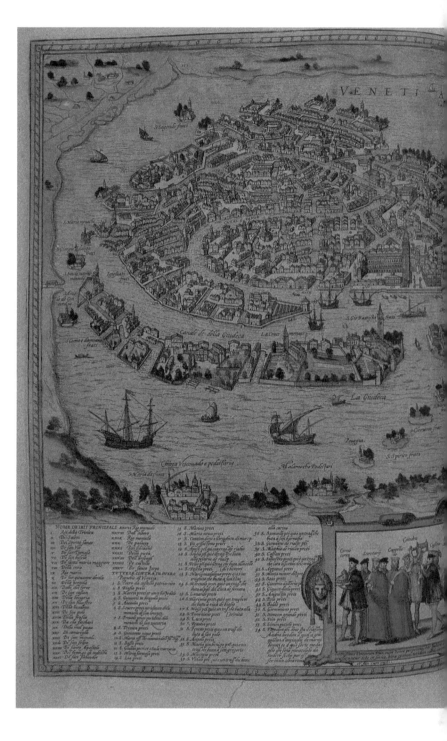

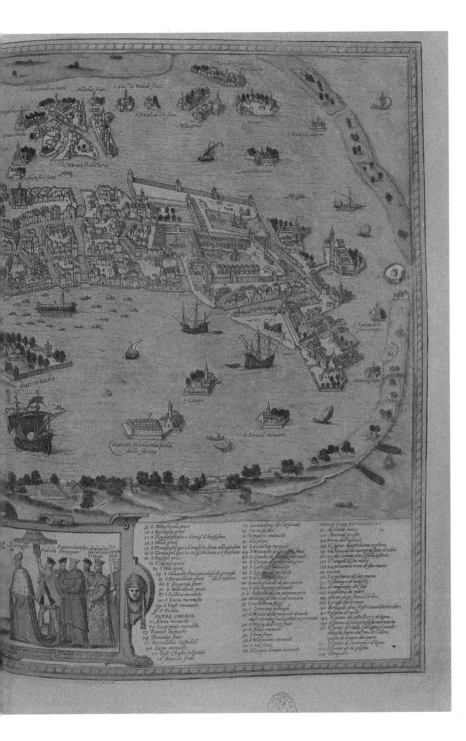

NEWMAN SPRINGS PUBLISHING
320 Broad Street
Red Bank, NJ 07701

First originally published by Newman Springs Publishing 2021

Cover drawing: Charcoal on paper, by Marsha Fazio

ISBN 978-1-63692-289-8 (Paperback)
ISBN 978-1-63692-290-4 (Hardcover)
ISBN 978-1-63692-291-1 (Digital)

Printed in the United States of America

Contents

Preface

*O*ne of the great Italian works of literature that I was assigned to read to complete my graduate studies at the Università Statale in Milan was Alessandro Manzoni's iconic *I promessi sposi* published in 1827. The work was not new to me: I was then living on a hillside above Lake Como where Manzoni sets part of his story, so I was used to hearing, for example, references to the *Lucía*, the typical lake boat named after the heroine in *promessi sposi*. In fact, over the years before I actually read the book, I had already assimilated much of its story. Although this historical novel, set in 1628, touches on politics and culture, even the Great Plague that struck Milan from 1619 to 1631, for me, the chapters dealing with the Monaca di Monza were the most captivating.

The frustrated, unhappy nun, the Monaca di Monza, had been forced into claustration, destined from the womb for life in the convent by her father, a powerful Milanese prince. I was soon to learn that Manzoni had modeled his forced nun after the real-life seventeenth-century Suor Virginia Maria de Leyva, information that concretized my subsequent research agenda: I would flesh out stories and histories about the forced monachization of young girls in Italy.

It did not take me long to come across the name of Suor Arcangela Tarabotti and the important work of Emilio Zanette who begins his 1960 biographical account of Elena Tarabotti with a terse declarative sentence: "Questo libro ha un'origine manzoniana," expressing succinctly that his book began with Manzoni. Zanette had had questions about the novelist's rendition of convent life in the seventeenth century, particularly the portrayal of the Monaca di Monza.

Distinctly qualified, Zanette, an early twentieth-century Venetian scholar (author of *Dizionario del dialetto di Vittorio Veneto*, among other works), had by chance, in the basement archives of a Venetian monastery, come upon the writing of Arcangela Tarabotti, *La semplicita' ingannata,* in which this seventeenth-century nun, a contemporary of Virginia de Leyva, accuses Venetian fathers of imprisoning their daughters; Tarabotti rails against the Venetian Republic for its complicity in sacrificing these innocent victims for "reasons of State." I was struck by Zanette's comment that the anger and fury rising from Tarabotti's pages could have well been written by Virginia de Leyva herself.

Hence, my labor of love begins.

The labor made itself known as I read through Tarabotti's works in their original Venetian Italian. The rewards were worth the work: Through her own words, I came to know the anguish of a young girl mewed up in a dingy convent. I became acquainted with her friends and associates through the nun's letter book. I saw late Renaissance Venice through Tarabotti's eyes, which I imagined would have been piercing, intent. And, finally, I came to know how this resolute, furious, erudite, manipulating, and proud nun—in complete confinement—had the courage to write her denouncements and the tenacity to see her works published.

Although my book is informed by many academic sources, it is written to appeal to anyone who loves history. I also present the subject's emotional reality through Arcangela Tarabotti's own words. The translations are mine, except when specifically cited. I wanted to tell the backstory of how an enclosed nun could achieve her literary goal, publishing scathing texts critical of the patriarchal society in which she lived. To that end, I present the friends and acquaintances Arcangela carefully cultivated, personages each with his/her own saga, as I bring to center stage these power players and their interactions with the confined nun. Most important, *Discarded Daughter* contextualizes the writer within her extraordinary environment, anchoring the nun to the historical, political, and cultural milieu of the day by underscoring preeminence of the co-protagonist of Tarabotti's story—seventeenth-century Venice.

I present heretofore untranslated text: Emilio Zanette's biography of Tarabotti, *Suor Arcangela monaca del Seicento veneziano,* has not been published in English. At the time of my writing, two of Tarabotti's texts were not available in English. All of Tarabotti's writing, however, must be read in its original archaic, often dialectical Italian, a project I undertook enthusiastically despite the challenges.

In *Discarded Daughter*, I have tried to capture the anger and aggression, the humility and hubris, and the single-minded will that allowed this cloistered woman to achieve her literary goals. And it is always Venice, antagonist and accomplice in the life of Arcangela Tarabotti—Venice of riches and beauty, of ghettos and walls, and of convents housing most of the well-to-do young girls of the city— that imbues her story, so it is with Venice I begin.

Marsha Fazio, May 4, 2021.

At age sixteen and a half, on September 8, 1620, Elena Cassandra Tarabotti took the veil, professing her final vows in 1623. Two decades later, in her book *L'inferno monacale* (Convent Hell), she describes part of the process:

> This "funeral celebration" is hardly distinguishable from actual funerals for the dead: The girl lies prostate, mouth to the stone floor. A black cloth is then thrown over her head and a burning candle is put at her feet, another placed near her head. From above, the litany is sung. All indications would suggest the girl is dead. She herself feels she is attending her own funeral.

PART 1

A World Apart: The Singular City, Tarabotti's Venice

The Virgin City: Divine Beginnings

The august city of Venice rejoices, the one home today of liberty, peace and justice, the one refuge of honourable men, the one port to which can repair the storm-tossed, tyrant-hounded craft of men who seek the good life. Venice-city rich in gold but richer in renown, mightier in works but mightier in virtue, founded on solid marble but established on the more sold foundations of civic concord, surrounded by the salty waves but secure through her saltier councils.

—Petrarch: Epistolae Seniles, iv, 3

The story of Arcangela Tarabotti is as much about the seventeenth-century Venetian nun as it is about the city in which she lived and died. La Serenissima—ethereal, surreal, majestic Venice of the 1600s—looked quite like the tourist attraction it has become or, better yet, has continued to be. Striated with amber light and luminous shade, Venice's ochre palaces lining her myriad of waterways called to visitors and sightseers—much as they do today. Slowly, from the eighth to the twelfth century, as Venice gradually emerged from the eastern empire and Byzantine control, she took advantage of her opportune position on the Adriatic, establishing trade routes, gaining naval supremacy, becoming the ideal city from which to launch crusades. Particularly the Fourth Crusade, which resulted in conquering Constantinople in 1204 and Venice's domination of the eastern Adriatic, stands as a marking point in history by which we can say the beginning of the Venetian Empire in its own right was established.

By the start of the 1300s, Venice had become a mecca of sorts for travelers journeying to glimpse the "Mistress of the Mediterranean," the shimmering alabaster city that Petrarch saw as "mundus alter," another world. As pilgrims gathered to embark from Venice for journeys to the Holy Land, streets filled with foreign visitors enchanted by the city's beauty and display of wealth. This "city of strangers," now center of trade and commerce, welcomed foreigners—especially those who could enhance commerce—forging a Venice that could boast an amalgam of residents, temporary and permanent, of varied races and religions; by 1500, almost 15 percent of the population was not of Venetian origin: Arabs, Germans, Persians, and Turks resided in communities set up by the authorities to accommodate them, while Jews, Greeks, Armenians, and Dalmatians established permanent residence in the lagoon city whose laws protected market transactions and encouraged trade and commerce.

Marin Sanudo, Venetian patrician writing in 1493, praises his Republic and the "powerful and rich people," according to Sanudo, who had established the lagoon city; the historian and diarist echoes the pride of Venetians, who by the fifteenth century could claim that their Republic, "built by Christians…had never been subjugated by anyone, as have been all other cities."[1] Indeed, it was left to Napoleon in 1797 to capture La Serenissima after her glorious, almost millennial, independence.

Elena Cassandra Tarabotti was born into early Seicento Venice, a city of contrasts as Thomas Coryat's firsthand description in 1609 relates: He tells of a luxurious city, awash with riches, but the English tourist also spotlights the torpid, tantalizing reputation Venice had earned, citing the city's courtesans, "at the least twenty thousand, whereof many are esteemed so loose, that they are said to open their quivers to every arrow." The travel writer describes "amorous calypsos" in queenly garb that attract visitors from every part of Christendom. On the other hand, he also observes that "gentlemen do even coop up their wives always within the walls of their houses… So that you shall very seldom see a Venetian gentleman's wife but either at the solemnization of a great marriage or at the Christening of a Jew, or late in the evening rowing in a gondola."[2]

Indeed, the protected position of Venice's patrician women, although well within keeping of seventeenth-century Italian socio-cultural dictates, contraposes with the libertine social atmosphere that permeated the city, *la libertá Veneziana*, giving rise to Venice's enigmatic reputation meshing together admiration for her astonishing beauty, urban sophistication, and enduring political system with her scandalous display of social freedom, all playing out against a setting of overt religiosity.

Just as Titian's *Pieta* is cast in a slanted darkening light, at once luminescent and golden, Venice's ineffable beginnings are cloaked in muted hues filtered through lore and legend. Unable to trace its roots back to the Classical era, and the only important city-state not dating back to antiquity, Venice would in many ways have her own Renaissance. Legends grew up around the origins of this city built entirely on Istrian oak piles sunk into the marshy islands at the head of the Adriatic Sea. One such story told of noble Trojans, who, after the fall of Troy, had settled the paludal land, thus rendering Venice older than even Rome. Indeed, the "Myth of Venice" dominated world opinion for centuries, prompting the Spanish ambassador to remark in 1618 that the city was the "greatest in dignity, power and authority in Italy today…for it founded itself, has always lived in freedom, and has never owed allegiance to any prince."[3]

Fueling the myth, another version of Venice's divine origins contributed to the mystique that had the city founded in 421 on the feast day of Mary's Annunciation, solidifying roots to Christianity and the city's privileged place, celebrating the day when Christ's spirit became a part of Mary.[4] The date became integral to the historiography of Venice's beginnings on this feast day celebrating when "the son of God was conceived in the womb of the Virgin."[5] Hence, this city that could not trace its roots back to the Classical era would create its own nativity: the veneration of Mary would come to identify Venice as the city of the virgin, based on the myth that Venice was founded in the fifth century precisely on the day celebrating the Annunciation, March 25. The Marian Cult, popular in other cities of the peninsula, intensified in Venice, nourishing the Venetian devotion to the Virgin, her veneration spawning spectacles and feasts—glistening barges gliding down the Grand Canal in jubilant panegyric celebrating the city's devotion and Christian heritage by honoring the Virgin.

Parochialism and patriotism embraced Venetian civic life with its most animated and fervent expression in the Feast of Ascension,[6] a pageant gloriously celebrating, as well as controlling, the image and Myth of Venice. Attended by the doge, the political head of State, this observance amalgamated politico-religious and civic spheres. By the fourteenth century, Venice had evolved its own brand of liturgical rites, especially seen in the festival of Candlemas,[7] one of the major celebrations honoring the Virgin Mary, focused on the reenactment of Venetian origins that supplanted, in many ways, liturgical focus on biblical history with a secular story of a city. This *partriarchino*[8] seamlessly merged patriotism and faith, state and religion.

Nowhere can we see a more emphatic example of this synthesis than in the remarkable ritual occurring on Ascension Day, the *Sposalizio del Mare* (Marriage of the Sea), a ceremony in which the doge drops a consecrated ring into the sea as a sign of the insoluble connection between Venice and its physical space, the adoring and adored Adriatic, in an enactment less to do with religion and much to do with politics, signifying Venetian hegemony of the Adriatic. The *Festa della Sensa* (Feast of the Ascension) culminated with these ceremonial words: *Desponsamus te, Mare, in signum veri perpetique domani. I wed thee oh sea in sign of perpetual dominion,* reiterating the patriarchal dominance, *patria potestas,*[9] in affirmation of the doge's sovereignty over his Neptunian bride and echoing the Venetian husband's legal dominion over his wife, affirming not only Venetian dominance of the Adriatic trade routes, but also supremacy over lands adjacent to the Adriatic Sea.

Linked to the Sensa, another ceremony—unusual, rather bizarre, and somewhat pagan—spectacularly affirmed the inextricable ties between the State and its religious institutions, in particular the nuns of Venice: the "marriage" of the doge to each new abbess of the Santa Maria Nuova in Gerusalemme (Santa Maria delle Vergini),[10] the oldest and one of the richest convents of Venice, solidified the doge's "groom" status and reaffirmed his rights of patronage to specified monastic institutions. Having its origins in the thirteenth century, this ritual served to invest the new abbess as well as underline the patronage of the doge who would place the ring of Saint Mark on the finger of the abbess, reasserting in this metaphorical marriage the position of the doge in relation to monastic institutions. Consummating in an elaborate wedding banquet, the ritual served to solidify an emblematic relationship, the abbess consecrating ducal authority, the doge recognizing the temporal powers of the abbess.

Aligning with Venice's divine origins and informing the Myth of Venice was the very real dazzling beauty of the "new Venus born naked in the midst of the sea,"[11] a bedecked and bejeweled city that flouted nature, built with the aid of divine intervention, a city so similar to the Virgin Mary and Venus, so perfect in its female likeness. The fourfold image of Venice that related to the four parts of the Venetian Republic—images that could not be severed from the political entity of the State—defined the interlocking structure of Venetian culture and politics: (1) justice or law represented the acme of political power; (2) Dea Roma, the goddess of Rome, signified a transfer of this power from Rome to Venice; (3) the Virgin Mary and the divine intervention responsible for founding the city in 421 on the day of the Virgin Mary's annunciation; and (4) Venus Anadyomene,[12] like Venice, born of the sea itself.[13] By the sixteenth century, the Virgin and the Venus gained in popularity and importance, signifying the impenetrable beauty of the Republic as well as the virginal, inviolate State of Venice itself. Luigi Groto, writing laudatory texts for the Republic in late Cinquecento, states that "Venice and Venus [are] both celestial, both mothers and both worthy of our holy devotion."[14]

Nevertheless, Venice's actual beginnings, although most likely lacking in divine intervention, were, not inconsequential: Refugees seeking asylum, fleeing from Barbarian invasions on the mainland, found safety in the swampy marshes of the lagoons. Establishing fishing communities, building wooden shacks, the first one popping up on the Riva Alto—the Rialto—these first inhabitants, in the sixth century, were sailors and fishermen. In fact, nature's earthly manna, the fish and salt of the lagoons, was to be the foundation upon which the splendid city would build its commercial empire. How the first settlers inhabited these marshes and built Venice out of the muddy Adriatic wetlands constitutes a tale perhaps even more impressive than the saga of divine intervention.

2

The Gordian Knot: Rome and Venice Entangled

*A*stonishingly and anomalously, from its legendary beginnings and throughout its subsequent commercial and political achievements, Venice would remain independent of foreign rule for over a millennium, invigorating the myth and widespread perception that the city-state was "immortal," partially owing to its perfected form of governing, evolved, for all purposes, from antiquity. Venetians, proud of their origins and achievements, counting on eternal independence from foreign rule, thanked and lauded the Virgin Mary but would require more than Marian devotion to become the eminent queen of the Italian Peninsula.

As medieval Venice gained power, the burgeoning city desperately needed prestige—the kind of status that Rome enjoyed. Thus, Venice would come to boast its own Saint Peter in the form of Saint Mark the Evangelist when, according to legend, Buono da Malamocco and Rustico da Torcello, two Venetian merchants, would confer La Serenissima with its very own patron saint, relics and all.

Tradition has it that in the ninth century, a fleet of Venetian merchant ships was forced to take shelter from a sea storm in the Arab port of Alexandria, at the time under embargo and off-limits to Venetians prohibited from trading with Muslims. Buono and Rustico, taking refuge in Alexandria and befriending a Christian monk, Staurizio, and a priest, Theodore, learned that the Coptic Christian Church of Alexandria was in imminent danger of destruction by the oppressing Muslim rule, the very same church that housed the bones of Saint Mark. The two merchants convinced the religious that Saint Mark must be saved, and the saviors should rightly be the Christian "sons" of the evangelist who is said to have converted the inhabitants of Venice and surrounding regions.[15]

After replacing the body of Saint Mark in the sarcophagus with a less important saint, the two merchants put the remains in wicker baskets, set them in a cart, and covered them with cabbage leaves and a load of pork, ensuring the Muslim guards would not touch the precious cargo. Having survived storms at sea and near shipwreck—complete disasters avoided by the presence of the saint—the relics of Mark finally arrived in Venice on a disputed date between 827 and 828, a "gift" to the doge, who had received word of the *translatio*.[16] Doge Giustiniano Particiaco generously rewarded Buono and Rustico, pardoning them for having entered an Arab country.

Venetians now had their status and prestige, whether in fact the remains of Mark or another had actually been transported to Venice.[17] Regardless, news of the *translatio* spread quickly. The city of Venice, now powerful and stable, secure and protected, constructed a relationship with Mark: the doges received their authority from Saint Mark just as the popes had theirs from Saint Peter.

Securing the church-state tie that had been reinforced by the doge's acceptance of the relics was a document that emerged in 1050, the *Translatio*,[18] proclaiming that Venice had the divine right to be the keepers of the saint's relics. Whether or not the body or relics were ever in fact transported from Alexandria is still subject to scholarly debate, but of consequence to our discussion of Venice's ties with Rome, this narrative could not be more important: the Venetian doge's relationship to the saint mirrored exactly that of the pope's to Saint Peter. Anyone entering the Basilica of Saint Mark today can still see the dazzling show of strength and power, a welcoming Saint Mark claiming his place in the Venetian Church, the glorious basilica telling a story—in gold and glass mosaic—of the eminence of Mark and the Blessed Virgin.

The autonomy of the doges, their political authority, and the *potestas* given them by God underscored the idea of descending political authority[19] granted to them as possessors of the body of Mark: The doge's power, divinely given, would supersede the law of the pope when necessary. Exacerbating antagonism between the Venetian Republic and the Holy See was La Serenissima's proximity to papal dominions and Venice's insistence on control of ecclesiastical patronage, engendering a relationship that could only be characterized as fraught with tension: periods of cooperation and compromise contrasted with extreme hostility, highlighted by papal interdicts that underscored pervading uneasiness and critical divisiveness. Particularly the Interdict of 1483 and especially that of 1606 shed light on the complex hostility between the Holy See and the Republic of Venice.

Territorial hegemony, especially in nearby regions of Ferrara and the Romagna where Francesco della Rovere, Pope Sixtus IV, was eager to expand papal domination on the peninsula, fueled the decision of Sixtus to place Venice under interdict in May of 1483. Demanding Venice withdraw its troops from Ferrara within fifteen days, the "warrior pope," who, after having initially approved of a Venetian attack on Ferrara, a decision now opposed by the powers of Milan, Florence, and Naples, switched sides, a *volta faccia* (about face), not uncommon in the ongoing Italian wars. When in 1484 both sides finally signed a peace treaty requiring Venetian withdrawal from Ferrara, Venice was allowed to keep possession of conquered lands in the strategic Polesine, the Po River delta.[20]

Over a century later, in a rapidly changing time of booming trade, sixteenth-century Venetian doges were to lock jaws with papal authority: Doge Marino Grimani (1595–1605) had passed laws limiting the power of the papacy within the Venetian Republic, going so far as to send, in 1603, his ambassador to visit Queen Elizabeth, now reigning over a Protestant England and whom the pope had excommunicated from the Roman Catholic Church. But it was Grimani's successor, Doge Leonardo Dona, stalwart defender of Venetian independence, who would precipitate a showdown between the Republic and the newly elected pope, Camillo Cardinal

Borghese, now Pope Paul V—friendly to Spain, traditional enemy of Venice.

The Venetian Republic, although insisting on its fidelity to the Roman See, had consistently quarreled over territorial jurisdiction; yet the political power struggle of the relationship also reflected a cultural confrontation: Venetians would defend their autonomy and their "republican liberty" at all costs. Thus, while Rome fought to maintain a centralized unity, it was inevitable that a clash of authority, cultures, and territorial hegemony would percolate and boil over into a crisis: Pope Paul V's Interdict of 1606.

Ostensible causes for Pope Paul to excommunicate the entire population of Venice concerned the Republic's insistence on trying clerical criminals in its civil courts and restrictions on clerical wealth including possession of real estate. Pope Paul, an expert on church law, forbade the Republic to hold religious services and celebrations except in cases of life or death, threatening to excommunicate Venetian rulers until they complied with church mandates to cease punishment of the clergy in civil courts and nullify laws that restricted clerical wealth and the building of churches. The pope's interdict catapulted fundamental and traditional notions and beliefs onto center stage: Italian humanists, scholars, and intellectuals debated the very foundation of Christianity, the church, and the overarching order of nature itself.[21]

Paolo Sarpi, contemporary historian, in his *Trattato dell' Interdetto*, asserted "no heresy has ever set foot" in Venice. Yet the city was a welcoming home to Protestants (Sarpi estimates ten thousand) and other "heretics," a city of "strangers" finding common ground in the Most Serene Republic.

Protestantism was a known, discussed topic of debate on the Italian Peninsula, Venice, as well as Lucca, home to a small minority of Protestant sects estimated at 0.5 to 2.0 percent of "philo-Protestants."[22] Sarpi, theologian and advisor to the Senate, held sway over politics in this electrifying era, decrying papal absolutism and advocating separation of church and State, both stances rendering him vulnerable to intellectual attacks as well as attempts on his life.

In April 1606, facing Venetian noncompliance, Pope Paul placed Venice and its commonwealth under interdiction, setting in motion acrimonious attacks and counterattacks, including that of the Venetian ambassador to Rome, Agostino Nani, who argued for *ragion di stato* (benefit of the State),[23] a philosophical appeal focusing on the potential sacrifice of *libertà* and the reputation of the Venetian Republic, an appeal that would drive Pope Paul to declare, "I am pope here, and I wish only obedience."[24] As a further reminder to the pope, however, the Venetian Senate noted that Venice had, in fact, been "born and preserved always free by the grace of God," initiating a defense that positioned the Republic under the superiority of God only.[25]

As the pope argued back against an autonomous and secularized State that he feared, Venice adamantly defied the interdict that was largely ignored by most of the Republic's clergy, eventually ending in mutual agreement, temporarily pausing the Rome-Venice conflict, and without admission of guilt from Venice.

In post-Reformation Venice, Pope Paul's Bull of Interdict would take on profound meaning, spawning heated debates and sparking discussions related to Christianity and the place of the church in an evolving world. The polemic, thanks to the printing press, played itself out in writing to a widespread and concerned European audience whose impassioned opinions dissected the issue, intellectually pitting Rome and the Venetian Republic one against the other.[26]

Now, at the end of what had become a yearlong propaganda war, it appeared that Venice's stance in defiance of the pope had resonated throughout Europe. Doge Dona, Venice's ninetieth doge, steadfast in his position, refused to accept the absolution of the pope when the interdict was finally withdrawn, stating, "To receive it is to acknowledge we are wrong."[27] The conflict between Venice and the Holy See emboldened the independent position of Venice; its stubborn stance had withstood the angry pope's interdict. Argued in print, discussed in literary salons, while diminishing the power of the papacy, the papal act and Venice's response had taken on broad cultural significance: the struggle between Venice and Rome brought to the fore entrenched historical differences—an innate anti-Roman bias, nurtured perhaps by Venice's unique historiography separating it from its sister-states on the peninsula as well as its practical interests, not unnoticed by the dominant European powers. The English ambassador to Venice Sir Henry Wotton, Anglican and eager to ignite the fire of conversion, stirred controversy, aggravating the papal-Venetian rift, taking up the cause of Venice. Feeding into patrician pride, Wotton lauded Venice "for antiquity, nobility, power, prudence, wisdom and marvel of its government, is the greatest and most glorious Republic the world has ever seen."[28]

In the years following the interdict battle, Venice would subtlety and steadily undermine the authority of the pope over its ecclesiastical affairs all the while reinforcing devotion to Christianity in typical Venetian piety.[29] Venetians appeared never more driven to demonstrate their Christian devotion in an environment of freedom, *libertà Veneziana,* from papal tethers. Facing down the pope, prevailing on every important issue did not, however, stem the tide of impending decline as Venice's position of "lord of the Adriatic" yielded to emerging English and Spanish commercial dominance. With both clergy and laity preoccupied with existential concerns of encroaching Hapsburg domination of the peninsula, now, perhaps more than ever, the patrician oligarchy needed to maintain control and authority to ensure the continued longevity of the Republic.

Patricians, guarding their time-honored privileged status, did not have an easy time falling in with the changing economic landscape populated by newly minted rich merchants, many of whom were neither Venetians nor Christians. In 1610, after a Senate debate, patrician oligarchs Nicolò Contrarini and Nicolò and Antonio Donà, expounding on *de intus et de extra* (two lower levels of citizenship), reminded fellow lawmakers that "foreigners, albeit of different religion and custom, have never been abhorred by this State; dwellings and store houses have been permitted for the Germans, Turks, Jews, and Marranos."[30]

3

Ragion di Stato: State Sacrifices and Political Rationale

Reason of State is a stable rule over a people and Reason of State is the knowledge of the means by which such a dominion may be founded, preserved and extended. Yet, although in the widest sense the term includes all these, it is concerned most nearly with preservation and more nearly with extension than with foundation; for Reason of State assumes a ruler and a State (the one as artificer, the other as his material) whereas they are not assumed—indeed they are preceded—by a foundation entirely and in part by extension. But the art of foundation and of extension is the same because the beginnings and the continuations are of the same nature. And although all that is done to these purposes is said to be done for Reasons of State, yet this is said rather of such actions as cannot be considered in the light of ordinary reason.[31]

Marin Sanudo, writing in the sixteenth century, commented, "While the Athenians, Spartans and Romans did not survive for more than six hundred years, this Republic has lasted for more than a thousand, because it was founded by Christians and given the most excellent laws in the name of Christ."[32] By the seventeenth century, the political and social stability forging the Myth of Venice had become a unique amalgam of liberty, justice, and endurance, attributed to divine favor and exceptional governing by its patriciate.[33] Seicento Venice would give the world its first public opera house[34] and could take pride in the brilliant Venetian School[35]—Giorgione, Titian, Veronese, and Tintoretto—thriving in a vibrant and flourishing cultural community. By this time, even after having survived the armies of the pope, Spain, France, and the Holy Roman Empire,[36] the Jewel of the Adriatic was not the power she once was: no longer the greatest European maritime force, having lost much of her mainland territory, rocked by the interdict battle, Venice was in decline.[37] Contemporary awareness and denial coexisted: Giovanni Botero in 1605 notes the "incalculable wealth of all good and delicacies" he found in Venice, highlighting, "There is such a variety of things here, pertaining both to man's well-being and to his pleasure," his account of immeasurable wealth ending with a commentary about the "splendor of her [Venice's] buildings… and everything else that derives from the industry and providence of men."[38]

Even though historiography points to 1508 and the League of Cambrai as the beginning of Venice's decline, we find that seventeenth-century contemporary notions vary as to the state and future of the Republic, for only seven years after Botero's sunny observations, Dudley Carleton, English ambassador to the Venetian Republic (1573–1632),[39] references Venice's decline in shipping and manufacturing as the Portuguese discover a route around the Cape of Good Hope to the Indian Ocean, this development posing a significant threat to Venetian sea trade—the observer well aware of significant loss of pride and power.[40] Pompeo Molmenti, in his monumental *Storia di Venezia nella vita privata*, writes of sixteenth-century Venice,

> A high conception of the greatness of their State was rooted in the minds of the patricians but rather as a matter of personal pride than as a source of counsel and aid against doubt and weakness. The further they declined, the more they imagined themselves like their ancestors, and, firmly convinced that the Republicwas an exemplar to all other nations, they paid no heed to other history than their own.[41]

The other side of the Venetian coin, however, indicated a slow but steady economic decline. Suffice to say that Venetians, aware of hegemonic reshuffling, were perhaps less aware of subtle changes that only later, history was to reveal, slowly saturated the Republic.[42]

Venetians cautiously looked around them and saw the Italian Peninsula systematically coming under control of Spain. Additionally, the ongoing Turkish threat characterized by the pendulum swing of victories and losses was to shake Venetian confidence. Not quite the "tottering State"[43]—still independent, relatively wealthy, and seemingly immortal, Venice slowly marched into the last complete century of her republican serenity, owing its existence to a particularly rigid societal stratification that reinforced and maintained a solid political environment. Crisscrossed by hundreds of lagoons, protected on all sides by water, with centuries-old history of peace and power, the sparkling city never having been invaded, Venice relied on its resistant system of varied levels of fixed social order.

Later observations about the slow-motion ending of the Republic reiterate historical theories of causality including disintegration from within of social institutions in tandem with outward forces of usurpers and invaders, expressed in the words of Pompeo Molmenti a century after Napoleon's conquest of Venice: "The decline was due chiefly to the conditions of the age and to the exhaustion of the political machinery, which, for a variety of inevitable reasons, was not susceptible of change."[44]

Looking back into the fourteenth century, we can already note that Venetians enjoyed relative complacency about their ruling class, whereas on the rest of the peninsula, city-states were in continuous struggle to maintain stable rule, contending with aristocratic factions vying for control.[45] The Venetian patrician ruling class could easily be defined and identified well into the sixteenth century, as penetration by hopefuls into this impervious caste was made difficult, with possible exceptions in times of war when the ruling patriciate would confer noble status to chosen families who did not possess sufficient hereditary lineage, but who could pay for the privilege.

By the close of the fifteenth century, we find about 5 percent of the Venetian population at the top of a solid pyramid of power and at the acme of social status: the ruling oligarchy, a hereditary group of adult males from a few hundred families and clans constituted the patrician class. Although patriarchal regimes were commonplace in European societies, Venice's hereditary aristocracy was a clearly defined entity, its parameters cemented into law, steadily closing ranks from the thirteenth through the sixteenth century.[46]

From the beginning, Venice thrived as a city of immigrants, even its great families having come from other parts of Italy and the Adriatic. Notwithstanding the irony, as early as 1297, with a series of legal measures referred to as the *Serrata*,[47] the ruling aristocracy became a restricted, delimited class: only those males who could show indisputable evidence of aristocratic ancestors having had seats in the government could now sit on the Maggior Consiglio (Great Council), the large governing body of the Republic.[48] Solidified by institutional barriers and legal prohibitions, the boundaries of nobility, formal legal definitions of class, were set.

Closing the Great Council, the *Serrata* over time progressed through the centuries, providing the Venetian nobility a high level of exclusivity to authority, preserving the wealth and much-admired stability of the Republic. Nevertheless, contamination—fear that the nobility could be infiltrated with "bastard" sons, for example—prompted new efforts to ensure the purity of the patriciate. Not even the *Libro d'Oro* (the Golden Book) established in 1506 could sufficiently safeguard the penetration of impure members into the elite estate. Requiring that names of all sons born to nobles be registered in the *Libro* within eight days of birth attempted to *tener al tuto emaculato et neto el grado et ordine de la Nobilità*[49]—to keep the status and order of the nobility completely immaculate and pure:

> They must give the date of the child's birth, and
> State that he was born in wedlock, and give the
> first and second names of the child and his mother,
> and they must also declare the nationality and sur-
> name of the mother, in order to establish whether
> the child was born of a woman permitted by our

laws as above, and they must also provide guarantors both of his legitimacy and of his age, as is now the practice, upon all the penalties laid down by our laws.[50]

But even these efforts did not stem the tide of the "pernicious and pestiferous" contamination of the patriciate, requiring the State to pass laws codifying class by age and gender to regulate social identity.

By the early Cinquecento, in order to guarantee that male babies were born of noblewomen, the *Libro* included the surname and birthplace of the mother as well; women born of noble families were valuable to the patriciate to maintain peace, unity, and stability, making proper marriages essential to the well-being of the State, and the *Libro d'Oro*—the registry of noble bloodlines—provided the legal documentation that defined the political class.

Aristocrats' mounting anxieties resulted in continual efforts to maintain political power and State serenity with further societal controls. In 1526, the Great Council ruled that within one month of every patrician marriage, a report be filed with the *Avogadori di Comun* in the presence of two witnesses from each side of the couple's families, with declarations upholding the "quality" of the father and status of the woman. The perfection of the Venetian political machine functioned to maintain hegemony of the exclusive ruling class—the aristocratic oligarchy.

Patricians occupied the top rung of a distinct, legally defined tripartite population division. These adult male *nobili* sat on in the Great Council and conducted affairs of State—some members very rich, others ducat-less, but all could boast of ancestors dating back to the thirteenth century. Addressed as *clarissimo* or *magnifico*, each Council member voted to choose senators in what Venetian diplomat Gasparo Contarini described in his 1543 panegyric as representing the exemplar Venetian governance: "One-hundred and twenty Senators were chosen from the ruling class, in elaborate lottery, fair to all."[51] This toga-clad elite consisted of a mercantile nobility of purest blood, esteemed throughout the peninsula and regarded with envy by most of the world.

Whittling down further the exclusive group of rulers was the selection of ten senators from the Great Council to comprise *I Dieci,* the Council of Ten. Originally founded in the fourteenth century, the Council gained permanent authority in the fifteenth century. Chosen by the senate, the *dieci* served one-year terms in a closed rotating cycle of oligarchs not eligible for continuous reelection and held supreme administrative power, from whose ranks the doge of Venice was elected.

As head of the constitutional monarchy, the Venetian doge ruled for life, lived lavishly, and had laws passed in his name. His powers, however, were limited by the influential families, whose members sat on the Great Council, appointed all public officials, and elected a senate. Contarini recounts how the figure of the doge encompassed the splendor of a monarchal ruler with limited powers, dominated by many, but representing the heart, "with the gravity and dignity of a king."[52]

At the Sensa festival, the doge, upon the sumptuous *Bucintoro*— the State ceremonial barge—sat on a red-velvet canopied throne as one hundred Venetian guild members rowed the magnificent galley through the lagoon before the marriage ceremony began. Such pomp and splendor reverberated throughout Europe, echoes of power and authority resounding as far as the court of Henry VIII. Indeed, when the English monarch ordered preparations for the coronation of Jane Seymour, his third wife, he insisted that she be floated down the Thames on a great barge to look like the "Bucentour."[53] And when Henry's daughter Elizabeth I was crowned, a Venetian observer was reminded of the Ascension Day when the doge and signory were symbolically wedded to the sea.[54]

The Venetian doge represented a figurehead, *primus inter pares* (first among his equals), somewhat of an anomaly in that he differed from contemporary absolute monarchs of the time. Limited in authority and duties, the doge was, however, given the titles of *il Principe* and referred to as the *corno* (royal crown). But to protect separation of powers and ensure the doge not exceed his authority, a document—the *promissione ducale*—clearly outlining dogeship duties and limitations was copied and distributed among the ruling hierarchy and read to the doge every two months.[55] Interestingly, Venice, anomalous in that practically every other medieval and renaissance city had surrounding protective walls, had no way of defining entrance and exit to its territory, except for sea boundaries. The doge, as ruler of the city-state, leaving his Palazzo Ducale, signified a type of "progress" entering the "outskirts"—actually the city itself, underscoring how the city of Venice consisted of its own realm.

Although he was the incarnation of the Republic and the face of Venice to the world, the doge possessed limited powers that were strictly curtailed by the senate. Even in his robe of gold and ermine, the doge was beholden to the senate, notwithstanding the fact that the effigy of the doge, stamped on Venetian coinage, guaranteed the Most Serene Prince equal footing with the pope, emperors, and kings. The ostensible curtailment of ducal authority, however, did not prevent the doge from wielding great influence, especially in the early years of the seventeenth century, as we saw, when Venice came into direct conflict with the Holy See.

The ecclesiastic power resided in the Venetian patriarch, the title given to the bishop of Venice—a title that still exists. Sanudo described the religious head as one who "dispenses justice…to the clergy." According to the fifteenth-century diarist, "He also has jurisdiction over nuns, Patriarch's jurisdiction… He takes precedence over everyone except the Doge who always goes first, whether on ceremonial occasions or not."[56] We should note that the Venetian patriarch was not appointed by Rome but instead was a Venetian whose interests and lifeblood were rooted in the patrician values of secular Venice; in fact, the position of patriarch, from mid-fifteenth century, was occupied by a patrician senator elected to the high clerical office. That the dominant clerical figure was chosen from the very same caste of aristocracy as was the senate blurred the clear division between the Venetian Church and the State while limiting papal authority within its territory.[57] Moreover, most patriarchs in the late Cinquecento and early Seicento were laymen elected from the governing patriciate harboring secular loyalties as well as ecclesiastical concerns. The overarching structure of church and State formed one body politic.

Directly below the patriciate were the *cittadini—cittadini originarii*. Although translated as "citizens," this group, actually a sub-aristocracy, occupied the uppermost tier of the middle elite, comprising in the sixteenth century 5 to 8 percent of the population. The *cittadini originarii* were full citizens whose lineage did not go as far back as the ancestry of the patrician class; they were not able to vote to elect the doge, but they did wield a good deal of power and influence. Deriving their wealth from mercantile endeavors, as did the patriciate, the *cittadini* often accumulated great fortunes. The proof required to enter this class centered on paternal lineage that clearly showed father and grandfather were *not* laborers who earned their living with their hands.

Even the *cittadini* had its precise order: one segment formed the Venetian bureaucracy in charge of keeping government gears humming; another subset provided the city with doctors, lawyers, and merchants. This more open class allowed, for example, immigrants involved in noteworthy commerce to petition for entry. The *scuole grandi* (the six largest groups) elected their own officials, a powerful sort of substate within the Republic. At the highest level of the *cittadini* reigned the grand chancellor whose lifetime position consisted in keeping government records and afforded him the privilege of attending State meetings. In fact, women of the *cittadini* class whose fathers were members of the elite *scuole* were permitted to marry patrician men.[58]

The rest of the Venetian population, the *popolani*, comprised close to 90 percent and encompassed a broad spectrum of the populace from the very poor to the well-to-do. With birthright as the overarching categorical consideration, Venetians, whether wealthy or destitute, self-identified according to traditional and legal parameters of stratification. How a city whose very existence relied on the rigid segmentation of its population could come to embody "Her Serene Highness" and epitomize *concordia* and *unanimitas* is a testament to the bedrock of nationalistic pride promulgated and reinforced by its patriciate.

In laudation of his government, Contarini admires the forefathers for having created a replica of the human body, metaphorically aligning the eye to nobility—all-seeing, in charge of directing the body to action; plebeians (*cittadini* and *popolani*) were the legs following where the eyes directed, coming together in mutual accord that guaranteed the survival of the whole.[59]

Remarkably, the majority of Venetians, without political power and prohibited from participating in government life, did have a place in their community provided to them by the *scuole*, a nexus where both patricians and commoners could come together in civic accord. Religious confraternities, the *scuole* were involved in church functions, charity, aiding the poor, as well as providing the manpower for Venice's elaborate civic processions in which representatives of every class of Venetians merged in solidarity, "living tranquilly in union"[60] to celebrate the Most Serene Republic.

Thus, to those who had gained wealth and status yet by law still devoid of political rights, the *scuole* offered prominent positions of relative power so "they should not altogether think themselves deprived of public authority and civil offices, but should also in some sort have their ambitions satisfied, without having occasion either to hate or perturb the estate of nobility."[61]

Without overt rebellion, almost insidiously, the very same sociopolitical construct that created and sustained the inviolable lagoon city—precisely the rigidity of her institutions underpinning longevity—would both consume and deplete the Republic. Venetians were, in fact, trammeled by their own sociocultural legacies inseparable from their politics and economy.[62] Steadily from the thirteenth, well into the sixteenth century, the patriciate had become a closed caste: only descent from a male noble would afford offspring entrance. Patrilineal descent was of dire concern to Venetian nobles; the Venetian oligarchy's endurance depended on the continuation of a constricted noble class kept vibrant through the bonds of marriage, familial alliances that were to become increasingly essential among clans.

Central to the *ragion di stato* and the maintenance of a perfect political system at the heart of the durable Venetian Republic was the necessary limitation of the aristocracy, the prevention of the controlling patrician class to grow in number. To that end, Venice, the Virgin Queen of the Adriatic, as Arcangela Tarabotti would write in her *L'inferno monacale* (Convent Hell), represented by its senate, supported and reinforced the endogamous exchange of dowries.

Social Constructions: Endogamous Marriages, Rising Dowries, and Unwilling Nuns

*I*n seventeenth-century Venice, as in most of the world—including the New World[63]—one of a father's duties was to provide for his daughter's dowry, much the same as familial obligations to clothe and feed offspring. Parents' resources usually dictated the amount of dowering, a practice existing well into the nineteenth century and still extant in parts of the world today. In England, for example, the dowry system endured well into the nineteenth century while in other parts of Europe such as Italy and Germany, the practice may have ended only after the First World War—if not beyond. In fact, we still find cultural traces of families dowering daughters in rural Italy, Spain, Portugal, Malta, and India.[64]

We can look at *la dote* (the dowry) from two perspectives: from the donor's point of view and from the recipient's. The donors in Early Modern Venice were not necessarily only the daughter's parents, but also relatives and nonrelatives alike could include gifts of money and property contributing to the welfare and future of the to-be bride, all having a stake in the girl's successful marriage.[65] When we view the *dote* from the recipient's standpoint, (the married couple's), the dowry is the bride part—what a woman brings to the marriage union. In some respects, it was the "right" of the daughter to receive her dowry, her portion of hereditary wealth and property, and it was the duty of the father to provide it.

Venetian society, on all levels, strictly adhered to endogamous marriages, marrying within one's social class. Indeed, marrying outside of one's rank had legal consequences, limiting or prohibiting possibilities of holding public office for contemporary and future generations. Since from the start of the sixteenth century, all noble marriages were recorded in the *Libro d'Oro*, the State could ensure pure bloodlines to preserve patrilineage heredity, a status that relied on preventing patrician offspring from marrying down: forming unequal alliances defiled *la purezza patrizia* and threatened sociopolitical equilibrium.

Although the family—linchpin of stability—was the default norm, it was also understood that not everyone could partake in holy unions. Even in post-Reformation Italy of the 1600s, where the sacrament of marriage had been elevated to a still-higher rung,[66] this holy union was not for everyone. Sons who did not marry should join the clergy, a simple solution of celibacy or marriage, but not one that always materialized in practice. What about those men who did not marry or join the clergy?

In Venice, bachelorhood was not discouraged, unmarried men often becoming heads of households overseeing younger siblings and family members.[67] With a son's independence from his *paterfamilias* taking place only upon the death of his father, a young man's economic independence came late in life. Venetian patrician male adults waited until an average of thirty years old to marry, some opting for bachelorhood, and of this group, 16 percent lived as heads of families. However, a threat to family practices and social order existed. The problem of keeping mistresses and fathering illegitimate sons, along with the larger danger of men secretly marrying, put into jeopardy family status and lineage. Thus, patrician men in Venice remained bachelors or married noblewomen or rich commoners. This latter segment comprised a growing wealthy merchant class often with more ducats than many in the established aristocracy.[68]

An upper-class woman was also socially and economically dependent on her natal family; but unlike her brothers, she would remain dependent for the rest of her life, exchanging one subordination for another when she married. If she were to become a widow, however, her position changed somewhat: legally independent, often reaping funds from jointures and her own dowry, the well-to-do widow enjoyed a degree of autonomy not relegated to her married sisters. Although a patrician man might "marry down" in respect to class if he were to profit from the benefits of having a rich, well-dowered wife, his female counterpart could not marry below without incurring the loss of status and honor, an ignominious situation to be avoided at all costs, driving noble families to seek aristocratic husbands for their daughters—an endeavor that would require a substantial dowry that not every family could amass. Indeed, the father of several daughters would be hard-pressed to find suitable matches for all of them.

On one hand, too many daughters posed a problem for families; but on the other hand, not having enough children to ensure that future generations would have wealth enough to maintain the family's political and social position—in a time of high mortality rates for infants—posed a likewise threat. The solution often lay in the common European practice of primogeniture, which limited the number of heirs, most of the testator's wealth to be inherited in perpetuity (as the law provided) by the eldest sons. Whether Venetian custom or pragmatic necessity to supply the Republic with more than one patrician son per family, Venetian landowners did entail their estates but did not favor the firstborn male in inheritance practices.

Although primogeniture was not a part of Venetian law or custom,[69] lands were entailed to male heirs. It is easy to see how fortunes could be dissipated through only two generations if all sons married, and all of their sons married—a predicament that in other parts of Europe was mollified by primogeniture practice, with younger sons remaining bachelors, joining the military, or becoming part of the clergy as the few respectable choices for celibacy. However, Venetian families, not coerced into primogeniture, typically chose one son who would marry and carry on the family legacy. Fynes Moryson, an English traveler living in Venice during the last decade of the sixteenth century, commented on how many Venetian men live.

In fratellanza, that is in brotherhood, without deviding their Patrymony but imploying it in Common, so many brothers live inone family or house throught all Italy, without any household Jarres, frequent among all other nations, espetially among bretheren. Indeede Commonly one of them only is marryed, so they are free from the cause of contention otherwhere frequently arising from diverse wemen of equall degree living in one house... In Itlay marryage is indeede a yolk, and that not easy, but so grevious, as bretheren no where better agreeing, yet contend among themselves to be free frommarryage, and he that of free will or by perswasion will take a wife to continue their posterity, shalbe sure to have his wife and her honour as much respected by the rest, as if she were their owne wife or sister, beside their liberall contribution to mantaayne her, so as themselves may be free to take the pleasure of wemen at large... For in these frugall Commonwealths the unmaryed live at a small rate of expences, and they make small conscience of fornication, esteemed a small sinne and easily remitted by Confessors.[70]

No law required that unmarried brothers leave their portion of the family estate to surviving brothers; usually the terms of the entails stipulated they keep shares within the family. The exclusivity of the ruling class relied on endogamous marriages to ensure the wealth and stability of Venice. For centuries, Venetian patricians and upper classes had practiced endogamy, typically without consideration of offspring's desires. Parental control over spousal choice permeated every level of society; children obedient to their parents' wishes and decisions informed the Venetian marriage process.

Daughters did not share in the estate division. One reason given by Leonardo Giambattista in his will of 1609 provides contemporary justification, "Everyone knows it is men who continue families and maintain their honor, and not women, who pass into other families."[71] In an attempt to preserve generational wealth through male lines of heredity, families considered the lives of daughters either by providing dowries upon marriage or spiritual dowries if they entered the convent. Family resources were stretched thin as patricians contended for the best possible marriages for their daughters, the achievement of which depended upon the amount of the dowry contractually and mutually agreed upon by the families of both bride and groom.

Typically, in patriarchal patrilineage societies, before the marriage of a daughter, a transfer of wealth or property from the bride's family to the groom formed the prerequisite of the union. In the city-states of Renaissance Italy, *exclusio propter dotem* (excluding dowered women from further family inheritance) guaranteed patrimony for male heirs while still allowing a portion of natal family wealth to the daughter when she married "so that agnatic masculine ties may be preserved, and that goods may stay in families through males and families and agnatic ties may long be preserved."[72]

Dowry amounts had been increasing for centuries in major cities of the peninsula, not only in Venice, making it a more and more expensive proposition for a girl to marry well, a circumstance that offered many perks to the family: having an eminent brother-in-law could secure the bride's male siblings prestigious connections. Indeed, the entire family would reap the benefits of a well-married sister, daughter, or niece, whereas a mismatch would have the opposite outcome, resulting in loss of the family's honor and regard, lowering its standing and opportunities.

The Venetian aristocracy and upper classes, entrenched for centuries within the dowry system and committed to endogamous marriages, continued to offer higher and higher prices to have their daughters marry equals or better, despite ecclesiastic and State authorities, who, in fear of impoverishing the very nobles that control the State and nurture its independence and stability, attempted in vain to cap dowry amounts through legislation. The Republic, however, recognized that widows and women over the age of twenty-four be allowed to offer amounts above the legal limits, with further exceptions permitting women from the upper bourgeois (now a wealthy class, often possessing more wealth than the unemployed nobles) to marry patrician men. Also, in the fifteenth century, marriage ceilings were eliminated from the disabled, recognizing the lower marriage-market value. Wealthy citizens and patricians, nonetheless, continued to compete, upping the ante, resulting in excessive rates of the marriage portion, with dowries soaring to as much as forty thousand ducats in seventeenth-century Venice.[73]

Questioning the economic binds put forth as rational justification for preserving patrimony, historians have noted that the stigma of hypergamous marriages informed family strategies: Venice's patrician men, in practice, married noblewomen, rich commoners, or mistresses, or they need not have married at all. Patrician women, on the other hand, could not marry down without staining the purity of noble blood, not to mention sustaining the concurrent embedded humiliation and social stigma; equally dishonorable, therefore unthinkable, was nonmarriage. Surplus upper-class and patrician daughters, together with ever-spiraling dowry costs and continued decline in economic opportunities put families in jeopardy of losing wealth and status. It is no wonder, with so much at stake, that daughters' desires were of little consequence—to the point of cloistering the girls at a lesser price (the spiritual dowry) than required for a dowry, thus allowing resources for one or more male heirs and perhaps a selected daughter or daughters, depending on finances and aspirations, to propagate bloodlines and ensure patrimony for the next generations. Families rarely scrupled to exploit their daughters.

The senate contrived every effort to deter dowry inflation—to no avail. Legally readjusting permitted ducat thresholds did not prevent families bent on arranging honorable marriages for their daughters, despite State apprehensions that excessive dowry payments would impoverish the very same ruling patricians. Although the rising marriage price was the driving force behind coerced monachization, the complex relationship between dowries and convents reveals perhaps more at play: The reality of escalating dowries cornered patrician families constricted by endogamous matches into a position, albeit socially constructed, leaving them with no choice but to cloister their offspring. Exacerbating the situation was social acceptance, often encouragement, of bachelorhood, resulting in a restricted pool of eligible husbands. With limited or no prospects to find earthly mates for all daughters, fathers turned to convents to secure an acceptable, often prestigious, alternative.

The dowry rationale provided a convenient justification to rid families of excess daughters, the underlying cause of which was the dowry system itself, in effect, culturally determined and socially shaped and sustained; how fathers and families managed their expenses was subjective. Questioning the economic binds put forth as rational validation for preserving patrimony, we should note that the stigma of hypergamous marriages informed family strategies, suggesting that monachization decisions, at the base, not only looked at economic considerations but also spoke to social aspirations.

Convents played an essential role in providing a dignified, often prestigious, place to deposit excess daughters, allowing families to concentrate legacy on perhaps only one daughter and select male heirs to ensure bloodline and patrimony survive into the next generations. These societal imperatives that drove family decisions also determined the fate of daughters. Customarily, willing or not, by the time a girl reached her midteens, she would be destined for marriage or the convent.

Forced monachization of daughters during the Renaissance in Catholic Europe became common practice among patrician families, committed to endogamous marriages and constrained by the dowry system. Particularly in Venice, La Serenissima, a city striving to maintain what had become a hereditary oligarchy, we see during the 150 years leading up to the seventeenth century a steady increase in the number of nuns enclosed in the thirty-nine convents within the city. By 1642, Venice would boast of having nearly 3,000 nuns. In a city that numbered 2,250 patrician women total, an astounding 84 percent of them were nuns, most of whom took the veil by force, having no religious vocation.[74]

The economic, cultural, and social dictates, from the late Middle Ages through the Early Modern period gave rise to convents that were basically receptacles for unwanted daughters, surplus girls. Those who entered against their will lived out their lives within convent walls, with little or no recourse to ever change their plight. At the same time that daughters were coerced by their families to enter the convent, there also existed within cloistered confines women who sought out the religious life that offered to those of the vocation a serene, terrestrial paradise, free from worldly temptations and corruption as well as an option other than marriage. However, we are hard-pressed to imagine that three-quarters of well-to-do young girls, typically under the age of thirteen—especially sheltered and protected from birth as were patrician daughters—could, without covert and explicit coercion, make an informed choice to live a life behind convent walls. For these girls, whose lives from childhood until death were to be spent in monastic institutions, convents were earthly infernos, creating for the cloistered girls and women devoid of religious calling a "living death."

In the lacework palaces flickering in gleaming waterways, within the opulence and decadence, the creative liberty and political rigidity of Venice, we are astounded to find that most patrician and upper-class young girls and women, rather than languishing in the lavish lives they were born into, were instead forcibly locked away in the convents of the Most Serene Republic, enclosed for life with little or no recourse to ever step beyond confining walls. This segment of hidden women, most of whom took the veil by force rather than faith, cast away in the scores of Venetian convents inspired the popular saying "maritare o monacare"—marriage or the convent. A third scenario, allowing unmarried girls to remain at home, was anathema to fathers and family: keeping at home unmarried daughters after the age of puberty with no prospects for an equally matched marriage presented social problems that were to be avoided at all costs.

Forced monachization of well-to-do and patrician daughters constituted normative family strategies that echoed political *ragion di stato*: sacrifices for the greater good of the Republic. Patriarch Giovanni Tiepolo (patriarch from 1619 to 1631) shows his awareness and understanding of the practice of forced monachization, acknowledging how this system sacrifices women:

Si sono confinate fra quelle mura, non per spirito
di devotione ma per impulso dei loro, facendo della

propria liberta, tanto cara anco a quelli che mancano dell'uso della ragione, un dono non solo a
Dio, ma anco alla Patria, a l Mondo, et alli loro piu
stretti parenti; che in quei strettissimi forni delle
lor celle, dove stanno a cuocersi la vita, et crucciarsi
con l'animo, ritrovandosi bene spesso molte di esse
a tale strettezza, che, mancandole il necessario cibo,
convengono pascersi solo di lagrime et di affanni.[75]

In this excerpt from a letter written to the doge and the Venetian
Senate, Tiepolo acknowledges that these girls are made to take the
veil not by their own accord, that they are deprived of their liberty—
which is a gift of God. He calls their living quarters "tiny little ovens
of cells" in which "their lives are cooked" as they pass the time "in
tears and sighs." Nonetheless, Patriarch Tiepolo goes on to defend
the practice:

Se duemille e piu Nobili, che in questa Citta vivono
rinserate nei monasterij ome quasi in publico
deposito [carcere]h avessero potuto o voluto altra-
mente disponere di loro stesse, che confusione! che
danno! che disordine! Quali pericoli! quai scandali,
et qual male conseguenze si sariano vedute per le
case, e per la Citta, e quanti riflessi di molestie, e di
indecentie alla publica pace e servitio.[76]

(But what would happen to 2000 noble girls if they
were not in the convents? What confusion! What
harm! What disorder! How dangerous! Those scandals and terrible consequences we would see for the
families, for the city. How it would result in inde-
cency and disturb the public peace.)

The fifteenth-century Latin proverb encapsulated the fate of
young women: "Aut virum, aut muram" (Either a man or the wall).
As well, a tidbit of popular culture reveals how the widespread practice of encloistering young girls was an accepted, yet problematic,
social phenomenon. In a comical song, written in the early sixteenth

century by Benedetto da Cingoli for the wedding of two nobles, we see seemingly lighthearted joking about the pervasive practice.

> Monacelle incarcerate
> Siamo state gia' molt'anni:
> Per uscir di tanti affanni
> Siamo al secol ritornate

> (Imprisoned little nuns
> We have now been for so many years
> To get away from so many woes
> We have returned to the world)[77]

The poem clearly acknowledged the popular leitmotif of forced monachization, presented in the format of "The Nun's Joke," poking fun at the sad social structure—ironically, and perhaps sardonically, since the poem was presented at the wedding of a daughter who was fortunate enough to escape the incarceration to which unlucky daughters fell victim.

The ballad continues to recount the story of nuns who escape from the convent and return to the world facing the rejection of their families—once again—and treated by them as mortal enemies. The girls continue, "Blind, deaf, adverse, and deceitful fortune is the blame," highlighting the misfortune of one sister, the unlucky one, not the one allowed to receive the fortunes of life; the misfortunate girl is discarded to spend a lifetime in pain and tears, while the lucky one is bedecked and bejeweled, and the enclosed girl wears a veil of black. The song continues to recount how, locked up in their cells, the little nuns "all naked, look at their white and beautiful bodies," lamenting how wonderful it must be to follow the holy dictum to "go forth and multiply." The lyrical ballad ends with the escaped nuns professing their commitment to be strong, to take on the filthiest of work rather than return to the convent: "We are determined to live joyful lives with husband in this world/you can help us with a dowry."[78]

Elena Cassandra Tarabotti, one such discarded child, would involuntarily become Arcangela Tarabotti, who, through her scathing texts, denounced the contemporary practice of forced monachization. As victim of patriarchal powers that defined family, State, and church, Suor Arcangela, enclosed and restricted as she was, objurgated the forces complicit in promulgating the practice, laying blame squarely at the door of family fathers and State powers guilty of committing unwilling girls to a life of *clausura*.

5

Patrician Iconoclasts: Accademia degli Incogniti

*I*f La Serenissima's familial strategies were to underlie the destiny of Elena Cassandra Tarabotti, it would be the lagoon city itself—and one of its most prominent patricians—that would play a key role in the fate of the Benedictine nun's literary longings. Without the intellectual, libertine environment of seventeenth-century Venice, neither Arcangela nor her patrician patron, Giovan Francesco Loredan, could have prevailed.

At least two centuries before the nun and the nobleman were born, Venice had already become a seat of learning, scholarship, and intellectual innovation. Fifteenth-century Venice, a city that no longer dominated trade, now dominated what can only be described as a thriving tourist industry; *villegiatura* (tourism) now overshadowed commerce in revenues. The magnificence of the city prompted Giovanni Botero, poet and priest, to comment in 1605 on the "incalculable wealth of all goods and delicacies" he found in Venice, noting,

> There is such a variety of things here, pertaining both to man's well-being and to his pleasure, that, just as Italy is a compendium of all Europe, because all the things that scattered through the other parts are happily concentrated in her, even so Venice may

46

be called a summary of the universe, because there
is nothing originating in any far-off country but it
is found in abundance in this city.[79]

Indeed, even after intermittent waves of bubonic plague, Venice
had remained not only one of Europe's most populated cities, but also
a world center of culture with a robust intellectual climate that dated
back to the Fourth Crusade when, after the fall of Constantinople in
1204, La Serenissima had served as a welcome port for Greek refugee
scholars who brought with them the classical languages of learning.
Then, two centuries later, when in 1468 the distinguished Byzantine
humanist Cardinal Bessarion[80] donated his extraordinary collection
of original classical texts to Venice, moving them from Rome, Venice
came to possess the core of her future *Biblioteca Marciana*, eventually
fulfilling Petrarch's dream of a public library open to all scholars.

With its marketplace economy, stable government, and capitalist base, Renaissance Venice could leverage her position and take
full advantage of innovative technology in the mid-fifteenth century,
as Johannes Gutenberg's printing system spread to hundreds of cities in Europe. By the end of the century, Venice was to dominate
the European publishing market and hold her supreme position well
into the next decades. It was humanist, turned printer, Aldus Pius
Manutius who would secure Venice's power of the press. Relying on
the city's unique population of Greek, Latin, and Hebrew scholars
(Greeks alone numbered almost eight thousand by 1494) Manutius
produced in this fecund intellectual clime *editiones principes* (first
editions), that included the works of Plato, Aristotle, Thucydides,
and Sophocles.

Having as its trademark the sign of the anchor and dolphin,
familiar to students of the classics, Manutius's Aldine Press converged
popular demand and capitalist investment to forge a groundbreaking
publishing industry that produced the first "pocket-editions"[81] of the
classics and sustained a dynamic print-music publishing enterprise.
The endeavors of Manutius produced small octavos, convenient in
size, clear in type, and low in price—a giant step offering to a wider
readership than only students and scholars the opportunity to read

the classics. In a market-driven campaign to advertise his productions throughout Europe, Manutius and his investors popularized literature and classical learning, a dissemination that some feared would halt the flow of would-be scholars beyond the Alps flocking to Italy since they would now have in their homeland their own Aldine editions. The great publisher, undaunted by fear, trekked on with his scholarly work. From a letter written in 1514, one year before his death, Manutius tells of his round-the-clock dedication:

> I am hampered in my work by a thousand interruptions. Nearly every hour comes a letter from some scholar, and if I undertook to reply to them all, I should be obliged to devote day and night to scribbling.[82]

The Aldine Press of Aldus Manutius was taken into the sixteenth century by Aldus Manutius the Younger, his grandson, a child prodigy who introduced a standardized system of punctuation, adding to printing innovations of his grandfather that would position Venice well into the seventeenth century as a cultural core of the Italian and European printing industry.

Decidedly, indubitably, in the aftermath of the Venetian Republic-Holy See showdown, in the decades following the lifting of the 1606 papal interdict, the lagoon city, having stood firm against clerical authority, became the peninsula hub where Counter-Reformation critics and religious skeptics could voice their thoughts; the intellectual politics of Venetian republicanism fostered an atmosphere unlike that of any other Italian city. Now in the early years of the seventeenth century, the creative, innovative cityscape of a culturally liberal, politically conservative republic, long a mecca for humanist scholars flocking to the Venetian-controlled University of Padua, attracted learned men, intellectuals, and libertines, creating a polestar for artists and academics eager to enjoy the relatively open air of *la libertà Veneziana*.[83]

Born into this city of tolerance found nowhere else in Italy, one young man was to dominate the publishing scene and to reign over the literati of the early decades of the Seicento, an aristocrat whose story intersects with that of the Venetian Republic—the nobleman destined to play a pivotal role in the literary life of Arcangela Tarabotti.[84] Giovan Francesco Loredan, descended from a long line of patricians with ancestors having sat on the Great Council since 1297 and blood ties to the Loredan doges, was born in Venice in 1607. Orphaned as an infant, he was brought up by his maternal uncle, Senator Antonio Boldù, who made sure his nephew received the elite upbringing consistent with his rank. From a position of power and pride, having been the beneficiary of a humanistic education, tutored by the Sicilian scholar Antonino Collurafi, Loredan began his political career in much the same way as did other noble young men inscribed in the *Libro d'Oro* of the Republic: at the age of twenty-five, the young patrician took his seat on the Great Council.

In addition to his important political positions including that of *Inquisitore di Stato* and member of the Council of Ten, Loredan, while still in his teens, had begun to gather around himself a group of literary figures who would soon comprise the liberal Accademia degli Incogniti, the prestigious literary academy he founded in about 1630 to "lasciar correr l'ingegno" (let loose the intellect). With Professor Cesare Cremonini's naturalistic Aristotelian philosophy providing the intellectual backbone for the viewpoints of these Venetian gentlemen, the Incogniti selectively eschewed church teachings and allowed themselves free rein to indulge in sexual pleasures. These Venetian intellectuals, for the most part, accepted Cremonini's tenets of the soul's mortality: "sins of the flesh" would not receive punishment.

Cremonini's motto, "Intus ut libet, foris ut moris est" (In private think what you want, in public behave as is the custom), allowed for the dichotomy between philosopher and Christian that libertines embraced, allowing them to separate philosophy from theology. Without overtly opposing Christian doctrine, Cremonini claimed that as a devout Christian, he was simply interpreting Aristotle; thus, with the support of his powerful Venetian cohorts, the eminent philosopher was able to avoid the condemnation of the Inquisition,[85] even while implicit in his teachings was the "sovereignty of instinct," illuminating a revised version of the Myth of Venice, allowing the sensual and political, the religious and erotic to coexist in the city that offered its visitors all pleasures, intellectual freedom, and relative autonomy from papal authority.[86]

The body politic reflected in the private and public lives of the Incogniti; the homosocial environment of the Accademia meetings provided a male-dominated nexus where the most popular discussions focused on female sexuality—the allure, vices, and dangers of women. Wielding influence through publications promulgating heterodox religious ideas, defending multiple points of view including ambivalent perspectives about gender, Loredan and the Incogniti dominated Venetian literary life of early to mid-Seicento. These ardent patriots committed to their Republic and the eternal Myth of Venice explored satire and eroticism, presenting arguments of the ongoing *querelle des femmes* (the female question), often publishing misogynist writings of controversial figures, unorthodox, libertine authors such as Ferrante Pallavicino.[87]

Pallavicino, a highborn Augustinian monk who eventually was beheaded at the age of twenty-eight, wrote such works as *Il Divortio celeste* (The Celestial Divorce) in 1643 in which he portrays Jesus as seeking to "divorce" himself from the Roman Church on the grounds of adultery and sin. Pallavicino's poetry turned on its head the popular Petrarchan style by celebrating carnal pleasure: a young man "loves for no other reason than…but to enjoy himself" and who finds that at "the end of his loving though is ultimately a bed."[88]

During the next decades, Giovan Francesco Loredan would reign over Venetian publishing, openly or in the shadows, producing iconoclastic works of history, poetry, fiction, and the burgeoning opera libretto—often anonymously. The Incogniti, this elite, quasi-secret cultural society, boasted about three hundred members who were classically educated, ardently patriotic, many libertine in thought, most belonging to the patrician ruling class.[89] Presiding over Venetian literary production and controlling the press in mid-Seicento Venice, Loredan and the Incogniti literati published impious works often relegated to the Index of Forbidden Books.[90]

Straddling between the legitimate and the prohibited, meshing patriotic conservatism with *libertinismo*, the Incogniti strove to support La Serenissima's focus on culture and learning while ever cognizant of the global role their city played in offering the pleasures of life, of all sorts, to its visitors. Accademia members relied on an Aristotelian foundation of thought allowing them their indifference to church doctrine and acceptance of sexual pleasures, all the while supporting their oligarchic Republic. And it was their Republic that provided reciprocal sustentation and protection for the Accademia's publications often issued clandestinely or anonymously, frequently erotic and obscene, in many instances openly anti-papal. Loredan and the Incogniti enjoyed government support as long as anti-Republic criticism was held at bay, which it was by these loyal patrician patriots of the Accademia.

The unique freedom of the Venetian Republic combined with its political stability and relative autonomy from the pope and the Inquisition announced to the world that men had a natural right to the pleasures of life, spurning any sort of deprivation, attitudes disseminated by Loredan's power over the press, often flouting the Index Librorum Prohibitorum.

The contrasts and contradictions inherent in the literature of the Incogniti, originating from a male-centric outlook on the world, cut directly into the *querelle des femmes* of the seventeenth century, with Loredan's own writings indicative of the focus on the "female question." In *Bizzarrie accademiche*,[91] widely published throughout Europe, Loredan's academic discourses included observations of how dangerous a woman may be to her lover, how unreliable her chastity could be, and how her silence was an impossibility, all the while acknowledging males' sexual needs. *Bizzarrie* achieved popularity for its light, playful tone and artful style presenting its male speaker as open minded to other views. However, under the guise of chivalric concern for women, what seeps through this writing is a patristic misogyny concerned with the danger a woman poses to her lover, the mobile nature of her chastity, and the accepted nature of men who must be permitted their sexual pleasures.

We glean from his writings that Loredan and his cohorts seem to have been living in a time and space where chivalry and courtly love (long since having disappeared) devolved into a form of Incogniti license. Loredan depicts a world in which a woman and her virtue found it difficult to survive, as he describes "poison darting from the eyes of the beautiful woman that takes away the lover's life," which in turn makes his face black, this blackness moving a lady to pity him and then bestow her favors. Loredan claims the appropriate color for the lover's soul is in fact black.[92] Emphasizing the destructive power of a woman's love, Loredan somehow manages to echo Petrarch, the injured lover. Whether an exercise in intellectual debate or a deeply held notion about all women, this stance held by Loredan and his fellow Accademians would drive Suor Arcangela to reply in kind.

When the text of Francesco Buoninsegni's *Contro 'l lusso donnesco satira menippea* (1638)[93] came to her attention, Arcangela composed an equally witty and satiric reply to the misogynist Menippean satire that lambasted excess female luxury. Published anonymously, with the help of Loredan, the nun's *Antisatira* struck at the political and religious foundations culpable in promulgating the anti-female agenda. Loredan would also be the dedicatee of Arcangela's last work—her letter volume, *Lettere familiari e di complimento*, published in 1650 with the Loredan coat of arms appearing on its frontispiece.

How the Incogniti libertine leanings could reside within the Accademia framework of strong nationalistic patriotism reveals a self-serving hypocrisy that presents a direct contrast to the Republic's view that women be virtuous, silent, and chaste—this in direct opposition to *querelle des femmes* discourse and Incogniti support of male pleasures. Such a rift allowed, for example, Loredan himself to praise and publish the writings of Suor Arcangela who pointed to the *ragion di stato* and the patriarchs of family and Republic as responsible for the "inhuman treatment of girls," while at the same time permitting the patrician to wholeheartedly support the practice of forced monachization, defending the incarceration of his own sisters.

Loredan and his aristocratic compatriots supported marriage restrictions aimed at concentrating wealth in the ruling class. And despite his willingness to publish Arcangela Tarabotti's *Paradiso monacale* in which the nun defended true calling as the only criteria for monachization, Loredan would deny a request from his own sisters to help them overturn their father's decision to lock them away in the convent. Arguing that without financial means to supply a suitable dowry for an equal marriage, the alternative of marrying below rank would "encounter universal contempt if you stain nobility with inferior alliances." Loredan insisted that "those marriages are always unhappy where the partners are unequal by birth but equal in poverty."[94]

The Incogniti, dedicated to saving, or perhaps rescuing, the Myth of Venice as the city dreamily floated into a State of economic and hegemonic decline, focused on the realm of culture to disseminate the message of eternal superiority, a message well-received even beyond the lagoons of Venice. Elsewhere, the Accademia was understood rather like a fraternal order whose members were tied together to give voice to the cultural and political debate of equality and to push the envelope of provocative literature—Loredan at the helm.

The Riva degli Schiavoni in Venice

Legend of the ocean calmed by St. Mark.
A fisherman gives the ring of St. Mark to the Doge of Venice

Ceremony celebrating the symbolic marriage
of Venice with the sea: The Doge of Venice on
the state barge, throwing a golden ring.

PART 2

"The Unlucky Sister": Elena's Years

Cittadini: The Tarabotti Family

*I*n 1604, the year Elena Cassandra was born, it is unlikely that Stefano and Maria Tarabotti, parents now to their fourth child and first daughter, would have had any contact with the literary elite of their city who would play a pivotal role in their child's life. But inasmuch as the post-interdict climate in the years to follow their daughter's birth would affect *cittadini* families like the Tarabottis, the relative peace enveloping the first decade of the seventeenth century permeated the lives of most Venetians.

The Tarabotti home was likely the heredity house in which Elena's father, Stefano Bernardo Tarabotti, as well as her paternal aunts and uncles, was born. Stefano was probably descended from a family involved in maritime activities, although we do not know for certain what his profession might have been. Elena's mother, Maria Cadena, descended from the Tolentini line; she was always addressed as "Madonna," signifying her elevated social position. When Maria died in 1640, she had already gained the respectful appellation of *clarissima signora*. Maria's father, records show, was also addressed respectfully as *missier*, *signor*, and *molto illustre signor*—titles that indicate a high social ranking. Indeed, Maria's father generously dowered his daughter who brought to her marriage with Stefano a considerable bride-portion relative to her social position.[95]

Stefano and Maria, solid upper-class *cittadini*, married in 1599, from which time through to 1613, the Tarabotti family would eventually grow to consist of seven females (six of whom survive to adulthood and four males, two of whom die in early childhood), Maria pregnant on the average of every eighteen months. Emilio Zanette, Tarabotti's biographer, remarks that "the family was predominately female, a rather sad State";[96] and we may conclude sad and ominous for little Elena, the eldest and only Tarabotti daughter to be monachanized.[97] Surely, the fact that the Tarabotti firstborn female had inherited *una zoppia* (a limp) from her father influenced Stefano's decision to place his daughter in a convent. We learn of the deformity from Arcangela's own writing. The only mention of her father in all of the nun's writing notes that she was *zoppa* like him.[98] The hereditary aspect of the child's limp suggests a form of skeletal dysplasia, a condition that did not inhibit Stefano from finding a suitable wife, but one that would, in the competitive upper-strata seventeenth-century Venetian marriage market, surely impede his daughter's marital prospects. Although even the richest families in Seicento Venice would have been hard-pressed to marry off six daughters, the remaining Tarabotti females were either married or remained in the household unmarried—an anomalous situation that might have been driven by Arcangela's protests, early on and later widely disseminated, as we will see in part 3.

At her baptism on February 24, 1604, the name of Stefano's grandmother was given to the Tarabotti daughter whose namesake was a woman of financial means.[99] Little Elena's paternal grandfather had inherited a sizable patrimony. However, in a time when the choice of a child's *padrino* was a significant one for the newborn's future life, the Tarabottis chose a rather undistinguished godfather for Elena. The *padrino* typically reflected the status of the child and family and therefore would have to be of equal or superior socioeconomic rank. The senate, as early as 1506, had acknowledged the practice of families selecting godfathers "for the sole purpose of creating obligations and making use of these people." More to the republican concern, though, was that such spiritual ties act as a bar to intermarriage. A *buon santolo*, as it was referred to, was a blessing; but Elena Cassandra's godfather, a certain Eustachio Matrico, was a shopkeeper of no particular importance.[100]

Marin Sanudo highlights "the three classes" of Venetian inhabitants that formed estates or legally defined status groups not categorized by the person's wealth or occupation but distinguished by the privileges they shared, how they functioned in society and State—all of the same *qualità* and *condizione*, legal terms found in Venetian official documents of the time. Paramount to one's position was the reputation of the family—a communal agreement about its quality and conditions.[101]

Not noble, yet in every way enveloped by the status conscious norms of the time, this upper middle-class family—as we might categorize the Tarabottis in modern terms—abided by the existing cultural dictates that conceived marriage as a union that should benefit the two families in terms of prestige and position. Francesco Sansovino, in *Venetia città nobilissima et singolare*, describing the wealth and opulence he saw in the palazzos of the great families, tells us much about the way in which even *cittadini* families lived:

> I have seen sold at auction the home furnishings of a noble condemned by an unfortunate incident that would have been more that a Grand Duke of Italy would wish. The same can be said of the middle and lower classes in proportion. Because there is no person so miserable, with *a casa aperta* (literally, an "open house, ready to welcome visitors) that he would not have chests and bedsteads of walnut and green draperies and carpets... Such is the *politia* of this city.[102]

The English ambassador Sir Dudley Carlton observed in 1612 what he labeled as "perpetual faction"[103] between the old families and the new ones, with the newer families larger in number although not necessarily in wealth and dignity. Maintaining middle-class status and moving up the permitted steps involved securing appropriate marriages for children, alliances that aimed to ensure generational economic and social stability. From the upper echelons of Venetian society, filtering down through and permeating the stratified *cittadini* class, was the primary place of family, illustrated by paintings such as Jacopo Tintoretto's portrait of the patrician Soranzo family, fifteen members total including grandchildren and their spouses flanking the family patriarch, Jacopo Soranzo, all appearing seriously aristocratic, proudly blue-blooded.

Looking more closely at the Tarabotti family composition, we see that two sisters, Lorenzina, third from last born, and Innocenza, last born, were both married at a relatively late age for the time—Innocenza at twenty-five to a widower seventeen years her senior, medical doctor Francesco di Camillo Dario; and Lorenzina at twenty-seven years old to Giacomo di Giovan Battista Pighetti, a Bergamasque lawyer eight years her senior (quite the norm).[104] In fact, it is Pighetti, prominent Incogniti member, who will play a crucial part in the abandoned daughter's life and to whom at least six letters of Arcangela's published *Lettere familiari e di complimento* were addressed. Interestingly, perhaps tellingly, in her extant work, including *Lettere* published in 1650 (at which time the enclosed nun had nieces and nephews), there is scant mention of her family. Although many forced religious maintained close ties with their families, we find little trace of concern, interest, or emotion regarding Arcangela's family members, understandable considering she could hardly have known two of her sisters. We do learn, however, of the profound rapport Tarabotti established with several of her *consorelle* and with the many literary contacts she nurtured. Of her early years in her natal household, Tarabotti is silent.

7

Sestiere di Castello: Arcangela's Natal Neighborhood

*B*y virtue of its physical position—different from practically every other Early Modern town and city—Venice had no protecting wall surrounding it. Marin Sanudo characterizes La Serenissima as a naturally protected city "amidst the billowing waves of the sea"; and then, putting the cityscape into perspective, the Renaissance historian describes Venice, dividing it into six districts, or *sestieri*: "three on one side of the Canal, and three on the other… On the near side, their names are Castello, St. Mark's and Canareggio; on the other side are Santa Croce, San Polo and Dorsoduro." The smallest of the six districts, Castello, had the prestige of housing the cathedral church, seat of the Patriarch of Venice,[105] and was, at the time of Elena Cassandra's birth, the *sestiere* in which the Tarabotti family resided.

Castello, located in the northeastern corner of Venice, in the parish of San Pietro, was by all accounts a working-class neighborhood. Home to the Arsenale, one of the largest naval complexes in Europe, this district quartered a diverse population: *sabioneri*—vendors of sand and pebbles for naval construction; sailors—both free and enslaved who rowed the *galeotti*; and members of the *cittadini* class, such as the Tarabottis. Although Venice's great age of sea domination had passed, the Arsenale was still an impressive site, "a beautiful and marvelous thing to see."[106] A plebian neighborhood, Castello was not without a scattering of *nobili*, families such as the Priuli, Balbi, and other names recorded in the *Libro d'Oro*.[107] Yet Arcangela's biographer, Emilio Zanette, notes that although Castello flouted families with noble cognomen, they were of "the third or fourth level branches."[108]

Churches and monasteries lined Castello streets, their facades of burnished ochre poised seriously against the dreamy Venetian canopy, some still standing today and functioning as religious houses, others repurposed over the centuries, still others, like the abandoned Church and Convent of Sant'Anna, closed and deteriorating. For the Tarabottis, as for most Venetians, neighborhood churches constituted a communal nexus, not only the site of religious devotion, but also a place of accepted socialization. Within the *parrocchia* was the Church of San Giuseppe that the family most likely attended on Sundays, given its proximity to the Tarabotti home. This relatively modern church by 1600 standards was built by senate decree in 1512, along with its adjoining convent, and entrusted to the Augustinians, in whose hands it remained until 1801 when Napoleon abolished both convent and church. Had the Tarabotti family looked up above the portal when they entered San Giuseppe, they would have seen the splendid Dal Moro tympanum depicting the Adoration of the Magi, a work that distinguished this parish church and undoubtedly filled its parishioners with pride as did the relics that Venetians were so passionate about: the church housed a collection of the consecrated remains of San Giuseppe, San Vito, Saints Giusto and Fiorenzo, and Saints Pietro and Claudio among its holy possessions.[109]

On feast days, the Tarabottis would have walked to the seat of their parish, the venerated Church of San Pietro, its history dating back to the seventh century when the first lagoon settlers occupied the island of Olivolo, as Castello was then called. Its Palladian-styled facade, denoting importance as the basilica of the Venetian patriarch, San Pietro boasted the presence of the patriarch himself on these special days. The Tarabotti family likely came to see Patriarch Vendramin pontificate from the antique basilica, the crowd immersed in an atmosphere of music and spectacle, pomp and glory.

It was the Convent of Sant'Anna where Elena would take her vows and live in *clausura* for life. Stefano Tarabotti conceivably chose Sant'Anna for its close proximity to the Tarabotti home, for this neighborhood church, by all accounts, was in a State of disrepair, or as Zanette put it, the edifice was *cadente* and *brutta*—"crumbling and ugly."[110] The church, with its convent, was founded by the Augustinians in 1242 and later passed into control of the Benedictines who by the ninth century had established itself throughout most of Europe as the exemplary order of monastic life. Today, the abandoned Church and Convent of Sant'Anna, closed to the public, looks sadly out on the Canal, bearing mute witness to its past, befitting of Suor Arcangela's characterization of her lifetime home as "a prison," the "Stygian swamp," and *L'inferno monacale* (Convent Hell), the title of her first work.

Yet Sant'Anna did have at least one redeeming feature and point of beauty: the extraordinary embroidered artwork of the Tintoretto sister nuns or the *tentorette*, as they were called—Suor Ottavia Robusti and Suor Pierina, who completed, after years of dedication, their impressive needlework in 1609. It was their famous father, Jacopo Tintoretto (1518–1594),[111] praised as one of the great artists of what has come to be known as the Venetian School, who placed his daughters in the modest convent. Zanette hypothesizes that Maria Tarabotti would have taken little Elena, only five years old at the time, to see the extraordinary embroidery work depicting the crucifixion that was said to have been designed by Tintoretto himself, echoing his work for the Scuola Grande di San Rocco. Further enhancing the allure of this story and giving the modest church a point of pride was the rumor that one of the sisters, Ottavia, had become blind as a result of years of intense, delicate needlework.[112]

On the day that Stefano and Maria Tarabotti likely accompanied their thirteen-year-old daughter[113] to the nearby Benedictine Convent of Sant'Anna, the family was doing exactly what others of their rank and class considered common practice: Well-to-do families typically sent their daughters to board in convents as *educandas*. Early Modern convents functioned as types of elementary schools for daughters of families who could afford to pay, providing the children with a rudimentary education—reading and writing, embroidery, and lace making.[114] The conventual education of daughters was by this time an embedded tradition going as far back as the seventh century:

> Devono essere allevate con tutto l'affetto, la bontà e la fermezza, affinché nella loro tenera età non siano macchiate dal vizio della pigrizia o della leggerezza e poi non possono affatto, o solo difficilmente, essere corrette. Si abbia nei loro confronti una cura tanto grande che non restino mai senza un'anziana, che impedisca loro di deviare da una parte o dall'altra, ma, sempre trattenute dalla sua fermezza ed educate nell'insegnamento del timore e dell'amore di Dio, siano preparate all'osservanza della vita religiosa.[115]

Fundamentally, the arguments made in these Seicento rules for female monasteries are twofold: The opportune time to impart learning would be when the girl is young, and the girls should be reared with affection, goodness and firmness, so that in their tender age they are not soiled by the vice of laziness or of easy morals which then cannot at all, or only with difficulty, be corrected. They should be looked after carefully so that they never are without an older woman to prevent them from deviating from one side or the other. The girls should be treated firmly, educated in the teaching of the fear and love of God, and should be prepared for the religious life.

Convent education for young girls, at the start of the seventeenth century, was a time-honored practice, especially among elite families who usually sent their daughters to board from ages nine through thirteen, oftentimes younger, most of them staying to take the veil. The *putte in serbanza* referred to the girls who would board side by side with those destined to become nuns. Both groups resided in complete monastic *clausura*, the *putte* returning to their families only when their education had finished or when called back to marry, many reluctantly remaining when parents could not forge satisfactory marital unions.

Upper-class families could boast of boarding their daughters in one of the many female religious houses noted for their aristocratic occupants, as Venetian convents were filled with well-bred girls and women. This type of education at the start of the seventeenth century was a sign that the family "had arrived" and, depending on the convent, often a prestigious social commentary. Boarding young girls also served another purpose: it was a sort of seminary for future nuns, voluntary or not. Some girls would return to their families and marry; others like Elena—future Suor Arcangela—would unwillingly take sacred vows and remain cloistered for the rest of their lives.

From Suor Arcangela's words of anguish and lament, years after she had been committed to the convent—"Oh Misery, oh torment of inferno for those unhappy girls that without any other belongings except the little dowry, poor in the richness of woes, are forced to be sealed in these cloisters!"[116]—we can imagine that on the day Stefano placed his daughter as *educanda* in Sant'Anna, the child was reluctant to enter. That Elena took her final vows several years after she would have been able to do so suggests the child's reluctance probably delayed the investiture.

Stefano Tarabotti made the first monthly payment to board his daughter on September 1, 1617.[117] Through 1620, payments for Elena total 115 ducats, and on September 12, 1620, a payment of 1,000 ducats *per dote di'Elena sua figliuola* (for the dowry of Elena, his daughter)—with further payments in the same year of 1,600 ducats.[118] The *dote* (spiritual dowry) sealed Elena's fate: after spending three years as an *educanda* until she was sixteen and a half years old,[119] the child was now ready to take her initial vows. During her *educanda* years, sporadic periods of no payments appear, suggesting that the child might have been at home with her family, possibly ill—a likely hypothesis considering Tarabotti's precarious health, to which we find numerous references in her writing.

As for any education the future Arcangela might have received before entering Sant'Anna, we cannot be certain; but we do know that Maria Cadena, her mother, was a literate woman, not at all commonplace for the time, as she left an autograph will evincing her ability to read and write. A distinctive marker of literacy, Arcangela's handwriting appears well above the typical penmanship of other nuns.[120] What we do know, however, is that the literary nun, through her own volition, became an autodidact succeeding in publishing in her lifetime works penned within the walls of a post-Tridentine Venetian female monastery.

8

Sant'Anna Convent: Lives Within Walls

*M*ost Venetian convents belonged to the oldest monastic orders, Augustinian and Benedictine, reflecting a steadfast culture of tradition that rooted these convents and affirmed Venetian embalmed resistance to new religious movements from abroad, the Carmelites not arriving in Venice until 1647.[121] For their daughters, patrician families preferred these established orders that emphasized a rigid life of contemplation and seclusion. Emanating from its foundation legends, Venetian convents manifested not only a symbolic importance in civic rituals, but also the practical necessity of housing the city's cast-off elite virgins.[122]

By mid-seventeenth century, there numbered thirty-plus female convents within city margins, about ninety nuns per religious house. The blue-blood daughters of aristocratic and upper-class families recreated within their confines a continuity of the societal stratification that existed without. The hierarchal dynamics of secular Venetian society penetrated convent walls, creating a clear bifurcation: choir nuns or veiled nuns at the upper level and *conversae* or servant nuns at the lower rung characterized the conventual system, promulgated and supported by the upper-class women's families whose daughters, sisters, aunts, and nieces resided in *clausura*.

Choir nuns' elite families paid significant convent dowries that allowed them to progress from novice to first professed status and then on to take full solemn vows as consecrated religious. The *con-*

versae, on the other hand, took simple vows, one time only. Coming from socially inferior families and bringing with them a lesser spiritual dowry than choir nuns, *conversae* were the laborers of the convent, performing the myriad of menial chores required to sustain female religious houses of the early seventeenth century. As maids and servants, these lay sisters allowed their more prestigious counterparts to dedicate themselves to pious duties.

Within convent walls, we see a microcosm or better yet a continuation of the secular society without. Class stratification penetrated the brick barriers: choir nuns were of noble birth, and their dowry payments to the convent were set high as to exclude most other women. The social divisions that existed without continued uninterrupted within, reinforcing Venetian convents' close ties with Venetian nobility, resulting in a symbiotic relationship that supported the political and social concerns of the Republic and would prove impervious to change.

However, change was the order of the time: from the mid-sixteenth century, significant and far-reaching modifications concerning convents and the lives of those within them were mandated by the reforms of the Council of Trent, held between 1545 and 1563 in response to the Protestant Reformation and significant changes in the confessional map of Europe. With the reforms and dictates of the Council, referred to as the Counter-Reformation, convents came under strict scrutiny.

Particularly in Venice, noted for its liberal treatment of nuns and having acquired a reputation for scandal, ecclesiastical and State authorities instigated rigid surveillance policies focusing on monastic enclosure, prohibiting nuns from stepping out of the convent in order to secure their total encloisterment and guarantee complete separation from the secular world. Such structural modifications as barring windows and making them smaller, as well as raising the heights of peripheral walls, would keep the nun inside. Other restrictions pertaining to control over reading material and visitors would keep the women free of the contamination from the outside world. Nuns resisted fiercely. Only gradually did some of the reforms take hold in a pervasive atmosphere of tension between enclosure and more open convents. From all accounts, the mandates remained on paper.

By the time Elena Tarabotti took her vows in 1620, decades after reforms, post-Tridentine normative dispositions on nuns and convents mandating strict *clausura* had been instituted and surveillance policies well in place. Nonetheless, essential mandates prohibiting forced monachization, requiring that all female professants be interrogated by church elders to certify that they were taking vows voluntarily and clearly understood the commitment, were difficult to institute even though it was forbidden for anyone to force a woman into a convent or deny a woman the right to enter. The subtleties inherent in coerced monachization of young girls would expediently be ignored as would another edict denying eligibility to women with chronic sicknesses, mental infirmities, or physical handicaps. In *Tirannia paterna,* Tarabotti decries the practice of offering to Christ.

> Not their most beautiful and virtuous, but instead the most repelling and deformed, and if a family has lame, hunchback and crippled or simpleminded [daughters], blaming these girls for the natural defects with which they were born, and condemning them for this to remain imprisoned for the rest of their lives.[123]

Ecclesiastic authorities, well aware of forced monachization, concerned themselves with Venetian convents, focusing on the security of its inhabitants, particularly their chastity. When Patriarch Lorenzo Priuli visited Sant'Anna on March 15, 1593, he noticed a small window that when opened could provide enough space for a man to sneak through. Knowing that where there was space for a man to enter, there was a nun without calling awaiting him, Patriarch Priuli ordered the immediate revision of the window, reducing its size to *quarta una e mezzo* with closing features requiring two different keys—one to open from inside by the abbess and the other to open from outside by the convent's confessor, in a way that wouldn't allow the window to open without a simultaneous concurrence of both abbess and confessor. Patriarch Priuli required the work be completed within eight days.[124]

The patriarch's orders were obeyed, but his successors would continue to complain about convents' lax rules, to mandate structural modifications, and to rail against the improprieties of its unwilling inhabitants. Notwithstanding ecclesiastical provisions, long after Priuli's edicts, Venetian convents were still posing problems. In 1674, years after Suor Arcangela had died and was buried in the convent in which she had been sepulchered for life, illicit entrance into Sant'Anna was still a preoccupation of the Bishop of Venice: Patriarch Morosini[125] observed that the convent's little windows continued to be a place where the interned communicated with the outside world. With female religious houses populated by girls and women without calling, one can well imagine the continued tension between the enclosed females' battle to live their lives and the church and State authorities' struggle to preserve power and stability.

Ecclesiastical administrators were aware of the young girls' plight, Patriarch Tiepolo referring to the Venetian gentlewomen enclosed in "public tombs." But the greater good, the *ragion di stato*, trumped any consideration for incarcerated girls and women: the more serious damage, the greater danger and scandal, must be avoided by institutionalizing thousands of girls. In *Paradiso monacale*, Arcangela comments on the rationale of *ragion di stato* and the sacrifice of Venetian females:

> Many [authorities] will have to repent closing their eyes in this way in favor of the interests of the State...filling these horrible cloistered tombs with miserable and innocent women.[126]

Tarabotti conflates societal practices and political utility, criticizing the politics that put above every other consideration "the defense, conservation and expansion of the State." Further distinguishing her work is the nun's ability to thematize gender injustice through an acute awareness of the political underpinnings of unequal treatment of women.

She notes a contradiction in practice pertaining to the notion that paternal and sovereign power is derived from divine origin, pointing out that liberal thinkers and defenders of the State support a more limited theory of government, yet they insist on absolute control and power over the family by the father. In *L'inferno monacale*, her "solution" to the problem, presented with Socratic irony and alluding to the "barbaric practices of the Turks and bloodthirsty Thracians," acknowledges how having all daughters marry would detrimentally expand the nobility and bankrupt it at the same time with so many dowries to pay. In her "modest proposal"—a century before Swift— she suggests instead of incarcerating the girls, killing all the boys as soon as they are born, leaving one for each family, which would be a lesser sin than burying alive the daughters. Finishing her stinging satire, Tarabotti feigns outrage: "And don't let me hear of your feelings and sentiments taking precedent over your political interests!"[127]

Obviously, to Tarabotti, the Myth of Venice was just that: a political and social construction that relied on incarcerating a large part of its population. In fact, the first of her two dedications that introduces *L'inferno monacale* is addressed to the Serenissima Republica Veneta and to "those fathers and relatives that force their daughters into clausura," blatantly accusing the governing body of Venice of propagating "paternal tyranny."

Addressing "The Most Serene Queen," Venice,

> You grant unconditional freedom to those of all nations, even to those who killed the Holy Son… from the very beginning, in these lagoons, fame and paternal tyranny sprung forth, hidden under the majesty of your Senators' robes, finally taking a seat in the Ducal Palace… The most noble lords have welcomed paternal tyranny, this monster from hell embraced by your noblest of citizens…that I have to fear that this book, written with my rudimentary pen will not be well received… However, I dedicate this, my first born to you, a fanciful whim of a woman's intellect.[128]

She concludes the dedication to the Serene Republic of Venice by expressing her enormous ingratitude to this Republic that is protected by the Virgin Mary…and as a caveat,

> My words are in no way intended to besmirch religion, but instead to rail against the fathers and families who violently put their daughters in coffins…
> I won't beg you to believe my sincerity, since in any case, for one who has lost her liberty, there is nothing more to lose.[129]

Patria Potestas: "Savage Parents"
and Lies of the Father

How can you inflict such torture on your own flesh and blood?[130]

*I*n her apostrophe to fathers, Arcangela Tarabotti, in *Tirannia paterna* (*Paternal Tyranny*), published posthumously as *Semplicità ingannata*,[131] argues that in appearance, good and evil look very much alike. However, in reality, we see the stark difference:

> In an attempt by you madmen [you fathers] to find
> good here on earth—just an illusion—you drive
> women into isolation, solitude, to endure life-long
> servitude and poverty, repugnant all of you for
> what you are.[132]

Focusing on the patriarch of the family, who possessed legal power over his wife and children, originating from the Roman law, *patria potestas*, Tarabotti is well aware of the system that governed family and regime: *paterfamilias*—the eldest male in the family—in early Rome, likely going as far back as 450 BC and the Twelve Tables, wielded total power over all in his household including daughters-in-law, servants, and legitimate and adopted children, not excluding decisions over the life and death of his children; legend has it that Junius Brutus had his sons executed for disobedience. The

Roman *paterfamilias* owned all property in his family; and his children, regardless of their age, could not own anything outright in their own names as long as the father lived. Along with these powers was the authority over who his children married. In the late Roman Republic, these legal duties took on a component of moral obligations, and throughout most of Europe during the medieval and early modern periods, the doctrine of *patria potestas* provided societies with legal and practical bedrock for family formation.[133] Just as in ancient Rome, the *princeps familiae* was master of the house in Venice: "Mothers contributed but fathers commanded."[134]

Francesco Barbaro in 1415 was working within the framework of *patria potestas* when he extolled the family as the basis for political rule in Venice, noting a woman's contribution to her family: "Let husbands give the orders and let the wife carry them out with a cheerful temper."[135] Indeed, it was the patriarch's responsibilities as head of household to provide for his children's care including their material and spiritual well-being. The husband was lord of his family as God reigned over the universe. Discord or infertility in a marriage was naturally interpreted as the fault of the wife.

Marco Ferro, historian of the eighteenth century, concurs that the original intentions of *patria potestas* were to protect children and guide them through to adulthood. The father was to provide correction and set on the proper path disobedient offspring, challenging authority anathema to social order. The wife, under the legal authority of her husband, was also relegated to the "power of correcting their children, even forcefully."[136]

The family patriarch must keep safe hereditary patrimony that followed patrilineage descent. To that end, a father's duty obliged him to find suitable spouses for his offspring, a responsibility that impelled him to dower his daughter(s); the preponderance of this obligation was such that upon a father's death, the responsibility of dowering daughters would be passed on to the girls' surviving uncles or brothers. Daughters, as Chojnacki reveals,[137] played a role in the marriage alliance as a powerful exchange medium in forging socially, politically, and economically advantageous unions. Both daughters and sons were expected to render complete obedience to their parents. Tridentine reforms—based on the theory of consent, requiring both man and woman willingly agree to marriage—did little to change Venetian upper-strata marriages: The Republic's 1596 decree passed by the Council of Ten required, for legitimacy, that patrician parents register their children's marriages at the Avogadori di Comun in the *Libro d'Oro,* or they would have no rights to sit on the Great Council. Thus, even though a man and woman were willing to marry, without the consent of their parents, the union would not stand up to Venetian civil law, which for all purposes trumped canon law.

Arcangela takes a somewhat psychological look at the patriarchal duty and decries the utter hypocrisy of fathers:

> You who expect [your cloistered daughters] to bow
> their heads at insults and turn the other cheek if one
> is struck, while you cannot stand a wrong look.[138]

We can argue that this personification of hypocrisy appears to be based on Tarabotti's own experience, perhaps referring to her own father's character—a supposition only, since Tarabotti mentions her father only once to tell us that she is lame (*zoppa*) like him.[139] Neither does she refer to her own experiences: her words do not simply reflect an autobiographical account of paternal tyranny but instead present an acutely incisive condemnation of practices, politically and economically motivated, that deprive women of their "God-given right to choose the course of their lives":

> You want to get her [the daughter] out of the house
> with as little damage to your pocketbook as pos-
> sible, without losing your money, the thought of
> which drives you crazy.[140]

She speaks directly to "you fathers," Tarabotti wise enough to know that the examples she presents are typical of the father who disposes of his daughters; the reasons are always the same. Her outcries rise to the emotional level of an inspired, impassioned preacher, mandating damnation for the evil sinners, pleading the case for all unwillingly incarcerated women:

> How is it possible, oh you deceivers, that you can keep in your breast a heart so cruel that would inflict torment on the bodies of your own daughters, who are of your own flesh and blood, with the danger that they can lose their souls. Their nature is so noble that Christ again would descend from heaven to hearth and return to suffer death on the cross to save just one of them... These poor girls whom you incarcerate would have been better off if their day of birth were their day of death.[141]

It is not for nothing that Tarabotti refers to fathers as "ruffiani"[142] (pimps), alluding to their trickery and deceit, the means they employed (rather than overt or physical force) to incarcerate their little daughters. Tarabotti dedicated her first published work, *Paradiso monacale*, appealing to the hierarchal triad of God, the Patriarch of Venice, and her readers, telling them clearly that she writes not from her own interests, but in the name of justice exposing, "le pretensioni ingiuste de gli huomini" (the unjust pretentions of men).

> All you relatives, fathers and family, of these girls, do not excuse yourselves by saying you were not aware of such particulars, with the pretext of wanting to keep these girls as glorious virgins, taking them away from the human trials and tribulations since you know that the world has been practicing this for centuries, as clear to you as the sun's rays.[143]

Although mothers are not Tarabotti's target, the nun acknowledges that they, "per compiacer al marito,"[144] go along with their husbands to please them, concur with every use of force and fear, and do in fact reap the benefits of their chosen daughter's worldly marriage. In a letter to her dear friend Betta Polani, Tarabotti announces the death of her mother (Tarabotti's), revealing a sincere affection and without any reprimands toward her.[145]

10

Convent Collaborators: "Sweet Words and Sugarplums..."

*A*complying church met the needs of families by accepting girls who brought the required spiritual dowry. A cooperative conventual system supported the enshrined practice of dowering daughters, but the intransigent tradition relied on the family patriarch and Republican corroboration—the weft and warp of forced monachization—without which the practice could not have endured.

Although the family patriarch wielded the power to banish his daughters to convents, he had help and collaboration. Through verbal persuasion rather than physical violence, the Venetian father, along with his collaborators, employed perfidious arguments to convince the little girl, as Tarabotti terms it, "to close herself in a cage."[146] Tarabotti begins her argument against religious superiors, fearing her pen is "flying too boldly,"[147] citing them as accomplices to the very deeds of the fathers, positing that they (religious superiors) should have as the center of their focus nothing but the service to God, to the letter of the pontifical orders, not State interests that allow women to become nuns without vocation.[148]

Arcangela notes that convents are run by prioresses and abbesses who, although dressed in nun's habit, were not called to veil by the Holy Spirit; they came to their position of power either by guile or good fortune, and instead of teaching and correcting, they turn a blind eye to the abuses and scandalous behavior. Indeed, the unwilling young nuns, now bound up safely in their cloistered confines, did present ongoing problems that were no secret to Venetians. Tarabotti blames the system, not the misbehaving nuns:

> You also know how many of these nuns, dissolving the ties of honesty, have stained their chastity, fleeing from the detested prison, have dishonored their homes and family and the house of God as well.[149]

However, flight was rare. In order to physically escape and live outside the convent, the nun would have to have had a supporting ally on the outside, as her family would not take her back.

In one recorded case, Suor Faustina managed to escape from San Giovanni Lateran in 1555, having as accomplice her lover, Francesco dalle Crosette, a convent employee hired to perform such chores as hauling water and helping to bake bread. The escape was discovered, and both parties interrogated, ending with the nun's return to the convent.[150] More frequently, however, were sexual transgressions such as that of Laura Querini, confined to the most aristocratic of Venetian convents, San Zaccaria, since the age of seven. Laura and her convent friend, a *conversa*, had made a hole in the confining wall large enough to permit two men, cousins— one for each nun—into the nunnery. When she was found out and interrogated by the patriarch, Laura blatantly foreswore her vows, admitting, "I spoke with my mouth, and not with my heart. I have always been tempted by the devil to break my neck."[151] The two men were exiled from Venice for twenty years, risking death if they returned. It is not clear if the nuns were punished at all since they were under the jurisdiction of the patriarch and abbess who possessed few options in light of the fact that the women were already imprisoned.

Clandestine correspondence between nuns and their lovers was a popular motif, jokingly satirized, for example, by the poet

Giovanni Francesco Busenello[152] who wrote of perfumed missives wrapped in gilded paper in dainty handkerchiefs delivered by willing accomplices. It was Patriarch Morosini in 1644 who exhorted the nuns of Venice to refrain from any sort of letter writing at all, as these romantic epistolary episodes were of great concern to the patriarch of Seicento Venice, questioning, in fact, if nuns should have been taught to write at all. As Tarabotti points out, nuns were given the bare minimum of instruction, held hostage to prescribed religious readings—all other texts prohibited.

Stemming the tide of scandalous behavior in nunneries was not only an ongoing endeavor of centuries but also a futile task. Boccaccio, writing in the fourteenth century, satirized those "who are so foolish as to believe that when the white veil is placed on a girl's head, and her body covered in a black habit, she is no longer a woman and is no longer subject to the desires of her sex as though she had turned to stone after putting on the nun's habit":

> Bellissime donne, assai sono di quegli uomini e di quelle femine che sì sono stolti, che credono troppo bene che, come ad una giovane è sopra il capo posta la benda bianca e in dosso messale la nera cocolla, che ella più non sia femina né più senta de' feminili appetiti se non come se di pietra l'avesse fatta divenire il farla monaca.[153]

Post-Tridentine Venetian convents, under the provisions enacted half a century before Elena was to take the veil, did not adhere to the Council mandates prohibiting coerced monachization, prohibitions that in practice were impossible to enforce. The subtle and insidious machinations employed by families to coerce unwilling, unwitting children to live in *clausura* were difficult to detect and regulate, especially with the cooperation and collaboration of professed nuns and the girl's own family.

Referring to the religious novice, "pure, naïve and simple," who "must cede to the cunning old ones [nuns] and their infernal court,"[154] writing in third person—"she" (the involuntary religious) Tarabotti complains,

> She must bow her head even to those not meriting. If she does not immediately obey, she is severely reprimanded by those, who like her, were married to Christ through the violence of force.

The older nun repeats the words heard so often by the novices:

> Sei novizza: a te, a te s'appartengono e dissagi... Tu, come ultima entrata in monastero, devi suplir per l'altre, ché così habbiam fatto ancora noi a' nostri tempi."[155] (You are a novice: as the last one to enter the monastery, you must bow your head before the others and must undergo the tribulations the way we did when we first came here.)[156]

Tarabotti's invective against convent superiors also recognizes that they too were put away involuntarily, but she insists that they should, as older, wiser women, have practiced true religious piety. However, the pecuniary concerns of both the convent and the father take center stage as the father and convent superiors bicker over money to be contributed to the adornment of the church, how much money he will provide for his daughter's food, and other monetary concerns that Tarabotti sardonically notes will "torment the purse of the old, tenacious man."[157]

Defiantly critical of the social, political, and religious patriarchal machinations that fostered the practice of discarding daughters, Tarabotti's first written works—*Tirannia paterna* and *L'inferno monacale*—were circulated among Venetian literati but not published in the author's lifetime. Composed between 1640 and 1642, both works are clear denouncements of coerced monachization and, as such, met with no success to bring them to press despite Tarabotti's attempts to publish these two iconoclastic works. She then wrote *Paradiso monacale*, a less polemic text now considered to have been penned precisely to achieve the goal of publication. In this tome, the nun shows deference for the convent as a "paradise" for those women with true religious calling, implicating just the opposite for those confined without calling. Determined to have her work put to print—and arguably considering publication of her previously written texts—Arcangela Tarabotti circulated copies of *Paradiso* among friends and acquaintances, garnering the respect and admiration from eminent literary figures that would enable her to request and receive copies of sought-after books and to seek advice from these prestigious figures, Giovan Francesco Loredan among the most prominent, and publisher of *Paradiso.*

As for *Tirannia paterna* and *L'inferno monacale*, they would not be published in the author's lifetime regardless of Tarabotti's persistent and ardent attempts that reached as far as France in her commitment to have her works see the light of day. Two years after the writer's death, *Tirannia* was published in Holland as *La semplicita' ingannata* (Deceived Innocence), a less provocative title, under the thinly veiled pseudonym Galerana Baratotti, an anagram of her name. This scathing denunciation of the role of the State (*ragion di stato*) in propagating the practice of forced enclosure also took aim at the family patriarch, the father, who betrayed his own flesh and blood through trickery and deceit, condemning innocent girls to a lifetime of confinement. The nun describes how the trickery begins with the father of the family, having most to gain from his daughter's monachization. His decision churns the wheels of the ensuing chicanery. Once the resolution is taken to cloister the child, a series of sweet persuasions is put into motion, as Tarabotti points out, "to knowingly deceive the girls."

> Betrayal is the most horrible monster that infiltrates and infects the peace and happiness of miserable mortals, cause of misery for these unfortunate beings, victims of false pretenses and false appearances of good will, bringing more evil and misery and torment because it comes so unexpectedly... the young girls are tricked and betrayed before they are of age to decide for themselves what kind of life

is best for them. Their parents send them to the convent before they are even aware of where they are to be imprisoned... Oh what a betrayal![158]

In *L'inferno monacale*, Tarabotti describes how the family goes on and on convincing the little one not to think about any other life except the religious one. The little girl's aunts tell her stories of the woes of marriage, the troubles and dangers of the world, quoting from Saint Jerome praising virginity as the more perfect State:

I will say it boldly, though God can do all things He cannot raise up a virgin when once she has fallen... He may indeed relieve one who is defiled from the penalty of her sin, but He will not give her a crown... The love of the flesh is overcome by the love of the spirit... I praise wedlock, I praise marriage, but it is because they give me virgins.[159]

Arcangela reveals just how far the elderly nuns, often in collaboration with the girl's cloistered aunts, would go to dupe the child—hanging sugared almonds and candied fruits on the trees of the convent courtyard to create a terrestrial paradise and con the children into believing the convent courtyard was a paradise on earth of magical enchantment. Through sweet words and sugarplums, the old nuns—they too, in their time, forced into the convent—tell the most fabulous fairy tales, employing every art of persuasion that not even the most famous of poets could match, all to convince the girl that the nunnery is an earthly heaven.[160]

Cleverly comparing the dissimulation to a "commedia" in *L'inferno monacale*, alluding to Dante's *Inferno* and presenting the convent as the stage,[161] Tarabotti's heartrending account of the treachery and deceit leading up to the child taking her vows reveals the psychological and emotional torture endured by these innocents. Not only her female relatives collude to coerce the girl into monastic life, but her male relatives and her own brothers, reluctant to forfeit patrimony and, as Tarabotti points out, their own pleasures, provide a complete familial cincture around the girl now encased in a sociocultural cocoon from which there is no escape. Tarabotti reveals that little boys, early on, are taught to be dishonest and even obscene, proud and cruel toward their female siblings, taking part in training the little girls to know they would become *sorelle* of the Church: *saranno monache* (they will become nuns) so that brothers could become wealthy—fathers proudly inspiring and condoning the treatment.[162]

The coercion continues with promises of carefree days full of games and play made to the youngest and more innocent of the girls, while the appeal to the more mature children was the enticement of comfortable rooms and fine food. Tarabotti discloses that instead of telling them the truth about how a religious life is rewarding, they promise that in leaving their natal home, here in the convent, your aunt will be more than a mother to you, highlighting the fact that Venetian convents were filled with female generational family groups. The elders insist that each girl can develop her own talents; and the convent has provisions for dancing, singing, music, and playacting—an appeal to some girls and women able and willing to take advantage of the contemplative life. Although Arcangela found little of this to be true, or at best limited in scope, for those with calling, the monastic life did in fact provide a tranquil ambient, and in the case of Tarabotti, ironically provoked the literary nun to realize her true calling.

Referring to the "lucky sisters," chosen to be terrestrial brides, and beginning with both mother and father ostensibly agreeing on which girl "will live in the light of the world and which other be miserably enclosed enduring a thousand pangs of pain and unhappiness," the stealthy coercion begins. Tarabotti bitterly asks,

> With what heart do you think that the one girl child sees the other sister destined to be physically married, and to revel in the delights and triumphs in the midst of luxury and grandeur?[163]

Tarabotti follows with an emotional account of the hypothetical secular life of the "lucky sister," pointing out the rough and ugly garments the unfortunate girl must put on, not even being allowed to keep her God-given natural hair. In fact, Arcangela herself would not submit voluntarily to be shorn and only after ecclesiastic persuasion finally relented.[164] Deprived of her hair and fine clothing, the unlucky daughter, now adorned in crude dress of rough fabric, protective bib around her bodice, could not turn a blind eye to her selected sister(s), lucky enough to remain in a privileged environment. Tarabotti explores the sibling's internalization of arbitrary selection by comparing the secular life of the chosen daughter to that of the enclosed sister, especially detailing the crude dress of "the ugliest of colors" that would cover her body, depriving her of the "gifts of nature." Hypothesizing how the girl must have felt—and arguably relying on her own memories—Suor Arcangela insists that these innocents must have considered themselves to be of little worth as they witnessed the extravagance lavished upon the select sister, the one to be well-married.[165] She asks how can parental injustice go so far as to treat four or five daughters, all of the same seed, birthed from the same womb, differently, choosing one and condemning the others to the "perpettuo laberinto d'un chiostro" (the perpetual labyrinth of a cloister).[166]

Along with the emotional and detailed account of parental preference, exhibited particularly in the pomp and splendor of the lucky sister's terrestrial marriage, Tarabotti offers scriptural support for her claim that it should be the firstborn who, rather than being cast off, should enjoy the privileges that the Old Testament cites is worthy of the more advantageous position.

That Tarabotti presents the marriage process to exemplify parental partiality is hardly surprising. As family mergers, Renaissance marriages took place in the public arena, and as such, they were often lavish affairs showcasing the wealth and status of the uniting families. When Arcangela writes that no expense is spared in preparing the bride for her wedding, she juxtaposes the deprivations of the brides of Christ, in contrast to "the gold, the gems that are given [to the terrestrial bride-to-be] to make her more beautiful, and even an expert teacher [is hired] to teach the girl artless style which will please the eyes and soul of all who look upon her."[167] Mentioning the silks and fine-colored fabrics imported from as far away as Syria, Tarabotti, in her acute sardonic style, cites the bride who was born of the same womb as the other less fortunate one—the spiritual bride—who will be clothed in funereal garb while the lucky sister "pompeggi[a] fra gl'ori e fra le gemme" (glories in gold and jewels). Supporting Tarabotti's observations about the social implications of the marriage ritual, Francesco Guicciardini, sixteenth-century Florentine historian, asserts, "There is nothing in our civil life that is more difficult than properly marrying off one's daughters."[168]

Tarabotti illuminates the effects of partiality and favoritism of fathers toward their daughters destined for earthly marriages and those to become brides of Christ. In fact, the well-to-do Venetian bride's family spared no expense, no luxury, to prepare the future bride for her wedding. Even the events preceding the marriage ceremony would consist of delightful times; and as Arcangela points out, even though two daughters share identical blood, one is treated with dignity and respect, while the other condemned to deprivation and obedience.

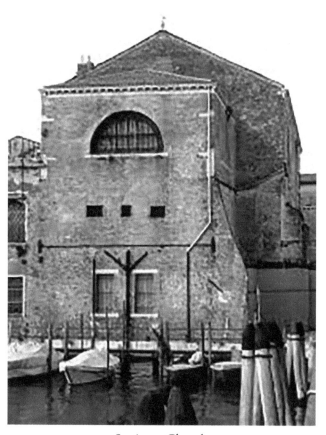

St. Anna Church

Jacopo Tintoretto—The Crucifixion

Palazzo Loredan

PART 3

"The Stygian Swamp": Internalizing Anguish

Becoming Arcangela: Taking the Veil

*A*t age sixteen and a half, on September 8, 1620, Elena Cassandra Tarabotti took the veil, professing her final vows in 1623. Two decades later, in *L'inferno monacale*, published after her death, she describes part of the process:

> This "funeral celebration" is hardly distinguishable from actual funerals for the dead: The girl lies prostrate, mouth to the stone floor. A black cloth is then thrown over her head and a burning candle is put at her feet, another placed near her head. From above, the litany is sung. All indications would suggest the girl is dead. She herself feels she is attending her own funeral.[169]

Tarabotti, along with two other young girls—one of whom became Arcangela's close friend, Renata Donà, eleven years old—dressed in virginal white, their long tresses flowing, kneeled before the priest who placed on each of their heads a corona of fresh flowers. The ritual continued as the girls recited scripted Latin dialogue—having memorized the ceremonial language that professed their willingness, their longing, to live the cloistered life:

> Cosi' ho diliberato nel mio cuore e faro' al Signore,
> di me, un sacrificio volontario, e confessero' il suo

nome, perche questo e' bene… Questa dunque e' la mia pace per sempre: qui' abitero' perche' mi sono scelta io questa casa.[170] (I have deliberated in my heart and will make this voluntary sacrifice to my Lord and confess His name… This, then, is my everlasting peace; here I will live because I have chosen this House.)

Indeed, post-Tridentine mandates prohibited forced vocation, "If a girl, who is more than twelve years of age, wishes to take the Regular Habit, she shall be questioned by the Ordinary, and again before Profession."[171] It would appear that through the elaborate verbal deposition, the letter of these reform decrees had been adhered to as Elena recited her dedication. But for this child, the process would play out as an ultimate tragedy with the convent as stage for a "funereal celebration." Noting that laments are useless, Arcangela writes that the girl—an unknown, unidentified protagonist—is now "buried in her own grave" with "tears and sighs to keep her company in the coffin," as she, "with desperate tightened lips endures her own entombment." The contrast between the willing, sacrificial words narrated and Tarabotti's account of what unwilling nuns actually endured appears more and more like the tragical farce within which framework Arcangela relates the investiture ceremony: "All the players recite eloquently…each to his part: Fraud, Pretense, Hypocrisy… Deceit and Betrayal."[172]

Minutes after vowing, the girl and her newly baptized *consorelle* are asked, "Che chiedete, o figli?" (What do you ask, children?) They reply, "Una sola cosa ho chiesta a Dio: di abitare nella casa del Signore tutti i gironi della mia vita, perche ho amato lo splendore della sua casa." (I only ask one thing of God: to live in the house of the Lord every day of my life, because I have loved the splendor of his home.) To this prescribed ritual reply, the confessor asks, "Have you firmly decided this in your heart, without having been constrained to do so, and with complete free will?" The nuns answer in biblical Latin, affirming they are making this sacrifice voluntarily, completing the syllogistic recital.[173]

The transformation of the postulants continues as the novices assume their new habits. The abbess oversees the girls as they shed their white garments to don Benedictine black ones, the novices now minutes away from the climactic moment of the ceremony: the tonsure, an emblematic procedure symbolizing the sacrifice of Christ. Scissors in hand, the abbess steps toward the waiting girls while the chorus chants, "Veil your heart and sleep your flesh, may your heart be veiled, and your flesh put to rest."[174] The singing stops. The abbess proceeds to cut off a chunk of hair from each head—this a gesture only, to be followed by the complete tonsure performed by the already incarcerated nuns, to the singing voices of the convent choir. It is revealing that Tarabotti would spend many words on this particular part of the investiture ritual representing the denial of vanity, meant to be the ultimate sacrifice of young girls: their flowing manes, often luxuriously beautiful, had been a part of their personas from early childhood. She is adamant about the representative value of a woman's tresses. Observing that canon law looks at shearing a woman's hair as a sign of submission, Tarabotti refutes this notion and insists that, instead, the female natural adornment represents freedom and superiority. [175]

Suor Arcangela, writing as a mature woman, twenty years after she herself had undergone the tonsure, would have witnessed in the interim years so many young girls compelled to *clausura* being shorn of a part of their identity. In *Paternal Tyranny*, published two years after her death, Tarabotti reasons that a woman is, in fact, born free and should not submit to having her greatest natural adornment shorn from her head. She asks how one can justify cropping a girl's hair, depriving her of her God-given beauty, citing the Bible and quoting Leviticus (Lev. 21:5) about God prohibiting priests from cutting off their hair. Although her biblical references are somewhat skewed, the thrust of her argument remains: "Hair is a sign of liberty." In direct address to "perfidious men," she challenges, "Why would you want to take away the sign of liberty from those [women] who are as free as you are?"[176] Tarabotti is not alone in depicting the profound emotional impact of this sacrificial ritual: As late as the eighteenth century, the French novice Mademoiselle de Rastignac "shuddered at the moment when the mistress of novices put the scissors to her hair," which was long, blond, and flowing. In this case, the nun's hair was put on a silver platter, emblematic of offering up her sacrificial locks—the classic adornment of vanity and femininity—representing complete rejection of the body.[177]

Hair continued to be a point of contention even after the unwilling nuns were consecrated. The thousands of highborn daughters, now confined and marginalized in the thirty-plus convents of Venice, found ways to confound ecclesiastical overseers who mandated that nuns' hair be cut on a regular basis; and "locks on the temples, and curls on the head" were strictly forbidden, citing ringlets and curls as "inventions of the devil."[178] Authorities ruled that hair should be hidden under low-worn headbands and decried the curled locks leaking out of forbidden fashionable head coverings. Not even the exceptional action of Patriarch Querini, in 1525—years before Tridentine enclosure decrees—could set a cautionary example for the pampered patricians. Upon inspection of the Convent of Santa Maria della Celestia, the patriarch spotted a young noblewoman sporting long braids. In a furor, with his own hands, he chopped off her locks, forewarning the others to keep their hair short and hidden. Nonetheless, for more than a century following Patriarch Querini's outrage, and after Trent, we still continue to see archival evidence of unending invocations not only against a show of hair, but also against its length and color.

Revealing more and more of their tresses, secular Venetian women had tossed off the veil as early as the fifteenth century, shedding the medieval head covering in favor of detailed styles of intricately woven lace that spoke of their status and wealth. Hair was preferably blond, "Venetian blond," a warm golden hue—married women wearing piles of braids upon their heads, unmarried women displaying long, flowing, and golden manes maintained through systematic bleaching with natural dyes such as vinegar and lemon. In *La Storia di Venezia Nella Vita Privata*, Pompeo Molmenti describes how the ever-chic secular Venetian women would sit in the sun on the roofs of their houses, areas called *altane*, in the process of lightening their hair, which they had treated with a variety of colorants including saffron, white wine, and ammonia, their tresses swirling over the broad brim of straw hats (*solanas*) that had had the crown cut out.[179]

From archival records of patriarchal visits to Venice's female religious houses, we learn that many enclosed women bleached their hair, kept it prohibitively long, and imitated the fancy coiffures of their lay sisters. The nuns' provocative hairstyles provided fodder for Incogniti literati, prodding Francesco Busenello, for one, to take alarming note of the cloistered coiffures: "caveletti fuora alla francese con le cordelle de color de fuogo" (little French-style curls and bright red strands) peeking out from headbands. With the aid of powerful aristocratic families, resistant nuns ignored all threats and exhortations: no amount of preaching and beseeching deterred those women who would maintain their inherited lifestyles regardless of cloistered conditions. For them, it would seem that the defiant Arcangela Tarabotti had it right when she wrote that after losing one's freedom, what more can be taken away?[180]

Striking back at Francesco Buoninsegni's treatise on the extravagance of female attire, Tarabotti defends a woman's right to vanity and luxury, to adorning herself and showing her female beauty. Buoninsegni's *Contra l'lusso donnesco*, which he first read to an enthusiastic audience of both men and women (the text published in 1638) sardonically attacks, among other female embellishments, wigs and hair ornaments; he accuses females of using "ingegnosissima alchimia," referring to the hair dyes as "very clever alchemy."

Peering out from the grates of the *finestrine*, behind which the nuns looked on at activities in the *parlatorio* and talked with visitors, the enclosed women caught up on the latest gossip and observed their free counterparts' dress, style, and manner. Without vocation, forced to live the religious life, it is no wonder that the well-born inmates rebelled in the limited ways they could, and keeping their hair and styling it was one way they would hold on to a lost life.

Three years after taking her first vows, Arcangela professed at an age several years beyond the prescribed age to do so, suggesting, along with previous delays in her monastic process, that her relatively late arrival at each juncture indicates Elena's tenuous position. As Zanette points out, the delay in Tarabotti's walk to the altar does provide food for thought, especially in light of what the reluctant child would, in her mature years, have the spirit and talent to reveal.[181] Arcangela, in her own words, tells that "non sapevo che cosa importassero quelle parole"—confessing so many years after the fact that she had had no idea how important these words (vows) actually were.

Even though the first "dressing" vows were the most important for family, it was not until the novice pronounced her final vows that she would be completely monachanized, before which—in theory, much less in practice—novices could leave the convent. In fact, Arcangela's close friend Betta Polani, who had remained in Sant'Anna as a novice for many years, did leave the monastery, called back by her family to marry, practically the only way a girl could exit. Once on the path to holy marriage, it was difficult not to complete the journey; Polani, except for the fact that her uncle called her out of the convent, would have taken her final vows.[182]

Leaving the convent in any other way would involve a series of circumstances relatively impossible to create for the *malmonacate* (the badly monachanized): the girl would have to depend on the largesse of her family, the very family that had put her in the convent in the first place, to accept her back home—a process that would necessitate the return of her spiritual dowry by the convent, creating an unlikely situation. Furthermore, for a nubile daughter with no marriage prospects, living in her natal home was beyond the culturally accepted norms of the city. Another scenario would involve the nun having a protector or benefactor who would support the girl in his/her own home and back the withdrawal process. Protests and rebellions, on the other hand, took more insidious forms as many *malmonacate* suffered from *umor malinconico* (a depressed state), cited as a typical ailment of nuns.[183]

Economic concerns never far from the front, the nun at the time of her final vows had to sign a notarized document that legally excluded her from familial lines of inheritance, eliminating the possibly of receiving economic benefits from family patrimony. And it is this fact that Tarabotti brings to light when she reveals the stark change in the girl's family who have, up until her complete investiture, been visiting frequently, bringing gifts, and speaking lovingly—all of which, Tarabotti recounts, comes to a halt after the novice takes her final, and indelible, vows, an act accompanied by putting her signature on the legal release of claims to family patrimony. The financial bickering that takes place even before the girl is confirmed had remained a bitter memory for Suor Arcangela, and one that no doubt she had witnessed played out repeatedly as new young girls came into the convent: the abbess and the father would haggle over expenditures for the child's food and lodging, the father trying to pay the least for his daughter, the abbess looking to receive the most for each new nun.

Arcangela's tirade against depriving daughters of their free will extends to the victimization that drives these girls and women to rebel with scandalous behavior. She shows sympathy for them and their indiscretions, not necessarily condoning convent defiance, but condemning the powers that had created the situation that fostered ignominious behavior. Tarabotti observes that these nuns without calling not only suffer in the temporal life, but also risk salvation in the next, having given lip service only to their spiritual vows. She decries the process as a defamation of God's will and defends her wayward sisters by situating the blame not on the deceived innocents, but on those who betrayed and coerced them into a life—perhaps even an afterlife—of eternal enclosure.

Clarifying that she is referring to the majority of little girls forced by their parents to take the veil, Tarabotti acknowledges, and does so often, that those few, the children called by the Holy Spirit, are blessed in their vocation. But, specifically, it is the "tyranny of men" responsible for the condemnation of innocents devoid of religious vocation.

12

Nuns, Hebrews, Slavery, and Chains: Life in Confinement

But you, with violence, insults and threats, want to chain the bodies of these women who were born free; you condemn them forever…to where they cannot be released from until their death…in a living hell…[184]

For as much as Arcangela Tarabotti succeeded in defining the socioeconomic and political basis for the practice of forced monachization, she also shed light on inmates' internalization of confinement in what sociologists now refer to as the "total institution" and its effect upon the imprisoned. The seventeenth-century Venetian nun—hundreds of years before modern social scientists like Erving Goffman[185] would characterize the "underlife" of the institutional world—detailed the effects of a constricting societal structure on the self. Indeed, Goffman's definition of a total institution as "a place of residence and work where a large number of like-situated individuals, cut off from the wider society for an appreciable period of time, together lead an enclosed, formally administered round of life" encompasses such diverse structures as boarding schools and monasteries. The contention that confining institutions, whether they be prisons or convents, are more similar to each other than not is a recurring theme that Tarabotti captures when she compares the State of her convent sisters compelled into a religious life to that of forced imprisonment "by men who deceitfully coerce innocent girls into a lifetime within the four walls of the convent where they live in an eternal prison...locked up forever in these dungeons."[186]

Continuing the thread of losing one's liberty within a societal structure, Tarabotti compares compelled *clausura* to biblical slavery, referring to "the unhappy Hebrews...conquered and exiled from their homeland," claiming that this same punishment has been cast upon "the unhappy nuns...while we cry over the servitude in which we find ourselves and regret our lost freedom."[187] This loss of self, a process of mortification, today would be categorized as an ongoing series of abasements, degradations, and humiliations endured by the incarcerated individual.[188]

Referring to Dante to bolster her argument, Tarabotti begins by pointing out that even dumb animals, not to mention sentient human beings, value their freedom; she quotes from *Purgatorio*:

> Now may it please you to approve his coming in
> search of liberty that is so precious as he who gives
> his life for it knows...

Arcangela defines the unnatural condition to which the female child is subject, "Gli orsi, le tigri, le vipere, I basilischi, et ogni piu' cruda, velenosa, et indominata fiera alimenta, e teneramente aman e suoi concetti, non distinguendo da maschio a femina," pointing out that even "bears, tigers,...and every one of the most poisonous snakes...tenderly love their offspring without distinguishing between the male and female of the species."[189]

It is no wonder that Tarabotti, upon pronouncing her vows "with her mouth not her heart,"[190] would experience anger and rage, not only for a lifetime of enclosure, but also, and perhaps equally as important, for the sacred vows she had been compelled to take and the concomitant profound obligations inherent in the religious sacrament—indelible promises uttered but not heartfelt. Such blasphemous covenants forced upon the vocation-less induced internal strife and guilt, not to mention fear of purgatory and punishment.

Any little girl born into a patrician or upper-class Venetian family would know early on that one of two life choices was the convent.

She would have visited her aunts and female relatives in *clausura* and would have been inculcated, if she were the firstborn (usually selected for the monastery) or the daughter(s) targeted for enclosure, with the need to sacrifice herself for her family and State. Giovanna Paolini, one such professed nun, reveals, "Haveva 15 o 16 anni quando mi fece monaca…et venni monacha voluntariamente perche' avendo delle sorelle assai, mi pareva che fusse necessita' che io venissi," declaring that at fifteen or sixteen, she became a nun because she had many sisters and believed it was her duty to voluntarily take vows.[191]

Exacerbating the effects of deprivation of choice, forced isolation from family, and involuntary exile from life as known, parental quibbling over expenses was not an infrequent negotiation by well-to-do fathers. Tarabotti fumes over the enslavement of these girls:

> Rather than being clothed in religious garments, they are wrapped in chains…in this Stygian swamp of a monastery…in which they are condemned to subservience and submission to the will of others.[192]

One can imagine that she had overheard her own parents, certainly other parents of unwilling girls, bickering over the expenses for the condemned daughters:

> After they have treated her worse than a slave—they haggle over the spiritual dowry, trying to save on her clothing and musical lessons, mothers going along with these hard lines for fear of their husbands who want to save it all for the privileged child who will get married. For this daughter, only the finest will do including garments adorned with Belgian lace, hand stitched and embellished with the most prized damask linen from Flanders; just two of these dresses alone would equal the price of all of the outfits and furnishing for a nun.[193]

Referring to the "lucky sister," chosen for a terrestrial marriage, Arcangela writes,

Even her most intimate garments are also rich with embroidery and lavishly trimmed with gold ribbons that tie around her legs. Her splendid silky little stockings are worth a treasure. She will have lovely slippers and gloves, bows and ties for each.

For her dress, the most precious pearls from the orient are sent for to wear around her neck, and big, shiny diamonds in the shape of a flowering roses will be placed on her finger; carefully crafted gold will hang from her ears—there is no luxury, delight or extravagance too superfluous or too grand for the terrestrial bride.

Instead, the other girl, the one buried in the tomb of the convent, must cover her legs with rough cloth and she has to get used to wearing poorly lined wooden clogs on her feet. Around her neck, she has to wear a bib, so unflattering that all of her natural God-given gifts are hidden.[194]

In her vehement denunciation of fathers who sacrifice their daughters, Tarabotti cites the Bible as well as pagan philosophers to support her argument, pronouncing pagans better than "you, who profess to be Christians…worse than ancient tyrants, because they, the ancients, [they] were not Christians." [195]She charges "fathers" with "original depravity" guilty of "grievous mortal sins, having done violence to innocent girls by depriving them of their liberty, granted freely to them by God," condemning these fathers to eternal damnation, similar to the punishments for the worst tyrants of history.[196]

We see a humanist attention to the Bible as well as to paganism, Tarabotti praising the ancients who, in addition to teaching a simple, austere life, actually practiced it:

In contrast to you, fathers who preach piety, seclusion from the world and poverty as a pretext for sanctimonious seclusion and frugality—all to satisfy your own desires and interests—and under the guise of fairness and justness, you spend your lives living dishonestly like a Sardanapalo [weak, depraved ancient Assyrian ruler who died in an orgy], and want your own offspring to vow to God and make holy promises that they will fight against their natural instincts and sensibilities which are difficult to repress even for the chosen, St. Paul.[197]

Tarabotti cannot help but compare the ancient tribulations of the "figliuoli d'Israele" (the children of Israel) with the tyranny of fathers that "supera tanto piu' quella de gli Egitti" (goes way beyond that of the Egyptians), lamenting that even the Israelites had hope to be free of their misery, contrasted to the forced nuns who are without any hope, left to endure eternal pain.[198]

A regard for the ancient condition of the Jewish people threads through Tarabotti's work, especially as her literary life began to intersect with the Accademia degli Incogniti. In fact, Loredan himself, speaking to the senate in 1659, condemned the overcrowded situation of Jews forced into the Venetian Ghetto since 1516, expressing his troubled concern, "They are without correspondence, without strength, without help, spirit, heart and will." That the liberal literati of Seicento Venice did not hesitate to form friendships with the segregated and persecuted Jewish population reflects the open intellectual attitudes of many freethinkers. Angelico Aprosio (1607–1681), an apostate Augustinian monk, for example, openly befriended the Jewish poetess Sara Coppio Sullam.[199] In fact, the Incogniti pushed the envelope to the very borders of Catholicism with their intellectual inquiries, not only concerning Greek philosophy, immortality of the soul, and study of the Old Testament, but also establishing relations with Venetian rabbi scholars and reading cabalistic texts—going so far as to claim, "To be a good Catholic, it is necessary to be a good Jew."[200]

13

Post-Tridentine Times: Eternal Enclosure

I t could be said that the Council of Trent, a series of three major meetings composed of twenty-five sessions taking place during the period between 1545 and 1563, offered too little too late. By this time, the confessional map of Europe had been irrevocably altered—Roman Catholicism remaining in Spain, Portugal, France, Poland, and Italy, while a form of Protestantism reigned in Norway, Sweden, Finland, England, and most of the Holy Roman Empire.

Responding to the Protestant Reformation and prodding from Charles V (Holy Roman Emperor), Pope Paul III, the Holy See from 1534 to 1590, appointed a commission to examine doctrine and reform, the selling of indulgences and clerical corruption high on the agenda. It was the unlikely, then tiny, city of Trent, now a part of Italy, in the Adige River valley, where the Council met, the Tyrolian city then under jurisdiction of Charles V. What took place in Trent had had its roots implanted centuries before, culminating with the catalytic event in 1517 when the Wittenberg professor Martin Luther nailed his theses to the Wittenberg Castle Church door—precipitating a thunderous upheaval that not even the soul-searching Augustinian monk could have foreseen.[201]

By 1563, as the Council came to a close, the rift between Catholics and Protestants on matters of doctrine had deepened irrevocably. Even after Tridentine reforms, Paolo Sarpi, Venetian statesman and historian, would observe that nepotism, a practice that Venetians claimed to abhor, was alive and well. The canon lawyer goes on to note that Pope Paul V "expects to enrich his family, and this is the main point of his administration." He cites annates as a form of covert simony and decries appointments to the Sacred College motivated by economic interests, declaring, "The things that have occurred have rather caused dissolution than reformation," referring to the proceedings of the Council of Trent.[202]

While the Council did mark a public awakening from a "dogmatic slumber," it also threatened the core of the Venetian Republic, its young patricians maintaining the State as the one proper vicar of God and his supreme agent. Of the internal reforms, the very last ones of the third and final stage (1562–3), in its twenty-fifth and last session, concerned convents—a touchy topic that had been the crux of serious criticism, satire, and derision for centuries. Oddly enough, it was this very last matter on which both Rome and Venice could somewhat concur: Venice had, on its own volition (for political, social, and economic interests) attempted to control its female religious houses decades prior to Tridentine mandates. At least thirty years before the great Catholic reforming council set out to revise doctrine and regulate monasteries, Venetian authorities had initiated their own reforms.

Nuns had been in the lagoon city since the seventh century, the first convent, San Giovanni Evangelista, having been founded on the island of Torcello by the Benedictine order. From the onset, these female communities were riddled with conflict: while they were places of prayer and purity, housing chaste cherubs of Venice, they were also enclosed female enclaves marked by a lack of discipline that fostered vice and scandal that not only blackened the reputation of the Most Serene Republic, but also put the city in jeopardy of salvation. After Venice's crushing military defeat at Agnadello in 1509, the city's nunneries, referred to as "bordellos"—its inhabitants as "whoring nuns"—were blamed for the ruin of the Republic by Girolamo Priuli, doge from 1559 until 1567, who, along with his contemporaries, regarded convent reforms as essential to the survival of the State.[203]

Doge Priuli was not the only one, nor was he the first or last, to metaphorically conflate the nunnery to a brothel, nuns to whores. Among notable contemporary writers, Pietro Aretino (1492–1556) stands out as the author of salacious, pornographic texts, one of which, *Sei giornate, Ragionamento and Dialogo*, suggests that the three paths in life open to women are those of nun, whore, or wife. With wit and blatantly coarse, irreverent dialogue, Aretino's racy humor and colorful narrative expose the perceptions of convents and nuns, as Nanna relates her experience—a graphic account of how this innocent child, the cast-off young novice, romps through sexual encounters that Aretino describes in full pornographic style.[204] Understandably, the work is not a documentary—nor was it meant to be—of conventual life, and taking either Boccaccio or Aretino at their word would miss the point. But the tales and dialogues of *The Decameron* of the fourteenth century and *Sei giornate* of the sixteenth have roots in the reality of convents of every major city on the Italian Peninsula, convents full of women and girls locked up for life; in the reality of natural postpubescents' sexual desires; and in the reality of church officials, protesting and pouting, able to do little to preserve the chastity or discipline of unwilling religious.

The nunnery situation drove the Venetian Senate as early as 1509 to pass laws concerning female religious houses. Authorities ruled that anyone entering the sacred boundaries of the convent must have a license to do so; anyone assisting a nun to leave the convent would be punished by imprisonment or exile. Not only the senate, but also the patriarch, now mandated strict reforms attempting to regulate notoriously undisciplined convents—Le Vergine, La Celestia, and San Zaccaria, noted for their aristocratic occupants and scandalous behavior the targets of these decrees. In 1521, the *provveditori sopra monasteri* was formed to oversee Venetian convents, its prime and most obvious concern, the ignominious infractions allowing the virgins access to the outside world—a transgression responsible for behavior ranging from innocent conversation to sexual contact between nuns and their worldly counterparts. By and large, Tridentine convent reforms fit the needs of the Venetian

Republic that had long been concerned with the State of their female religious houses.

Before Elena Cassandra Tarabotti entered Sant'Anna Convent, compliance to mandates and strict reforms had been set in place, with dedicated oversight that would regularize convents and manage discipline within their walls. Although meeting intransigence from nuns and convent superiors, change, however, was the order of the day: from the mid-sixteenth century, significant and far-reaching modifications concerning convents and the lives of those within them were mandated by the reforms of the Council of Trent to keep the nun inside, the world outside.

Documentation of centuries of patriarchal visits to Venetian convents testifies to the ongoing problem of convent control and the sedulous attempt to curb noncompliance. Several years before Tarabotti entered Sant'Anna, Patriarch Vendramin on November 18, 1609, visited the modest convent on a routine inspection, records of which show a litany of infractions concerning permeable points of contact between the brides of Christ and the outside world. For instance, the patriarch noted that the convent's confessor prepared for mass in the sacristy—quarters that nuns could access—driving Vendramin to mandate that the priest relocate and only one key be made available. Male access to convents was a necessity: not only confessors and priests required entry, but also doctors, delivery personnel, and a variety of workmen needed to enter the enclosure. Even when supplies came in through the *ruota*, a kind of lazy-Susan turntable acting as the conveyance through which objects could pass in and out of the convent, nuns would take the opportunity to converse with the supplier (male or female) on the other side of the small space.[205] Vendramin ordered the *ruota* to be walled in, and the tiny grated windows only used for the purpose of confessing by priest and nun. Additionally, two different locksmiths must prepare the entry keys to convent doors.

In line with the usual conventual structure, Sant'Anna had two visiting rooms, *parlatorios*. In the smaller of the two rooms, the nun superiors could conduct business concerning the daily maintenance of a house full of one hundred or so women. When necessary, this room also furnished as the meeting place for public officials and convent superiors. The larger *parlatorio* provided the space where visiting laypersons, after having obtained special permission from the *Provveditori sopra Monasteri*, could converse at specified hours with the enclosed nuns through the *finestrine*.

Even these small windows, under the patriarch's renovations, would be secured with *trombe* (curved iron bars) and then closed with wooden shutters (*gelosie*) fastened with screws that could not be removed.[206] Especially convent windows, obvious points of penetration, were to be placed high enough so that neither the nuns nor laypersons could see one another—a requirement that mewed up the inhabitants, ensuring that every view to the outside be shored up. Constantly attempting to prevent worldly contamination, authorities ordered the nuns' cells available for spot inspections by the abbess at any time, all door locks removed. What the nuns often kept in their quarters would consistently reap the outrage of patriarchs.

Chickens, for example, kept in convents did not surprise anybody, given that the one hundred or so inhabitants of each house would require hundreds of eggs per week. What did alarm Patriarch Vendramin on one of his unannounced visits to Sant'Andrea Convent were the chickens found in the nuns' cells, kept as personal property. Circumventing mandates against keeping "either bitches or dogs" as pets, nuns, it seems, took to chickens, prompting decrees against keeping "birds, doves, hens and other poultry" as private property.[207]

Physical entrance into the convent vied with intellectual infiltration as major concerns, the latter dealt with by restricting reading matter to approved religious manuscripts only. All other documents were to be confiscated and the nuns having such material to be punished, usually by losing *parlatorio* privileges.[208] In 1596, upon his inspection of Sant'Andrea Convent, Patriarch Priuli ordered that "books, clothes, writings, unseemly paintings, dogs, birds, nor other animals be taken out of nuns' cells.[209] During Arcangela's confinement in Sant'Anna Convent, eighty-nine recorded incidents provide documentation for transgressions taking place in Venice's female religious houses—a number that is probably the tip of the iceberg.[210]

Nuns balked and disobeyed in a tension-fraught atmosphere that had patricians, fathers of the enclosed girls, giving a silent nod to infractions while upholding the tradition and need for enclosure. Nuns' pertinacity in preserving their way of living persisted to present significant roadblocks to reform, hurdles that delimited enforcement. One hundred years after the specific reforms regarding convents, the bishop of Mantua in 1661 acknowledged that "*suore* are women and women who very unwillingly see themselves retained."[211]

14

A Liminal Space: The Parlatorio

*D*espite Tridentine *clausura* reforms a half century before Tarabotti was born, convent walls were breached from within and without. Nuns, now living in monastic structures with smaller windows shielded by thickly spaced iron bars, doors with exterior locks only, and heightened peripheral walls, fiercely resisted ecclesiastical attempts to limit their interaction with a world from which most were involuntary separated. Defying mandates wrought to ensure total disjunction, the patrician and upper-class inhabitants of Venetian convents continued to intermingle, albeit from behind the grille, with visitors coming into the *parlatorio*, the reception room of the convent, a liminal space providing the cloistered women with a nexus between enclosure and the outside world.

Nuns regularly exchanged letters and gifts and visited with friends and family coming into the *parlatorio*. From behind the *fine-strine* bars separating this social juncture from other parts of the convent, the nuns would observe events taking place in the large meeting hall and speak with visitors who often introduced the enclosed women to friends and acquaintances. Arcangela Tarabotti, for one, would exchange books, discuss drafts of her works, listen to gossip, and receive visits from prominent figures of the day, creating a sort of salon within the *parlatorio*.

Convents became centers of civic life, the *parlatorio* frequently the scene of marriage negotiations and contract signing. Traditionally, after nuptials, the bridal party would pay a visit to the convent, sharing the event with cloistered female relatives in an atmosphere of festivity, visitors unheeding prescribed hours reserved for such occasions. By mid-Seicento, authorities had prohibited men from frequenting the *parlatorio* on weekday afternoons, and not at all on holidays. Nonetheless, the magistrates continued to cite infractions in many female monasteries as men defied orders and visited, especially on weekends and holidays, during the times reserved only for women. They would gather at the doors of the *parlatorio*, in the convent courtyard.[212]

All visits should be only by close family relations possessing official permits from the Provveditori, permits that they seldom obtained. Prohibitions from magistrates were no obstacle: with established connections to convent magistrates in charge of prosecuting such breaches, women religious were able to maintain social contacts; they would not be cut off from the world. Housing the better part of Venice's female patriciate, the convent was tightly woven into the political and economic fabric of Venice. Nowhere was gossip and catching up with current events more diffuse than within the public space of the *parlatorio*, where it was the fashion for the highbred and well-heeled to gather, to see and be seen. This nexus between the forced sisters and their world left behind survived for centuries, the nuns resisting prohibitions. Despite authorities' attempts to curb visits, entertainment, festivities of dance and music not necessarily sacred and devout, the *parlatorio* was to remain an attraction for the enclosed as well as for the public. Painters of the next century depicted the elegant *parlatorio* gatherings, the most famous, Francesco Guardi's *Parlatorio di San Zaccaria*, painted in mid-Settecento, depicting the Venetian convent's prime position in the city's cultural map, its elite nuns tied to powerful families including those of the doge himself.

The nuns frequently made use of interlocutors—go-betweens to deliver messages and provide them with the latest gossip and news and to maintain a network of friends and acquaintances. Authorities attempted to stem this practice, investigating the nuns' finances, since they had to pay the intermediaries for this service. From behind the grates, blue-blooded women would meet with their tailors, ordering prohibited clothing in popular designs "alla francese." Abbesses and prioresses defied explicit prohibitions and admonitions for excess expenditure on flour and wheat for pastry baking, convents persisting in offering sweets, food, and drinks in the *parlatorio*. As well, nuns would exchange gifts, perhaps their handiwork and pastries exchanged for special foods, establishing and maintaining contacts beyond the enclosure. The girls and women, most of whom came by force without religious calling, in a desire to partake and mimic the normalcy of lay life, found that in recreating former lifestyles, enclosure seemed less restrictive.

The beauty and elegance of the city's young patrician nuns encased in the elite convents did not escape the eyes of the Early Modern world: Pietro Casola, a fifteenth-century Milanese ecclesiastic, arriving in Venice to embark for Jerusalem, visited several convents, because, as he notes, "they are widely famous." About his visit to San Zacharia, he writes, "There are many women there, young and old, and very eager to be seen." On his visit to the prestigious Convent of the Virgine, he writes, "They say they are very rich and not shy about being looked at."[213]

Although the intermediate zone of the *parlatorio* was strictly for close relatives of the nuns, this space, along with two other structural features of the convent—the gate and the church—comprised physical symbols of the borders separating two worlds, the sacred and the profane. Tridentine mandates allowed for not more than two gates, carefully controlled to ensure that deliveries into and products leaving the convent did not create social interaction opportunities. The *parlatorio* and the gate both came under strict control after Trent to monitor outsiders' access. But it was particularly the *parlatorio* that became a site of anxiety and alarm, since it is here that the nuns could speak to outsiders, albeit from barred *finestrine*, and overseen by chaperones.

As the nuns' families and friends gathered in this convent *salotto* or reception parlor, the cloistered girl was not at all sheltered from the fashion and luxury of seventeenth-century Venice. The enclosed girls and women would receive visitors: elegant ladies and fine gentlemen; they partook in the festivities of bridal parties, concerts, dance recitals, all a part of *parlatorio* events connecting the nuns to the outside world.

15

High Style in Holy Places: The Sociosemiotic Language of Venetian Nuns

T aking vows, the young girl leaves behind her former name and sheds her secular clothing, rejecting a previous life and denying the body, as she leaves her baptismal name and temporal attire outside convent walls. However, Venice's hidden daughters, doubly marginalized, housed in convents throughout the city—girls and women, most of whom came by force—strove to partake in the lives left behind. Maintaining and mimicking former lifestyles, they might also gain a modicum of control over their circumscribed lives. In response to the unnatural conditions of enforced enclosure and mandated restrictions concerning mundane aspects of their daily routine, the young novice's self-worth and personal value, undermined by subservience and subjugation, seethed at the surface.

Arcangela tells of the *gravissimi scandali* (serious scandals) emanating from the restlessness and anxieties of the involuntarily imprisoned.[214] She clearly understood that for a professed nun, the obligation was to believe in the Santa Romana, the Catholic Church, as she had solemnly sworn to do. But with candor and perhaps not lacking a sense of guilt, Tarabotti reveals doubts that "agitar l'intelletto in speculazione," referring to the internal tension of the vocation-less professants, their mental anguish resulting from the tension between a duty to obey sacred vows that battles with a desire to exercise free will. It is no surprise then that many of these forced inmates develop "secondary adjustments" as they forge habitual unauthorized arrangements in their social establishment.[215]

In fact, many nuns resisted in the few ways they could. They recreated within their confines a continuity of the culture and societal norms that existed without. Among the limited ways patrician women, now morphed into nuns, could speak out and shape their social persona was through their clothing. The language of fashion becomes a powerful metaphor to emphasize the symbolic/semiotic strength of dress, particularly forceful in the study of women deprived of a means to project individual identity, social status, and connection to a world from which they were plucked prematurely.

Thus, for many women religious of Venice, the luxury of fine clothing and extravagant accessories brought with it personal power and control, an imitative declaration of participation in Venetian life and a pronouncement of social status within their confines. If fashion is driven by the dualistic forces of distinction and imitation, a theory put forth by Geog Simmel,[216] the case of enclosed nuns illustrates this notion in their desire to dress as chicly as their lay counterparts—the Venetian upper-class women who were considered the most elegant women of their time, trendsetters of the day.

Although Massimo Baldini, in his *Semiotica della moda*, insists the language of attire is not always articulate and could be misunderstood,[217] I would argue that there was little room for misinterpretation in seventeenth-century Venice, all speaking the same sartorial dialect, a sort of folk taxonomy of symbols. Clearly, color, fabric, and style of dress announced the wearer's station in society and enunciated vocation and marital status.

And in Renaissance-Baroque Venice where we see perhaps the most bombastic and articulate language of dress in all of Europe, women, in particular, with limited possibilities to participate in cultural or political spheres, found social expression through attire. In fact, a Milanese cleric visiting Venice in the seventeenth century would remark that Venetian women, "those who are able as well as those who are not, dress very sumptuously."[218] Indeed, women from the poorer, middle, and upper classes participated in an outward display of self: with cloth constantly recycled and reused, even the less affluent woman could keep up with new styles; she could dress to the hilt by trading or renting clothes from dealers, mostly other women entrepreneurs in the trade business.

Through dress, a woman could enunciate the wealth of her husband, the status of her family, and her own standing in the world around her. This language was so potent a social tool that regulations were enacted during this period as never before. Although sumptuary laws go back to antiquity, sixteenth-century Venice saw a flurry of new statutes attempting to regulate, especially, female dress. Justification of this legislation ranges from a desire to prevent political upheaval and maintain social stability to economic considerations and trade protection.

Prohibitions such as those against using gold and silver cloth for garments could not, however, deter fashion-forward Venetian women who circumvented the statute by, for example, inventing the slashed sleeve to show exquisite gold or silver lining lurking beneath the dress cloth. Determined fashionistas would not be deprived of their elegance. When the slashed sleeve was legislated against, the gold or silver cloth began to peek out from the cuffs in much the same way that noblewomen peered out from their window perches. The patrician women of Venice were indeed a sheltered species, appearing in public on their way to and from church or in gondolas with their husbands at dusk. "Gentlemen do even coop up their wives always within the walls of their houses... So that you shall very seldom see a Venetian gentleman's wife," remarks the English visitor Thomas Coryat in 1609, describing La Serenissima, awash with riches and smug in its splendor.[219]

Copious records of patriarchal visits to Venetian convents over a period of hundreds of years document the doges' and patriarchs' strict monitoring of female religious houses. Records of admonitions, rules, decrees, and injunctions issued by ecclesiastics to keep nuns in line—and constant upbraiding, pleading, mandating—seemed only to foster nuns' microrebellions of immoderate display.

Beginning with their most intimate attire, uncompliant nuns initiated the flouting of strict prohibitions by slipping into embroidered, lace-trimmed silk camisoles instead of regulation woolen undergarments, marking a personal revolt and assertion of agency and womanhood. Even the corset, mandatory under the elaborate dress of secular women, saw its way into monastic houses and onto the bodies of professed nuns.

Along with fancy undergarments came a remarkably revealing décolleté for which Venetian women, from patricians to prostitutes, were renowned. Fashion-forward nuns, eager to keep up with secular style, adorned themselves in prohibitively low-necked dresses, almost falling off their shoulders, a mode that can be traced from the fifteenth century and lasting well into the seventeenth century. Such scandalous and sacrilegious show of skin prompted Patriarch Priuli, in 1592, after his checkup visit to the Augustinian convent of Sant'Andrea de la Zirada, to rule "that neither the breast nor any other body part should be exposed."[220]

Also finding their way through convent gates were dresses of the richest fabrics—shot silks (iridescent); velvets; gold cloth; damasks; brocades in opulent colors of vibrant green, coral red, and regal black; and the extraordinary Venetian brocatelle with red, yellow, and silver wefts.[221] In the archived inventories of nuns' belongings, we find listed items such as fur muffs of zibeline, ermine, marten and fox, ermine-lined coats, and purses trimmed in gold. Patriarch Vendramin, in 1619, was outraged at the "maneghetti di seta sottile" (refined silk sleeves), "calze a gucchia" (embroidered stockings), and "scarpe alla romana con cordelle/fettucce di seta e cose simili" (Roman-style shoes with ties of silk and other such things). The patriarch also found nuns sporting gold filigree chains, knotted at the throat; silver and gold broaches; and necklaces of pearls.[222]

Coerced religious, even in the enclosed courtyards of convents, continued in their deeply entrenched habits of luxurious dress. No amount of intimidation, including excommunication, could control what a large sector of nuns would wear and how they would live within their constricted circumstances. The continual prohibitions over decades, lasting for centuries, attest to the will of the women and lax enforcement of authorities who were well aware of forced monachization, deemed a social and political necessity for the stability of the Republic of Venice. Who of the doges, Council of Ten, elite patricians did not have a daughter, niece, aunt, or sister within the walls of these prestigious female houses?

Although doges and patriarchs worried and fretted, mandated and threatened, the sartorial sins of nuns went largely unpunished. Even when punishment such as confinement to one's cell was initiated, the well-connected women's influential and powerful families would intervene on their behalf.

One of the most extraordinary visions of haute couture in holy places must have been the sight of sumptuously dressed women religious clopping around on their chopines, also called chapineys, and in Italian *zoccoli*. This footwear, an extreme version of the wooden clog, often "three fists high," as English traveler Coryat[223] noted, had been a shoe fashion favorite in Italy dating back to the fourteenth century, falling out of fashion in most Italian cities by the seventeenth century; however, in Seicento Venice, these high wooden platform shoes were still must-haves for ever-elegant rich women who reached new heights, actual and metaphorical, towering over their servants whose heads they held for support as they promenaded to church and home again.

The higher the shoe, the longer the dress, the more flowing fabric, the more pearl and gold trim—the more precision a tool for a woman's self-promotion. Reaching heights of several feet, *zoccoli*, as symbolic representation, and the special prerogative of nobility, spoke superiority, prestige, and wealth of the many silenced women. Coryat remarked that "I have heard that this is observed amongst them that by how nobler a woman is, by so higher are her Chapineys."[224] In a more biting, sardonic vein, Francesco Buoninsegni, in his harangue against women's attire, *Contro'l lusso donnesco satira menippea*,[225] sees fit to vilify the *pianelle* (platform shoes) of Venetian women as he lambastes female fashion, a popular motif of the ongoing *querelle des femmes*.[226]

With his Neoplatonic positions idealizing women as the chaste targets of male spiritual love, Buoninsegni, as well as his Incogniti cohorts, delighted in a tongue-in-cheek misogynistic display of literary skill, rendering absurd female fashion, and by implication the ridiculous nature of women. Yet it was Loredan and his Accademia that commissioned Tarabotti's reply to the Sienese satirist. In *Antisatira*,[227] Arcangela comments that although men are scandalized by the *zoccoli* their wives wear, they themselves walk on tippy-toes just to seem taller (referring to the heeled footwear in fashion for men at the time) as she defends women's prerogative to dress as they will. In like manner, the unlucky noble daughters, involuntarily in *clausura*, boldly articulated their station in the microcosmic societal sphere of the convent, mounting themselves on the height of foot fashion. Inside post-Tridentine fortified walls, as well as outside, highborn women defied ecclesiastical tirades and sumptuary mandates, oftentimes risking wobbling right off their *zoccoli*.[228]

In the novice nun's conventual trousseau, the brides of Christ stored collections of gold and silver jewelry, bejeweled ornaments, and lavish accessories like silk shawls. The patrician nun also brought with her diamonds and pearls, rings, gold enamel, and silver earrings. Time and again, patriarchs issued more and more specific prohibitions against tonsorial transgressions. Upon a spot check of San Zacharia, Patriarch Vendramin, in 1619, witnessed nuns in fishnet stockings, a sight that resulted in a specific order against wearing such hose. On another visit, he observed the nuns sporting fancy shoes with silk laces tied up their legs—"scarpe all Romana con cordelle di seta e cose simili." This infraction caused the patriarch to issue a prohibition specifically against "shoes of the Roman kind with silk strings."[229]

Especially dress sleeves were of ecclesiastical concern: intricate detailed sleeves could be detached from the body of a dress, allowing for fabulously innovative combinations of dresses and sleeves. Some of the nuns' most prized possessions were their lace, silk, brocade, gilded, and jeweled sleeves that prompted the patriarchs to rule against "the use of sleeves of the fine fabrics."[230] As ecclesiastic convent inspections continued to reveal an ever-growing catalogue of infringements, the expanding list of injunctions grew more and more specific. Finding that nuns liked to wear their silver and gold broaches, patriarchs ruled against wearing this type of jewel. Seeing the accessorized women with ears enhanced by diamonds and rubies, patriarchs issued decrees prohibiting nuns from wearing earrings. Forbidden as well were all other embellishments such as pearls and enameled jewelry.

Venetian nuns, most of whom had no religious calling, appropriated by their families while still children to cloistered institutions, straddled two worlds, two identities, juggling monastic seclusion with public interaction, maintaining autonomy through the cracks in a far-from-rock-solid environment. Living life on the margins of a society and city that should have offered them more, rebellious nuns managed to maintain the semblance of their inherited lifestyle beginning with the very garments—of their choice—that they would put on their bodies; with the embellishments of beauty that announced their birthright, and the show of luxury and modernity that refuted seclusion and separation, they aligned themselves with their secular sisters to defy patriarchal mandates forged to deprive selfhood and autonomy.

As the hierarchal dynamics of secular Venetian society penetrated convent walls, characterizing the conventual system, so did the ramifications of the *querelle des femmes*, which reveal the general, growing anxiety about what is a woman and what is her relationship to society, fostering heated literary and intellectual discussions inspiring debates that positioned protofeminists as well as overt misogynists to rail against such things as the "vulgar display" of feminine fashion excess.

Laura Cereta, female humanist of the late fifteenth century, expressed her distain for elaborate female dress: "Empty women, who strive for no good but exist to adorn themselves…women of majestic pride, fantastic coiffures, outlandish ornament, and necks bound with gold or pearls,"[231] her words underscoring the ongoing tension concerning what a woman wears. Francesco Buoninsegni in typical misogynist writing of the time derides female fashion excess and the "vacuous women who waste money on consuming the luxuries of attire." In defense of female choice, Arcangela Tarabotti, from behind convent walls, contends, "Il lusso e' morale" (Female luxury is moral).[232] That female luxury *is* moral, an argument she poses in *Antisatira*, takes on a wider scope as Tarabotti expands the discourse in her emphatic response to Buoninsegni, which becomes a social critique defending women against the tyranny of men. She regenerates the polemic of fashion and dress into a strong defense, not only of a woman's right to dress as she wishes, the more embellished the better, but also the right women have to an education, to social and intellectual inclusion.

That a Benedictine nun could take up her pen, not to write devotional poetry or pious treatises, but to defend the freedom of nuns and their secular sisters, displays astounding courage and fortitude. Tarabotti justifies a woman's right to excess, adornment and luxury, as she assails the hypocrisy of those who would deprive females of the very same vanities that they, men, themselves display. Her arguments are twofold, the first of which focuses on just this hypocrisy. The second goes to the heart of the debate as Tarabotti aims at the crux of the controversy: men denigrate women's fine clothing and jewels for no other reason than their own (men's) avarice. She presents the argument of hypocrisy, noting that men are "perfumed and powdered in the French style,"[233] the likes of which are extremely costly, rising to amounts that could easily "support someone for six months."[234] If men can adorn themselves, why can't women? The question penetrates the core of the feminist polemic and ongoing *querelle des femmes*, Tarabotti going so far as to challenge Buoninsegni as she writes against "il lusso degli uomini" (the excesses of men), pinpointing men's vanity about their beards and mustaches that they "treat with precious oils."[235] Indeed, upper-class Italian men, conscious of their social status, like their female counterparts, dressed in clothing of fine fabric, their doublets and breeches of exquisite design, reflecting the rising influence of French fashion on the continent that did not go unnoticed by the patricians of Venice.

Tarabotti aims her diatribe at the appropriate target, reprimanding men, who, after having studied the ways in which they can marry a well-dowered woman, now would have these same women, their wives, "dress as the virgin herself."[236] Hitting the mark, Tarabotti sums up Buoninsegni's acrimonious satire against female attire and pompous display as having one motive only: to diminish the status of women. In an era when the great Queen Elizabeth I had sat on the

English throne, defending herself as a woman, stating that although she was born "cloven not crested," she had the "heart and stomach" of a king, it is no surprise that a writer, decades after the Virgin Queen's death, would address the "female question." What is astonishing is that this author, not an erudite queen, nor even an educated noble—but a simple Benedictine nun enclosed in a modest Venetian convent—could have the *fegato* (the guts) to declare, "Women have the right and the duty to cultivate their own vanity."[237] The debate and obsession about female attire, from patricians to prostitutes, suggest that we are looking at more than outer garb.

Il Parlatorio: the visiting parlor of the convent

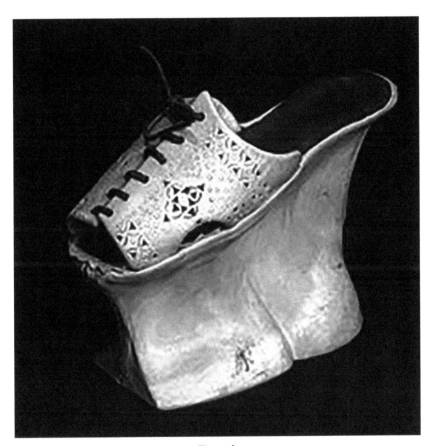

Zoccoli

PART 4

"I Have No Sword...": Arcangela's True Vocation

16

From Aristotle to Boccaccio: Wicked Women in the World

Conosco il mancamento delle femine ancor' io: siamo imperfette, conforme all' opinion d' Aristotele. (I am well-aware of the defects of our sex: we are "imperfect" according to the opinion of Aristotle.)[238]

*T*arabotti continues her reference to Aristotle with a tongue-in-cheek admission that "you perfect animals are superior to us in deceit, cunning and cruelty. It is crazy to praise oneself; but I cannot adhere to the opinion of those sublime scholars, whose enormous amount of false conceptions is an outrage against the female's innocence and goodness."[239]

Suor Arcangela makes reference to Aristotle's proclivity for superior/inferior dualities distinguishing between male, the superior, and female, the inferior—the former "associated with active, formative and perfected characteristics," the male form complete, while the female is created from "passive, material and deprived," wanting the male to become complete.[240] Underscoring the male semen as the generating cause with the female devoid of seminal fluid, contributing only nutrition in the form of menstrual blood to offspring, Aristotle bases his argument on the notion that nature aims to create the most perfect, complete form: the male, whose work to create other males should be accomplished by inseminating the female, and only when this process is stymied by lack of generative heat or adverse conditions is the imperfect female created.[241]

The Aristotelian view of woman as a mutilated, deprived, or incomplete male, essentially relegated the female into the "mistake" category, a theory somewhat assuaged by Saint Thomas Aquinas, the thirteenth-century theologian, asserting that God did not intend for the female to be a failure of nature, as both male and female are necessary for procreation. Acknowledging that the event that produces the female occurs through an incomplete process, Aquinas argues that the female herself is not incomplete per the plan of nature.[242]

As Greek theorists construed it, woman's biology informed her psychological characteristics, rendering her more soft, malleable, docile, as well as moody and duplicitous, desiring completion in the sexual act with a male. It was the womb where responsibility for woman's nature was firmly placed. Her "hysteria" ("womb" in Greek) defined woman as prone to chatter, deceit, irrationality, and lust—all concurring together at times to exhibit signs of hysteria or emotional instability.

Although Aristotle's teacher Plato had envisioned his *Republic* where distinctions involving male/female superiority-inferiority disappeared and women as well as men could be educated and lead, Plato's imagined Republic never did establish itself in the real world, the inferior states of women very much remaining the norm, forming the foundation of medieval thinking.

Roman law that reiterated much of Greek philosophy concerning women molded medieval culture: *infirmitas sexus*, the notion of women's weakness of mind and body, justified Roman statutes prohibiting women from holding office or functioning as *paterfamilias*, even excluding them from having the right of guardianship of their own children. The concept of *tutela* or guardianship extended to a protective control over women as the weaker sex, with terms such as *fragilitas sexus* and *imbecillitas sexus* defining women's fragility, feebleness, and helplessness—placing, for example, testimony of a man over that of a woman.[243] A woman's need of protection certainly constituted a viable argument; yet other factors, particularly pecuniary concerns of a patriarchal society, have also been put forth as rationale underlying laws diminishing women's responsibilities. Among those asserting substrata motives other than the protection of women is historian Suzanne Dixon who postulates that *tutela mulierum* protected the inheritance rights of males rather than safeguarded the "weaker" female.[244]

Since ultimate power was vested in the *paterfamilias,* his *patria potestas* lasting a lifetime regardless of the age or status of his offspring, women by default had limited autonomy: laws concerning inheritance as well as those referring to dowries and divorce affected female subordination to male authority. In the later republican and imperial periods, women acquired somewhat more freedom while significant disabilities remained. For example, Roman law acknowledged only agnate heirs; even though a mother could bequeath property to her children, she could not establish a successive female line of inheritance. Women could not hold public office, their presence significant only within household and family.[245]

It was the Codex Justinianus that would establish the basis for civil law in Western Europe. Later known as the Justinian Code, this compilation of Roman law and legal interpretations ordered by the Byzantine emperor Justinian I, reigning from 527 to 565, was received and revived as foundation of civil law, the new dawn of Roman law starting in Italy in the late Middle Ages with the teachings of Justinian's Code at the University of Bologna. The Code remained the bulwark of Italian civil law influencing such legal scholars as Prospero Farinacci, the sixteenth-century Roman lawyer, whose work *Praxis et Theorica Criminalis* would inform the legal proceedings of his time.

Farinacci maintained *infirmitas sexus* as the rationale for limiting women's responsibilities. His work, thirty-five years in the making, first published in 1589 included a defense of lighter sentencing for women, citing their diminished reasoning powers. Farinacci interpolates ancient laws with much of his argument becoming the fundamental blocks upon which the constructs of criminal and civil subjugation of women were based.[246] Along with French jurist and humanist André Tiraqueau, writing on family and marital law (*De legibus connubialibus* [1513]) justifying females' legal disabilities,[247]

Farinacci, influenced by the French *juriconsult* Tiraqueau, animated subsequent centuries of legal scholars.

Referring to ancient texts—the Bible; works of Aristotle, Homer, Plutarch; and the Church Fathers—Early Modern scholars participated in the *querelle des femmes* debate of the day, arguing that the claim for women's inferiority is firmly placed in the Bible.[248] The Bible as authoritarian support defending women's subordinate status and subsequent repression was a commonplace among scholars who relied on the void of actual text translation to sustain their arguments: post-Tridentine prohibitions severely limited Italians' access to the vernacular Bible. Historian Massimo Firpo's comment that use of the vernacular would erase language barriers "that safeguarded the clergy's exclusive dominion over religious matters" targets the apprehension of the Church.[249] In 1596, the Index of Prohibited Books banned all vernacular translations that had been previously available, albeit in limited and incomplete forms, from 1471. Also banned were writings that quoted from the Bible. This limited access to the Latin vulgate posed a problem for most Italians, unschooled in Latin, who would not have been able to read it.

Scripture has traditionally been cited to defend women's submissive and subservient role. Both the Hebrew Bible and the New Testament feature creation accounts, looking at Genesis 2 to interpret woman's relationship to man, Eve having been created from Adam and for him. Genesis 3, interpreted by Christian theologians, put responsibility for the Fall squarely on Eve's deceit, with further consequences that required Jesus to sacrifice for the "original sin." From Genesis 2:21, for example, scholastics interpolated a woman's lessened mental ability. From Genesis 3:16, after the Fall, woman was trebly cursed with the pain of producing offspring, constant sadness, and subjugation to her husband.[250]

The first complete Italian vernacular Bible, stamped in Venice in 1471 and translated by Nicolo' Malerbi, a Camaldoslese monk, obtained significant circulation. Antonio Brucioli, humanist scholar with Protestant sympathies, in 1532, published a version of the Bible translated from Hebrew and Greek texts, the first to be taken from these original sources. Although this translation enjoyed successful clandestine circulation among philo-Protestants, it was eventually banned on the list of Forbidden Books. The Church's long history, dating back to the first millennium,[251] of anxiety and tension about Bible translations came to the fore after Trent when "the mother of and origin of all heresies"—the Bible translated into the common tongue—was placed on the Index Librorum Prohibitorum by Pope Paul IV in 1559.[252]

Possession or reading of vernacular translations of the Bible (including Brucioli's)[253] warranted the penalty of excommunication.[254] In 1548, Brucioli's books were confiscated and burned, the author fined fifty ducats and exiled from the city for two years; he was again prosecuted in 1555 and imprisoned for three years for his heretical writings before the sentence was commuted.[255] Italians had no, or severely limited, access to the very text whose contents were cited as ancient, historical, authoritarian support for scholars' misogynist claims.

Commonplace medieval themes concerning women, although by the seventeenth century having come to a forum of discussion and debate, still, as we see, required voices loud and clear to redress anti-female literature. Arcangela's consistent argument, which not only defended female equality but also placed women on a higher rung, found in Giovanni Boccaccio's *De mulieribus claris* (*Famous Women*) support as well as controversy. The early humanist presented the first compilation in Western literature of biographies devoted entirely to women and in many ways forecast the coming era of more open discussion, presenting, for example, women with talent and intelligence able to participate in public life. Boccaccio, in his lives of one hundred and six women—mostly from Greek and Roman antiquity, but including Eve and several more contemporary such as Joanna, Queen of Naples—with one foot firmly planted in his medieval world, does present women such as Semiramis, Cleopatra, and Agrippina as powerful leaders.[256] Since Arcangela references Eve, Semiramis, Cleopatra, Lesbia, and Messalina, most likely, she had read Boccaccio's work, as Letizia Panizza surmises from the nun's references all found in *Famous Women*.[257]

Arcangela argues there is no use for men to remind us of supposedly "wicked" women, since every rule has its exceptions; and besides, these women have outstanding qualities as well, fully worthy of *lodi eterne* (eternal praise). She suggests that contemporary women be considered as models for women alive on earth: "Quante donne vivono, e viveranno sempre con glorioso vanto di virtudi eccellenti" (How many women there are and always will be who can boast of the most glorious virtues).[258]

Yet even by mid-Seicento in Venice, few women, virtuous or otherwise, were able to take advantage of the Renaissance humanists' focus on education that did not provide the same rebirth of learning for women as it did for men. Although girls and women of the upper classes began to receive instruction in the rudiments of reading and writing, and in some cases advanced tutoring in the humanities, the aim of this education was to make them better wives and mothers and to prepare aristocratic women for their marriages and/or potential reign. While educating a man became more geared to the service of his city and State rather than to the service of God, the woman's question became more pronounced, as females were not engaged in public activities.

During the period from about 1350 through circa 1650, some women of exceptional learning and scholarship rose to power within the framework of unsettled attitudes and existing laws. Noblewomen like Isabella d 'Este, "the first woman of the world" in her own time, could become patrons of the arts and rule: Isabella d'Este, Marchioness of Mantua, in absence of her husband, the Marquess of Mantua, Francesco Gonzaga, took his place while he was imprisoned. Even the misunderstood Lucrezia Borgia, illegitimate daughter of Pope Alexander VI who manipulated her as a pawn in hegemonic alliances, was a well-educated Renaissance woman, in her own right patron of the arts, confidante to such eminent scholars as Pietro Bembo.[259] Both women fulfilled their duties of reproduction, giving birth to presumed heirs while becoming patrons of artists, writers, and scholars.

Catherine de Medici ruled as regent for France's King Henri II's successors, adopting the emblem of Artemisia who honored her dead husband, Mausolus, just as Catherine did in exerting authority during the years between the death of her husband and the rule of her sons. In England, the void of male heirs allowed the English queens to inherit power, Queen Elizabeth on the English throne for almost half a century. Nonetheless, although the great English queen referred to herself as "prince" who possessed "the body of a woman but the heart of king," she knew her opposition, on one occasion acknowledging that if she were "crested, not cloven, my Lords, you had not treated me thus."

17

Women and Letters: A Feminine Space

We have all read the letters of Cornelia, the mother of the Gracchi; and are satisfied, that her sons were not so much nurtured in their mother's lap, as in the elegance and purity of her language.[260]

B y 1650, the year that Arcangela published her *Lettere famil-iari*, women had been writing letters for centuries about a vast array of topics. The epistolary genre, dating back to Cicero and Seneca, reenergized by Renaissance humanists,[261] presented an acceptable space in which women could write, a non-threatening "female" niche giving women a voice and affording them a literary outlet. Written in the vernacular, often without intermediary, letters would record financial transactions, certify marriage arrangements, provide accounts of household business, and propagate relationships.[262]

The very essence of the letter form, the multiplicity of the missive, whether formal or familiar, sets the genre apart from other modes: the letter is always in the present relative to past and future, much like spoken discourse, with its pronominal language—I/you—predicated upon the relationship between sender and addressee(s). Delivered by courier, coach, or rider until the nineteenth century, letters provided a means of private conversation between writer and recipient divided by distance, spawning a paradoxical *apon-paron* (absent-present) interface, a nexus of orality and writing. As literacy practice, the letter effectuates communication in its role as receptacle and transmitter of text, acquiring meaning as it is embedded within cultural contexts. Hence, considering the fundamental function of the genre, it comes as no surprise that letters are among the earliest writing formats, extant missives dating to 500 BCE.[263]

Cicero, the foremost Latin letter writer of antiquity, in the first century BCE addresses a missive to his friend Curio, in which he explains epistolary forms:

> You are aware that letters are of many kinds; but there is one kind which is undeniable, for the sake of which, indeed, the thing was invented, namely, to inform the absent of anything that is to the interest of the writer or recipient that they should know. You, however, certainly don't expect a letter of that kind from me. For of your domestic concerns you have members of your family both to write and to act as messengers. (Cicero, Fam. 2.4.1).[264]

He continues to talk of letters that are personal and funny, letters that are weighty and serious, noting the difference between public and private letters, referring to the style of his own missives as intimate and conversational, observing that the letter, in fact, replaces conversation when distance separates the interlocutors. His model for the familiar letter saw new light in Italy with Petrarch's rediscovery of Cicero's *Epistolae familiares* in the fourteenth century, a finding that would rehabilitate the literary genre of the epistle.

Beguiled by Latin literature, Petrarch, from early boyhood, dedicated himself to studying luminaries of Greek and Roman antiquity, revealing in his "Letter to Posterity" why he was so attracted to the ancients:

> Among the many subjects which interested me, I dwelt especially upon antiquity, for our own age has always repelled me, so that, had it not been for the love of those dear to me, I should have preferred to have been born in any other period than

our own. In order to forget my own time, I have constantly striven to place myself in spirit in other ages, and consequently I delighted in history; not that the conflicting statements did not offend me, but when in doubt I accepted what appeared to me most probable, or yielded to the authority of the writer.[265]

Petrarch's study, dedication, and continued infatuation with Cicero in particular were to have rebounding repercussions on Western civilization when in 1345 the Italian poet, scholar, and humanist uncovered Cicero's *Letters to Titus Pomponius Atticus* in the fifth-century Biblioteca Capitolare at Verona. Painstakingly, Petrarch copied the treasure trove of manuscripts using amanuenses, but often through scarcity of competent copyists, toiling in his own hand:

And yet I must confess that I did finally reach a point in my copying where I was overcome by weariness; not mental, for how unlikely that would be where Cicero was concerned, but the sort of fatigue that springs from excessive manual labour.[266]

Bemoaning his liminal state between what he termed "the dark ages" and a new era still to come, the great Italian scholar carefully crafted letters to the ancients such as Cicero, Virgil, and Seneca[267]—the letter form now a conveyor of information, personal thoughts, emotions, and motivations. Intended for a wider audience than an addressee, Petrarch's letters are self-fashioned in his imitation of classical writers; through the vehicle of the familiar letter, he was to provide the epistolary literary model that would endure for centuries.

In addition to humanists' revitalizing classical epistolary discourse, we also see in the fourteenth century, particularly in the peninsula's economically developing areas, Tuscan, Lombard, and Venetian merchants who found it a practical necessity to communicate information about finances, family, and general affairs through letters.[268] The *carteggio commune* and *carteggio da Melis*, the former, letters between the principals of companies, and the latter, commercial documents such as *lettere di cambio*, were both written in the vulgate rather than Latin. With the emerging acceptance of the vernacular, in great part thanks to the illustrious triad of Italian literature—Petrarch, Dante, and Boccaccio—writing became more accessible to those who were not schooled in Latin, the heretofore language of learning, authority, literature, church, and law.

In this period too, we find women emerging as letter writers, whether driven by necessity or bolstered by the fact that "letters do not blush,"[269] women, through this medium could speak, almost at will, defying cultural norms and mandates that for the most part relegated them to silence.[270] Finding a voice and a medium to communicate in the Tre-Quattrocento, women of the upper-middle and patrician classes would write in their own hand or possibly delegate these duties to better-skilled scribes, for even daughters of wealthy families usually received only the rudiments of reading skills and oftentimes not even the basics of writing instruction.[271] They often circumvented the obstacle—lacuna of learning—as did Caterina da Siena, author of one of the first women's letter collections,[272] dictating long, complex letters full of lively mysticism and politics to her *consorelle* or to the monk, Fra Raimondo.[273]

Autograph missives were not the only practiced form: letters could also be collaborative endeavors, the "writer" having his/her words penned by amanuenses, scribes working for those who could not write or could not write proficiently, dictating their texts to those with superior skills. It is estimated that one-fourth of all letters sent in the Renaissance were written by secretaries.[274] On occasion, women who were socially and economically so positioned could learn the basics as did the wife of the Florentine Francesco Datini—Margherita, as an adult, learned to write (taught by her notary friend, Lapo Mazzei) in order to communicate with her husband during his frequent business trips to Prato, necessity often the catalyst for women to pick up the pen.[275]

From Alessandra Strozzi to Isabella d'Este, many Early Modern women worked through their lives, corresponding with family and doing business through written communication that reveals, in the case of the former, a devoted mother's concern about her sons' position in life and their welfare. In the fifteenth century, in her own hand, apologizing for her limited skills, writing out of necessity to her sons doing business in Spain, the Low Countries, and Naples, Alessandra asks pardon for her handwriting and unrefined style: "Non guatare al mio bello scrivere: e s'io fussi presso a voi, non fare' queste letteracce; che direi a bocca e fatti mia, e voi e vostri"[276] (Don't look at my lovely writing, for if I were near you, I would not have to compose these badly written letters; I would tell you about myself, and you would tell me about yourselves in person). Nonetheless, Alessandra wrote to her sons from the time they were young men until her death in 1471, her missives spanning a quarter of a century, seventy-three of which survive representing a formidable collection of letters written by a fifteenth-century women.[277]

In the case of Isabella d'Este,[278] born in 1474, the future Marchioness of Mantua received an exemplary humanist education that enhanced her natural gifts and intellectual precocity. Becoming proficient in Latin and Greek, able to recite Virgil and Terence by heart, Isabella was an accomplished singer, musician, and dancer, not to mention trendsetter and fashion icon of her day. With extraordinary intellectual and political skills, she played an important role in Mantua, taking control of the military, keeping the city free from invaders during her husband's imprisonment in Venice. Not only a keen political administrator, Isabella was also a foremost collector of the era's finest artwork: housed in her *studiolo* were the masterpieces of the most noted artists of the Renaissance. We see in her letters[279] (182 extant, now located in the Mantuan State Archive) how this erudite woman skillfully exploited the epistolary form, going so far as to use the missive as instrument of political power play and artful self-presentation. Counseling Francesco della Rovere, Duke of Urbino, the marchioness advises him "to try everything possible to avoid open warfare. All terms to avert conflict should be weighed by you and such caution must be more praised than censured."[280] Politically savvy, Isabella writes that she will support him, no matter his decision, knowing that the duke was bent on war. In a letter to Leonardo da Vinci, the marchioness implores the great master to paint her portrait, an endeavor Leonardo was not to realize.

Hearing that you are settled in Florence, we have begun to hope that our cherished desire to obtain a work by your hand may be at length realized. When you were in this city, and drew our portrait in carbon, you promised us that you would some-day paint it in colors... We beg you to keep your promise by converting our portrait into another figure which would be still more acceptable to us.[281]

By the Quattrocento, the epistolary genre had become a pop-ular form of writing, especially for Italian women, whether it be the *lettera formale* (the formal letter) or the *epistula familiaris* (the infor-mal letter to friends and family). During roughly the same period that Alessandra Strozzi was keeping her sons close to her through let-ter writing, and Isabella d'Este, from Mantua, was ordering paintings from artists in distant cities, Laura Cereta (1469–1499) was penning her Latin missives, some more similar to moral epistles, often to fic-tional or veiled addressees, clearly using the letter format as conduit to publicly circulate her treatises, broadcast her literary persona, and defend herself against detractors. Cereta, a classically educated humanist, not only portrays her scholarly learning, but also pres-ents herself and her relationships to a wide readership. Mixing the mundane with the erudite, writing in Latin, emulating prominent contemporary humanists, Cereta demonstrates her literary dexterity, commenting on a broad array of contemporary topics. For example, she writes here of her intricate needlework, a typical feminine activ-ity, while clearly broadcasting her narrative talent:

With rough and trembling hands, I designed, orna-mented, and embroidered a tunic for the nursling baby Christ child, which was to be as precious as pearls. For trembling necklaces hung around his face with gleaming brilliance, from which hair like threads of silver flowed down, which were sur-rounded by violet rosebuds on a bed of verdant grass. And little scales of many colors stood stiff

with thread of gold, sewn under a knotty bough
twisted and tawny with thorns, and the seal one
adorned the curving orb. [282]

Cereta's missives attest to her literary skills and depth of thought
as she expounds her ideas about women's education and intellectual
aptitude, claiming that although she herself is talented and educated,
she should not be considered an anomaly, citing as Boccaccio does,
women of power, intellect, and ability. Interestingly, Cereta looks at
women as a group, employing humanist critique:

> I should think that the tongues should be cut to
> pieces and the hearts brutally lacerated of people
> whose minds are so wicked and whose envious rage
> is so incredible that they deny in their ignorant
> rantings the possibility that any woman might mas-
> ter the most elegant elements of Roman oratory.[283]

With fierce invective, Cereta goes on to lambaste those females
who disparage educated women, accusing them of jealousy, frustrated by their empty lives and thwarted desires to attain for themselves an education. This diatribe against women who would malign
other women showcases Cereta's cultivated style, directly imitating
Juvenal's sixth satire,[284] as she takes full advantage of the epistolary
space to publicize her treatise and self-worth in this acceptable female
forum. Writing about familial matters, her own personal relationships, and current humanist topoi such as the nature of greed, the
Islam menace, death and bereavement, her letter volume of eighty-
two missives, *Epistolae familiares*, although circulated and widely
read in Italy during the Early Modern era, was not published until
the seventeenth century.

Laura Cereta along with Isotta Nogarola[285] and Cassandra
Fedele,[286] also writing in the fifteenth century, exemplify learned
female intellects engaging in the popular epistolary form to comment on a variety of Renaissance motifs—scholarly women whose
letter books were published (Cereta and Nogarola) or widely circu-

lated (Fedele) paid the price, whether it be foregoing married life or discontinuing dedication to studies. Impediments created by the patriarchal society notwithstanding, Early Modern women writers who aspired to become a part of the res literati would have to weather not only de rigueur literary critique, but also public censure, social ostracization, and attacks on their credibility as authors of their own works.

By mid-Cinquecento, the familiar letter written in the vernacular had gained currency, writers recognizing the common language native to the population as the medium most suitable for a more intimate tone and more accessible to a wider range of readers.[287] In good part responsible for the ascension of the familiar letter's popularity in Italy was Pietro Aretino whose letters published in 1538[288] reinvigorated the popularity of the familiar letter, offering a fresh look at this centuries-old discourse form. Aretino's letters in Italian ensured a broad readership, including some women who could now enter the literary circle without classical humanist credentials.

As we saw in chapter 5, aided by the expansion of the printing industry, an ever-more-encompassing readership would now have access to affordable books, tomes that appealed to a diverse audience. Aretino, Venice's "secretary to the world," gained fame and notoriety as *il flagella dei principi* (the scourge of princes), for his stabbing condemnations, lighting the fuse of the powerhouse that is the public letter. In his missives, he acknowledges receiving gifts of money, revealing the reciprocity of patronage and underlying social corruption—not without overtones of blackmail. Hinting at broken promises, for example, Aretino writes, "Accenna alle promesse non mantenute, come per esempio una pensione di 600 scudi, promessa da Francesco I, la quale è difficile incassare" (Mentioning promises not kept, for example a pension of 600 scudi, promised by Francesco I, which is difficult to collect), referring to the pension promised him by Francis I, King of France. Aretino exposes and participates in a culture where corruption—everyone on the make and on the take—flourished, he himself often at the mercy of benefactors, not hesitating to overtly accept gifts for favors such as laudatory mention in his published pieces.[289] One of the few writers to make a living through printed publications, Aretino, in conversational style, unmasks the hypocrisy of his time: addressing his work to members of various social levels—from the emperor Carlo V to popes, to the queen of Poland and the duchess of Mantua, to students, courtesans and secretaries, merchants, soldiers, and prostitutes—Aretino liberates the letter, allowing it to go wherever, to whomever, the content often explosive.

On the heels of Aretino's publications, in 1544, Vittoria Colonna, who had published her highly acclaimed Petrarchan-style poetry, presented to her readers a collection of spiritual missives, *Litere*.[290] As a prolific letter writer, Colonna kept up relationships with notables of her day, not the least of whom was Michelangelo Buonarroti. Several decades later, in 1580, a published letter book would represent a deliberate and savvy use of the familiar letter format: Veronica Franco's *Lettere familiari a diversi*, a volume of fifty undated missives, situates the woman writer as creator of her own epistolary image: the reader views the writer through her varied relationships, thoughts, ideas, and emotions expressed in an ostensibly private format clearly in the public forum. This self-fashioning allowed Franco to circumvent traditional ecclesiastical and cultural obstacles preventing woman from teaching as she gives advice to both men and women, instructing and admonishing. Franco, the literary courtesan, through her familiar letters converses with the public, thereby blurring the binary relationship between writer and addressee, allowing the epistles to stand as literary creations.[291]

Writing in the next century, Arcangela Tarabotti made good use of the power of letters, publishing her missives when she had already become a well-known figure and vocal participant in the debate over women, a debate that elicited defense of women as well as condemnation in the form of misogynist writing. Tarabotti had come under attack after publication of her *Antisatira*, detractors overtly questioning her authorship. Defending her integrity with the publication of *Lettere familiari e di complimento* (*Letters Familiar and Formal*) (1650), she fires back, vehemently charging accusers, several of whom had once been her supporters, with patriarchal prejudices as she strives to put an end to the criticism: the letters represented a personal account and clear demonstration of her talent, bolstered by evidence of her involvement with eminent literary figures.

Tarabotti hardly throws caution and calculation to the wind in composing her missives, for, although we might think of letter writing as unartful, extemporaneous composition, this was not the case. On the contrary, the *sprezzatura*[292] that Castiglione praised (natural grace and spontaneity) was often achieved through mediated literary artifice. The writing, eventual collecting of the letters, and final publication of the volume were not merely the result of the author rummaging through copies of her cache, collecting papers, tying a string around them, and delivering them to the publisher. Rather, these works were often self-edited, the writer selecting which letters would see the light of day. We can assume Tarabotti, as other epistolarians, carefully chose missives to be included in the published volume, attention to consciously presenting herself to readers, considering carefully the public persona that would leave little doubt she unquestionably authored her published works. Arcangela vindicates herself appealing to readers through the letter book, defending herself while exposing her attackers—heretofore supporters—as hypocrites.

> Let them say what they like, let them prattle on, since, in a short time, the world will see in a volume of my letters, if it is true that gossip about my writing.[293]

We should note that post-Tridentine dictates in Counter-Reformation Venice strictly controlled the act of letter exchanges by nuns, limited only to close relatives and censored by the abbess or prioress. Nuns charged with guarding the doors were obliged to hand over to the abbess all incoming mail and to receive from the abbess all outgoing correspondence.[294] Testimony to porous walls and powerful friends, Tarabotti's connections to influential Venetian figures protected and permitted her to operate in defiance of current tight restrictions on convents. Arguably, it was Arcangela Tarabotti's ties to such luminaries as Giovan Francesco Loredan that held sway over the religious superiors who seemed to turn a blind eye as the literary nun proceeded to transgress the divide between public secular life and private cloistered life, scaling confining structures to encroach upon the outside world. Tarabotti distinguishes herself as a polemic nun, veering from the religious writings of her *consorelle*, when she publishes these nondevotional letters in her own lifetime. She defies *clausura* prohibitions against even writing a letter, an accomplishment that speaks to her persistence and courage, although she herself acknowledges, "Che ad ogni modo non resta che perdere a chi ha perduto la libertà"[295] (For in any case, there is nothing left to lose for one who has lost her liberty).

18

The Querelle des Femmes:
"The sleeping pen is awakened"[296]

The topic is irritating... A lot of ink has been spent on the quarrel over feminism.[297]

*W*riting in the twentieth century, Simone de Beauvoir begins her treatise *The Second Sex*, acknowledging the centuries-old debate about a woman's worth and her place in the world, a debate, it can be argued, that began as early as Eve, with the book of Genesis functioning as the principal source in Western civilization that defined the character and identity of women. As we have seen in chapter 16, early Christian theologians maintained that all women share in Eve's original sin and are therefore responsible for the subsequent loss of paradise and the fall of the human race—exegesis that has been argued in both directions. From Aristotle's writings on virtue ethics,[298] to modern feminist literature, we can say that the woman question—regardless of the amount of ink spent—has never ceased being fodder for polemic discourse.

When Arcangela Tarabotti takes pen in hand to begin her bold literary defense of women and blatant condemnation of the patriarchal culture that would deprive them of their free will, Italian female writers such as Isotta Nogarola, Laura Cereta, and Cassandra Fedele had already paved the path for learned women to write and publish.

As Italians like Boccaccio began to look at "exceptional women," the *querelle* often focused on the extraordinary achievements of atypical females who by their uncommon successes proved that women are capable of attaining power and reaching intellectual heights.

Indeed, a number of contemporary women did succeed in proving themselves exceptional. Typically, these Early Modern women were born into educated noble families who could afford to provide a sophisticated level of learning for their offspring. Hence, female participants in the *querelle* belonged to high-placed families who allotted to their daughters the instruction required to engage in intellectual discourse. One such daughter, Venetian-born Christine de Pizan (1364–1430), is credited with initiating the *querelle des femmes* in the public forum.

Transferred to France at an early age, Christine de Pizan was raised in the atmosphere of the French court where her father held office, summoned by Charles V to be his secretary and astrologer—a position akin to medical doctor. As a child, Christine was exposed to regal life and given an education equal to that of her male counterparts, scholarship that well prepared her to take up pen and engage in epistolary debates with eminent male authorities.

With her denunciation of *Roman de la Rose,* one of the most widely read contemporary works of the French language, written in sections during the late years of the thirteenth century, Pizan in 1401 became involved in the public debate—a heated epistolary exchange with formidable intellects of the day about the merits of *Roman de la Rose.* Pizan specifically targeted Jean de Meung's satirically vicious attack on women and, in Pizan's view, his immoral portrayal of love and romance. She declared the poem "an exhortation to vice" exemplified by the ending—the taking of the Rose by force.[299]

Widowed at twenty-five, Pizan supported her family through her publications as a professional writer. In the early years of the Quattrocento, she wrote prolifically commenting on political topics and popular humanist topoi with references to her own autobiographical accounts as well. In 1405, she published *Le Livre de la Cité des dames* (*The City of Ladies*), today her most well-known work for its protofeminist modernity. Inspired by Boccaccio, Christine begins the book narrating how she was contemplating in her study, wondering why the male authors of the books that line the shelves "all speak with the same mouth and all arrive at the same conclusion: that women's ways are inclined to and full of all possible vices."[300] In dialogue format, she presents three allegorical ladies—Reason, Justice, and Rectitude—who converse with Christine, inviting her to build a city of famous past and present virtuous women living in a world created by men. This world imagined by Pizan is one in which women can be whatever they would like to be—educated as men if they so choose:

> The man or the woman in whom resides greater virtue is the higher; neither the loftiness nor the lowliness of a person lies in the body according to the sex, but in the perfection of conduct and virtues.[301]

> If it were customary to send daughters to school like sons, and if they were then taught the natural sciences, they would learn as thoroughly and understand the subtleties of all the arts and sciences as well as sons.[302]

What Pizan ignited, scholarly women after her gave energy to. Intellects like Isotta Nogarola (1418–1466) were fortunate to be born into prominent, noble families. Nogarola was even more blessed by her widowed mother's decision to provide the finest humanistic education to her daughters as well as her sons. Isotta, along with her sister Ginevra, was tutored by Martino Rizzoni, disciple of the prominent humanist scholar, Guarino Veronese. Nogarola's classic education provided the budding humanist with fluency in Latin and academic credentials in the study of classical philosophy, the Scriptures, and theology.[303]

A half century after Pizan, Nogarola takes up the female identity discourse, writing letters to prominent scholars such as Antonio Bonromco when she was just nineteen, determined to earn the patronage and esteem of highly regarded humanists. Isotta succeeded in having her work praised, garnering recognition by those who read her treatises; then furthering attempts to establish herself within the scholarly enclave, she wrote to the famous classicist of her day, Guarino Veronese, who had already been sent Nogarola's essays by an intermediary. Her first letter, penned in 1437, went unanswered, a nonevent that in Verona did not go unnoticed: gossip and ridicule ensued. How brazen was this woman to dare contact such a lofty person in hope of receiving a reply! She wrote again to Guarino a year later:

> Why…was I born a woman, to be scorned by men in words and deeds? I ask myself this question in solitude… Your unfairness in not writing to me has caused me much suffering, that there could be no greater suffering… You yourself said there was no goal I could not achieve. But now that nothing has turned out as it should have, my joy has given way to sorrow… For they jeer at me throughout the city, the women mock me.[304]

This attempt did elicit a reply from the esteemed educator, her second letter filled with disappointment as she notes Guarino's past encouragement that had been related to her through an intermediary and the ridicule she endured as a female entreating entrance into the academic realm. Additionally, what have been determined as false accusations of promiscuity and incest were lobbed at her—typical censures cast at those few women who were aberrations in their own society, her anonymous accuser claiming that the wise saying "An eloquent woman is never chaste" holds true for the behavior of educated women.[305] Isotta Nogarola dedicated the rest of her life to religious studies—neither marrying nor taking vows, living a celibate existence in her mother's house.

More successful in receiving replies from distinguished humanist philosophers was Laura Cereta (1469–1499)[306] whose writings, although in Latin epistolary prose, reminds us of the letters of Alessandra Strozzi and Isabella d'Este in their honest and straightforward tone. Born into a venerate Brescian family, Cereta began her learning years in typical fifteenth-century upper-class fashion: she was sent to a convent at age seven to learn the basics of reading and writing. Her later missives reveal that she couldn't sleep at all, suffering from insomnia during those convent years, her sleepless void filled with nighttime writing. At the age of nine, she came home to help care for her siblings, during which time Cereta's doting father—attorney and magistrate—taught his daughter Latin and Greek.

Married at fifteen to a prominent Venetian merchant—and widowed eighteen months later, her husband having succumbed to the plague—Laura Cereta was to live only until thirty years old. During her short life, she was a prolific epistolarian, leaving us with abundant documentation, including a volume of letters that reveal her personal family relationships and struggles for a literary career. After her husband's death, she dedicated herself to her studies and literary production, a vocation that generated accusations that her father had written her work, attacks that sparked the learned scholar to pen her own self-defense and to inveigh against the lack of educational opportunities for all women.

In 1488, Cereta wrote an epistolary essay that portrayed talented women, echoing and amending Boccaccio's *De claris mulieribus*. Her work presented not only outstanding women of the past, but also contemporary women, including her predecessor, Isotta Nogarola. Cereta defends the right of women to have access to an education, beyond the rudiments of reading and writing, in a letter addressed to "Bibulus Sempronius,"[307] possibly a fictitious creation of the writer. Her theme is that intellectual, learned women are not exceptions as Boccaccio would have it, supporting this claim with a catalogue of intelligent women, eschewing mention of sexual activity that the fourteenth-century writer had highlighted.[308] Defending learned women, Cereta attacks the addressee for singling her out as an exception, thereby offending and degrading all other women. She goes on to show that she is indeed not an aberration, beginning her invective in no uncertain terms:

> Your complaints are hurting my ears, for you say publicly and quite openly that you are not only surprised but pained that I am said to show this

extraordinary intellect of the sort one would have thought nature would give to the most learned of men...you should be blushing... Why should the condition of our sex be shamed by your little attacks? Because of this, a mind thirsting for revenge is set afire, because of this, a sleeping pen is wakened for insomniac writing. Because of this, red-hot anger lays bare a heart and mind long muzzled by silence.[309]

Although Laura Cereta's contemporary, Cassandra Fedele (1465–1558),[310] lived a much longer life than her literary counterpart, Fedele's production came to a halt at age thirty-three, one year before she married, and ended for all purposes her epistolary practices. However, during the last decades of the Quattrocento, this Venetian humanist was the most renowned woman scholar of her time, achieving fame and recognition before the age of twenty-five. Quite the celebrity, Fedele earned widespread popularity as an accomplished orator, delivering, for example, the welcoming public oration for the queen of Poland, Bona Sforza, upon the monarch's arrival in Venice. At the University of Padua, in 1487, Fedele, poised and confident, delivered an oration on the liberal arts to an audience of European scholars.[311]

Cassandra Fedele was born into the *cittadini* class of Venice, her father, although not patrician, well-respected among the aristocracy—the family enjoying their fellow Venetians' prestige and respect. Angelo Fedele taught his daughter Greek and Latin, Cassandra becoming fluent in both by the age of twelve, at which time he sent his prodigy child to study with Gasparino Borro, a Servite monk and acclaimed scholar, "the greatest jewel and glory of the Servite Order" as Cassandra would describe him.[312] With the erudite monk, she studied not only Greek and philosophy, but also the sciences.

By the age of sixteen, the child prodigy would "perform" for eminent scholars who "tested" her knowledge—these renowned humanists astounded by her learning. At twenty-two, the erudite young woman took part in debates with the most prominent intellectuals of the University of Padua—she herself, as a woman, unable to obtain a degree or hold an academic position. In 1487, Cassandra was invited to be a part of the Court of Isabella and Ferdinand of Spain, an invitation that she eventually declined when war broke out, postponing until peace ensued. Although the request to join the royal Spanish court and related correspondence with Queen Isabella continued until 1495, Cassandra never did leave Venice for Spain.

The fresh and lovely polymath, who as an elegant young woman charmed as well as impressed her audience, acknowledged in 1492 that an educated woman would have to choose between a scholarly profession and the servitude of marriage—but could not have both. Accordingly, in 1499, at the age of thirty-four with a stalled literary career—stymied by protocols and laws of her time—Cassandra married Gian-Maria Mapelli, a Venetian doctor of medicine, after which time she retreated from academic life.[313]

Upon her death in 1558 at age ninety-three, a state funeral was held and her coffin carried through the streets of Venice. Cassandra Fedele left us with a full letter volume published in the seventeenth century, the most extensive—two hundred missives—of Renaissance women humanists. Her correspondence with eminent women of her time includes letters to Queen Isabella of Spain, Eleonora of Aragon, and Beatrice Sforza. Although writing in the style of fellow humanists in the mannered Latin of Cicero and Seneca about academic themes of the day, Cassandra added to the *querelle des femmes* discourse with her distinctly female voice, focusing on topics of womanhood and the weakness and deficiency of her sex, acknowledging, for example, in a letter to the Marquess of Mantua, Francesco Gonzaga, that she had chosen "manly pursuits" rather than woman's traditional work. To a courtier of Louis XII, she writes that she is a scholar "to the extent that our sex permits such a thing." It comes as no surprise that this talented and ambitious woman, to assuage male trepidation and circumvent women's sneers, portrays herself as a diminutive, innocent to her readers, referring to her letters as *literulae* (little notes) and to herself as a *virguncula* (little maiden), epistolary ironic self-deprecation not uncommon in women's letters of this era.

Almost a century later in Venice, Arcangela Tarabotti would take up the cause of women, putting pen to paper to assail the patriarchal powers that limited women's life choices including access to education. Certainly, emboldened by the scholarly women who had blatantly added their voices to the "woman question," Tarabotti takes part in the broadened demand for equality for all of her sex. Differentiating Tarabotti from her predecessors was the nun's self-acknowledged lacunae in learning. Neither was she the daughter of a doting father who would confer upon his female child the gift of an education—rather just the opposite, as we have seen in Stefano Tarabotti's coerced enclosure of his eldest female offspring to the Convent of Sant'Anna. None of these impediments, however, prevents Arcangela from lacing her work with intertextuality: the autodidact weaves throughout her writing references to contemporary and classic literature suggesting the confined nun had read not only both the Old and New Testaments of the Bible (she quoted these in received Latin) and Dante's *Divine Comedy*, but also works of her relative contemporaries—Lucrezia Marinella, Moderata Fonte, Lodovico Ariosto, Torquato Tasso, and Battista Guarini.[314]

Writing to the Illustrissimo Signor Giovanni Dandolo, prominent patrician descendent of a centuries-old Venetian noble family, Suor Arcangela boldly states that

> The sex which should be called most bestial rather than strongest has become like a mole, unable to see because of its own pretension and temerity, and does not know and evilly works to condemn the female who has been exalted by Wisdom above the choir of angels.[315]

Tarabotti speaks truth to power, intertwining allusions to Dante's *Paradiso*[316] to support her argument, continuing the debate—now her battle. The nun's polemic stance takes the "woman question" to the political and socioeconomic arena of mid-Seicento Venice—a forum that offered a fertile field to cultivate the popular motif of the *querelle*, as Arcangela dares bring the discourse to an emotional level with her first written texts, *Tirannia paterna* and *L'inferno monacale*, considered too provocative and polemic, even in Venice, for publication.

19

Paving the Way for Arcangela:
Fonte and Marinella

*A*rcangela Tarabotti's invectives against a political and socio-economic system that would require families to commit their daughters to lifetime *clausura* are pointedly targeted at those who wielded power. Hence, Arcangela lays blame squarely on the shoulders of men, fathers, patriarchs, and ruling patricians. As obvious victim, the nun is uniquely situated to lend her voice to the *querelle* arguing for equal treatment of women; by the same token, she is tenuously positioned on a precipice from which she can clearly see the "inhuman" treatment of innocents—and from which she could easily fall into an emotional vortex, she herself suffering as pawn and prey to patriarchal powers. Nevertheless, the literary nun delivers her censure in the name of all women, Arcangela never personalizing her own torment as she fires accusations that echo the unheard anguish of her *consorelle*. In *L'inferno monacale*, she sets her sights on "Satan's ministers":

> Considerate voi qui un poco, o ministri di Satanasso, che sforzando le vostre figliuole ad entrar ne' monasteri, siete partecipi di tutte le loro attioni scandolose: qual riparo siate per impetrare nell'eterno e

spaventevol giorno del Giudicio, quando la Sonora trombe si fara' con orido rimbombo sentire all universe?[317]

Directly addressing—in the *voi*, familiar plural—fathers responsible for forcing their little girls to enter the monastery, she accuses them of taking part in all their daughters' "scandalous actions," warning all fathers that they themselves will be accounted for on the frightening day of judgment when the trumpet will sound with horrible echoes that will be heard throughout the universe." [318] Tarabotti's mordant metaphors dispatched zealously attest to underlying outrage, but the nun adroitly channels her own emotions into acute denunciations, targeting the inherent causes driving the perpetuation of a despicable system.

Arcangela Tarabotti's manifestation of anger and outrage differs in tone from her immediate Venetian forbearers, Modesta da Pozzo (writing as Moderata Fonte) and Lucrezia Marinella, with whose works the nun was probably acquainted.[319] Both of these Venetian literary women step by step cleared the way for Tarabotti to raise her defiant voice from behind convent walls. Moderata Fonte (1555–1592), born into the *cittadini* class of Venice, like her female literary predecessors, showed early signs of precocity and like them had nurturing family support that fostered the child's learning.[320]

Fonte had been dead for almost half a century before Arcangela put pen to paper, but the nun's precursor had set the way for Tarabotti by veering in the direction of delineating tangible consequences for men's blindness toward the value of women. Fonte, as does Tarabotti, elaborates on the perfunctory themes of women's equality and men's mistreatment of females, beginning her *The Worth of Women* (*Il merito delle donne*)[321] with the de rigueur elegant panegyric of the lagoon city. Fonte parts ways with paradigmatic discourse toward the end of the work, noting that women are suffering as a direct result of men's positioning themselves as their superiors; and as such, men could and do substantiate their mistreatment of women. Writing in the popular narrative frame of dialogue, Fonte has seven "noble and spirited women, all from the best known and most respected families of the city…united by breeding and taste"[322] gossiping and discoursing in a Venetian garden, chatting about life, men, and marriage. The spirited interchange among the women—some married, others widowed, some unmarried, young, and old—reveals each one's thoughts about a variety of topics, most compelling of all, their views about the opposite sex.

Helena (newly married) comments to Leonora at whose home the encounter takes place:

> If men knew what you were thinking when they saw you walking past in the street—if they had the least suspicion of how much ill will you harbor against them—I'd have to start fearing for your safety.

Denying any antipathy, Leonora retorts,

> Men have good cause to honor me…nothing of what I've said has been intended to offend good men, rather, it's all been directed toward converting bad men—if only they'd listen… I feel for the many suffering women I see around me, one made unhappy by her father, another by her brother, another by her husband, still another by her son, and so on across every relationship one person can have with another.[323]

This exchange is emblematic of the discursive volley, a dialogue playing on a seesaw of opinions with one woman taking exception to another's comments, all reasonable and rational in their lively repartees.

There is also much lighthearted humor in Fonte's text, which should not diminish the topics she touches. For example, after a brief discussion in which dowries are mentioned, Leonora sardonically comments, "O quante…farebbon meglio, inanzi che tuor marito, comprare un bel porco ogni carnevale, che starebbon grasse tutto l'anno, avendo chi le ungesse e non chi le pungesse del continuo"[324] (Oh how much better it would be if instead of a husband, they bought a nice pig at every carnival; they would stay fat all year long having something that would provide grease instead of continued displeasure). Fonte's allusion to dowries continues with inference to forced monachization as Leonora notes the maliciousness of fathers "whose cruelty toward their daughters has been such that they have wretchedly deprived them of their honor or their life."[325]

Couched in bobbing, seemingly spontaneous, verbal banter, the women's dialogue succeeds in gently bringing to the fore the societal practices of dowering and coerced claustration. The author also chimes in to the *querelle* topos of women's exclusion from education and their subordination to husbands. In total disgust, Cornelia[326] blatantly asks,

> Wouldn't it be possible to for us just to banish these men from our lives and escape their carping and jeering once and for all? Couldn't we live without them? Couldn't we earn our own living and manage our affairs without help from them?… Come on, lets wake up, and claim back our freedom, and the honor and dignity they have usurped from us for so long.[327]

Tarabotti's precursor and another upper-class married woman who had access to the Venetian literary community was Lucrezia Marinella (1571–1653),[328] a contemporary of Suor Arcangela. Lucrezia was born only sixteen years after Fonte, she too daughter of well-to-do Venetians—*cittadini* class like Fonte—her father a celebrated medical doctor, philosopher, and learned scholar, author of several medical treatises, known for his *Ornamenti delle Donne* filled with recipes for women to highlight their blond hair and improve their facial skin tone and general instructions pertaining to health and beauty. Marinella acknowledged receiving her father's support in her education and was neither coerced into marriage nor forced into the convent. Of her private life, we have few details; but we do know that Marinella too was a prodigious learner, which is evidenced by her writings that demonstrate erudition and expertise.

Marinella's literary life begins in 1595 with an epic poem in ottava rima; but in 1600, in stark contrast to her previous works, she published a provocative piece of secular prose in reply to the misogynist essay "Dei donneschi difetti" (about women's defects) written by Giuseppe Passi. Marinella's "La nobilta'et l'eccellenza delle donne co' difetti et mancamenti de gli uomini" departs radically from her previous lyric and narrative poetry on religious topics. She indignantly responds to Passi's overtly misogynist diatribe that warns men against the wicked ways of women, advising young men about the "truth" of women and cautioning against desiring them, making a case for male friendship—the more noble alliance—all of which had the effect of placing marriage as undesirable.

In her treatise, Marinella argues for the superiority of women, in many ways summarizing the fundamental *querelle* arguments as she constructs her theses with astonishing philosophical and rhetorical skill, providing an explanation for men's misogyny and the subsequent exclusion of women from the political arena. Although her arguments are not new, her comprehensive, detailed compilation of these moral and philosophical positions set Marinella apart from her predecessors. She defines the defects of the male sex and accounts for their evil motives, attributing the shortcomings they find in women to men's own defective nature. She also rejects the "equality" argument, insisting that the souls of women are more noble. What comes to the fore in Marinella's treatise is her erudite, skilled reply to Passi's work as she deconstructs, one by one, his rather hackneyed—even for the early Seicento—claims.

Writing in this fertile literary period in Venice, Arcangela Tarabotti takes up and continues with the popular *querelle* motif. What sets the dissident nun apart from her predecessors and contemporaries, however, are noteworthy: she is cloistered, in a confined state to which her family—precisely her father[329]—had condemned her. Also, if little Elena Tarabotti had shown signs of precocity, we know nothing of it; we know she did not have the support and encouragement of a doting father who would offer educational advantages to his daughter. Moreover, while her brilliant and erudite forbearers saw the ills of a patriarchal society and corresponding repercussions that females endured, their own personal involvement with men and mal-treatment—although in some cases significant—cannot compare to the physical and mental torments that Tarabotti, living in her "con-vent hell," internalized and depicted in graphic detail.

Zeroing in, Suor Arcangela pinpoints the essence of the argu-ment: "liberty," a right given to men and women—not by the Venetian Republic, but by God, to all humans: "Frà tali eccessi di colpe, tiene il primo luogo l' ardire di coloro, che con pregiudicio del libero arbitrio da S. D. M. concesso, tanto a' i maschi, quanto alle femine."[330] Speaking of men's subjugation of women, Tarabotti writes, "Among such egregious evils, first is their audacity to jeop-ardize the free will that God has given to both men and women."[331]

In *Tirannia paterna*, Tarabotti condemns the Republic, a cen-sure she addresses to the "Serenissima Republica Veneta" (To the Most Serene Venetian Republic) in her dedicatory introduction to *Tirannia*. With an apostrophe, spiritual and reverent in tone—"You, the Most Serene Queen"—she calls attention to the fame Venice enjoys as "the beautiful city that offers unbounded liberty to people from all nations, including those who crucified the son of Your Most Holy Protector, the Virgin Mary."[332] Tarabotti continues her sardonic dedication, addressing, "Vostro gran Senato,—Your great Senate—that, by incarcerating young virgins,…You hope to be eternal, beau-tiful Virgin, Queen of the Adriatic."[333] With fearless irony, she offers her book to "the Most Serene Venetian Republic":

> Ben si conviene in dono la "Tirannia Paterna" a quella Republica nella quale, più frequentamente che in qual altra si sia parte del mondo, viene abu-sato di monacar le figliole sforzatamente. (The gift of *Paternal Tyranny* is well suited for a Republic that, more than in any other part of the world, practices the abuse of forced monachization of their daughters.)

Although convents did give rise to literary nuns, having the time and relative freedom to write, the context of their work remained in the religious-spiritual sphere. We see nothing like Tarabotti's secular polemic writings daring to point a finger at political powers. Arcangela Tarabotti's unique situation gives the nun's argument passion and urgency as a vocal proponent of women's rights, she herself an innocent casualty, suffering perhaps the most horrific manifestation of patriarchal power—lifetime imprisonment.

20

Living to Write: Arcangela's True Calling

*A*rcangela Tarabotti died of consumption on February 28, 1652, in the Convent of Sant'Anna di Castello, leaving behind five published works[334] from which we learn of her deep desire for recognition as an intellectual and writer. Although from 1620 through 1643 very little is known about the literary nun's life, we can assume she spent time reading as much as she could, her formal education, as she acknowledges, having been minimal. Tarabotti, although never accepting her "internment" in the convent, did make the very best of her plight, and it might be argued, if such arguments can be made, that perhaps without her early and harsh condemnation to the convent, Elena Cassandra Tarabotti might not ever have been driven to contemplate on and then put into words the underlying causes of female confinement and women's disparities.

Suor Arcangela's literary awakening, according to Zanette, probably took place when Tarabotti was about twenty years old. He suggests that the fury and anger had built up in the young girl over her involuntary claustration, until finally her wrath reached the surface, pouring into *Tirannia paterna*, her first work, put to press as *Semplicita' ingannata* under the thinly veiled pseudonym Galerana Baratotti, two years after her death.[335]

The dates of Tarabotti's publications are deceiving in that they do not correspond to the time frame of the actual writing. Suor Arcangela had circulated copies of *Tirannia paterna* (*Paternal*

Tyranny), her first written book, and *L'inferno monacale*, considered her second work, from 1640 through 1642. These early texts are fierce denouncements of coerced monachization, defiantly criticizing the social, political, religious, and patriarchal powers that fostered the practice; *L'inferno monacale* contains a strong autobiographical undercurrent, detailing the process of taking the veil from the point of view of an unwilling girl, devoid of vocation. Tarabotti was well aware that the content of this work was dangerous and knew it could not be published in Venice. However, also polemic—uncovering the political, economic, and social powers that upheld and reinforced compelled claustration—*Tirannia paterna*, the author's premium work, was the focus of Arcangela's battle to publish.

Meeting with no success in her attempts to publish these two iconoclastic works, Tarabotti wrote *Paradiso monacale*, a less polemic text now considered to have been written to achieve the goal of publication. In this tome, Tarabotti shows deference for the convent as a "paradise" for those women with true religious calling. Determined to have this work, and arguably considering publication of her previously written texts, Arcangela Tarabotti circulated copies of *Paradiso monacale* among friends and acquaintances, garnering praise and admiration from respected literary figures, culminating with its publication in 1643 when the nun was thirty-nine years old. Much less polemic than her two previously written works, *Paradiso* lauded the convent as a true haven for those with spiritual callings, "oprando volontariamente, per Amor di Dio" (working voluntarily for the love of God).[336]

While recognizing the convent as a paradise for those with vocation, Tarabotti begins the book with her consistent motif, the glorification of women:

> Iddio Benedetto ama tutte le Creature, ma particolarmente la Donna, e poi l'huomo, bench'egli non lo meriti, e per ispiegare di che qualita' sia l'amor suo verso questo ingratisimo animale, basta il dire, che l'immortal Creatore l'ama veramente da Dio.[337]

She asserts that "the Blessed Lord loves all Creatures, in particular women, and then men, even though they [men] do not merit it." Although *Paradiso* was palatable and acceptable enough to make it to press as her first published tome, in it, Tarabotti did not hide her convictions, positions held and expressed in her first written work, *Tirannia paterna*, the heterodox content of which rendered it unpublishable. In *Paradiso*, as in her previous and subsequent works, Suor Arcangela decries forced monachization while vehemently defending those who voluntarily choose the cloistered life, celebrating "fanciulle, che doppo aver pregato Dio longamente... sentono accendersi nell'anima un santo furore et affetto verso la Religione"[338] (those young girls, who after having prayed to God at length...feel the rising saintly spirit of love in their souls towards religion).

Through her adulation of voluntary religious called to God and the cloistered life, Suor Arcangela succeeds in contrasting the sacrilege of forcing spirituality and confinement upon the unwilling without vocation. She confesses her own spiritual shortcomings in the opening, "Soliloquio a Dio" (Soliloquy to God), calling to her "amato sposo" (beloved spouse) to help in her weakness and "non-iscandalizarsi dell'umana fragilita'...," not to be offended by this human frailty.[339]

Even though the powerful Loredan contributed an introductory letter to *Paradiso,* Arcangela still came under negative scrutiny that cast doubt on her authorship, some citing the erudition displayed in her work as proof that the unschooled nun could not have penned it.[340] With her dedication to "Eminentissimo Signor Cardinal Cornaro," and to the noble Giovanni Polani, as well as a dedicatory poem written by Lucrezia Marinelli, one might think that the nun's integrity would not be challenged. However, the congenial literary climate of the day was adumbrated by political concerns of Venetian patriarchs anxious about the social stability of the Republic and eager to ensure its continued longevity—durability rooted to a ruling, wealthy oligarchy of a relatively closed caste of patricians that relied on entrenched socioeconomic practices, not the least of which was monachization of daughters.

Sometime in 1641, Arcangela had gotten hold of a copy of Francesco Buoninsegni's Menippean satire, *Contro 'l lusso donnesco satira menippea*, published in 1638.[341] With hyperbolic ridicule, Buoninsegni premises his argument on woman's *antico peccato* (biblical sin), making her responsible for depriving "our first parents of their innocent nudity." He declares that women have transformed the punishment for their crime (having to be clothed) into a triumph of luxury.[342] From this historic place of support for women's inferiority, Buoninsegni, not without wit and turn of phrase, proceeds to condemn women for their vanity, frivolity, and even ignorance: we cannot dissuade women of the vanity of dress until we "undress" them of their ignorance.[343] Tarabotti's rebuttal to Buoninsegni's misogynist text took the form of a defense by respectable married women (*illustrissime signore*) whom the nun claimed had petitioned her to write a reply.[344]

When Tarabotti's response to Buoninsegni, *Antisatira in risposta al "Lusso donnesco,"* was published anonymously in 1644, her rebuttal caused a clamor, especially among several heretofore supporters, who now, with the nun's defensive attack on men, did not see to praise the boldness and trepidation they so admired when her furor and sarcasm were aimed at religious institutions and political practices. Targeting men, Tarabotti set out to disclaim, one by one, Buoninsegni's accusations against women—their frivolity, love of fashion, and vanity—by turning the argument on its head and showing, for example, how men are *more* frivolous and vain than women: they follow fashion, donning garments of plush velvet, damask cloth, and lace-trimmed linen; they are fond of wearing English hose, small shoes, and intricately embroidered waist sashes among other accessories.[345] Besides, she argues, women's clothing provides testimony to their modesty and not to their guilt of which they are innocent. She counters Buoninsegni's accusations of women's ignorance by laying blame squarely on the shoulders of men, who deprive women of an education, thereby divesting them of means to defend themselves. Her reply to Buoninsegni's attempt at comedic ridicule that harkens back to historic arguments supporting women's inferiority marks an important step in social criticism in defense of women against male subjection as Tarabotti morphs the polemic about fashion into a significant critique of men's treatment of women.[346] The outcry against *Antisatira*, mostly from her former supporters, continued to put Arcangela in a place from which she had to constantly defend her writerly integrity, a defense she would publish in the form of her letter book, *Lettere familiari ed di complimento*, in 1650.

Through *Lettere*, Arcangela defends her authenticity in retaliation against misogynist critics and former supporters who, after publication of *Antisatira*, openly questioned the legitimacy of her authorship. Testimony to her ambition and relentless drive, Arcangela Tarabotti's *Lettere familiari e di complimento*[347] presents us the opportunity to explore the author's uncanny ability to forge and nurture strategic alliances among "the most illustrious and most excellent"[348] members of literary, social, religious, and political spheres of influence who facilitated the publication of her manuscripts. Chronicling a close association with eminent men and women, recording the trajectory of her literary career, Tarabotti cleverly faces detractors head-on, flouting her literary successes and taking to task critics whom at one point she thanks for the compliment paid her (implying the work was too well-written to be her own).[349] The content of *Lettere* reveals sophisticated strategies of self-representation, a rhetorical exercise that makes public the nun's temperament and talent. Suor Arcangela is clearly in the business of identity construction, affirming and defending her intellectual honesty and literary worth in this auto-edited and selected collection of formal and informal missives.[350]

Inextricably entwined in Tarabotti's self-defense and self-assertion in this letter book is the narrative discourse, a dialogic that sheds light on the enterprising nun's relentless drive to have her "offspring"[351] come to life in print. Arcangela's letters provide documentation of the author's single-minded quest to legitimize her intellectual worth and concretize her writerly identity by putting to print *Tirannia paterna*, her finest literary issue.

Tarabotti appended to her letter volume an encomium, *Le lagrime di Arcangela Tarabotti per la morte della illustrissima signora Regina Donati* (The Tears of Arcangela Tarabotti upon the Death of the Most Illustrious Signora Regina Donati), dedicated to Arcangela's dear friend and *consorella*, Regina Donà (Donati), who died in 1645 at age thirty-six. Regina, the little girl who took voluntary vows at the same time as young Elena, became a beloved friend of Arcangela who was inconsolable upon her friend's passing. In this eulogy, Tarabotti praises her convent sister and highlights Regina's true spiritual, not coerced, vocation. She refers to Regina as a "queen" and "a gift worthy of being donated to God," playing on the deceased's given and family names. Tarabotti goes on to tell the story of Regina, how she cloistered herself for love of God when she was a young girl, how she gave up palatial surroundings for the humble convent, how "no man would have been worthy of possessing this precious jewel."[352] Tarabotti praises Regina's physical appearance, "Her tall stature, regal presence, and noble bearing were beyond mortal ways," then goes on to delineate how Regina was "submissive and responsive to the commands of her superiors," adherent to the vows of "Obedience, Poverty, and Chasity."[353]

Suor Arcangela details how this "queen," born into riches, loved poverty, how she abstained from drinking, gambling, and gluttony, even as a young girl, never giving in to temptation of "satisfying herself at lunch or dinner."[354] Arcangela lauds Regina for her inner strength and courage, her modesty in dress, and her complete devotion to God. In sum, Arcangela Tarabotti describes the perfect nun, her beloved friend whom she honors and mourns. Not detracting from Arcangela's grief and admiration for Regina Donà, the decision to include the panegyric as a separate work with its own title page in her letter book also served to satisfy ecclesiastic authorities and to mollify any offensive content of Tarabotti's letters, thus smoothing the way for publication of *Lettere*.

In a missive addressed to "His Excellency, Enrico Cornaro," a friend and liaison between the nun and Incogniti members, Arcangela asks him to procure for her a poem by Giovan Francesco Busenello, giving Cornaro the eulogy for Regina in exchange, hoping he will pass it along to others capable of helping her put to press *Lettere*.[355] We see in another missive addressed to an unknown "Illustrissimo ed Eccellentissimo Signor N,"[356] Suor Arcangela imploring "on bended knees" the recipient, a person who wields influence and power, to obtain licenses from the State and the church authorities to publish her letter volume, urging the high-ranking addressee to please help to have her work "legitimamente comparir nel teatro del mondo"[357] (legitimately appear on the world's stage). She buttresses her request for help to publish by putting into play "quell' anima santa"[358] (that blessed soul) (of Regina Donà). Tarabotti believes that Signor N. will not deny the request to seek licenses for her work when he sees at the end of the letter volume the glorious praise of her beloved friend. With the help of the influential Signor N. as well as with that of Loredan—and with the posthumous assistance of her dear *consorella*, Regina Donà—Arcangela Tarabotti succeeded in putting to press her *Lettere familiari e di complimento* in 1650.

One year later, Suor Arcangela would present a powerful *j'accuse*, systematically and logically dedicating a scathing attack to the anonymous author of the tract *Che le donne non siano della spezie degli uomini*, which sardonically asserts "women are not members of the human species."[359] Although somewhat of a joke, at the expense of women, the anonymous treatise cited Scripture to provide "proof" of females' irrationality, a deficit that deprives them of the ability to form logical decisions, ultimately "proving" they have no soul and cannot receive salvation.

In the last work published in her lifetime, in 1651, under the thinly veiled pseudonym Galerana Baratotti (she also used Barcitotti), Suor Arcangela demolishes in *Che le donne siano della spezie degli uomini* (Women are of the same species as men) the anonymous author's specious contentions, dismissing them as eisegesis. In a series of arguments that alternate the author's "*inganno*" (falsehood/deceit and truth) with Tarabotti's "*disinganno*" (truth), the nun, with wisdom and wit, decomposes each "deceit" of the anonymous author, retaliating in kind with the "truth," demonstrating her shrewd and subtle command of the topic by revealing the author's misinterpretations of Scripture.[360]

In this, her last work, Arcangela inserts herself into a spiritual debate about the human soul of women, a debate taking place in the public sphere. She goes toe to toe with Venetian scholars—an exceptional undertaking for a female, unprecedented for a cloistered nun.

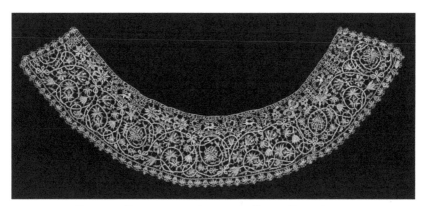

Needlepoint (Punto in aria) Lace Collar, 16th–17th century.

A Venetian gondola with gondoliers arriving at canal steps
where many noblemen and women wait on the quay.

For centuries, Venetian naval and commercial
power was unrivalled in Europe.

PART 5

Empowerment and Identity: Networking from the Nunnery

Material and Spiritual Exchanges: Lace, Matchmaking, and the French Connection

*T*he tranquility of the convent did not calm the storm raging in Arcangela, nor did it quell the desire for recognition as a serious member of the literary community. Although her works circulated among the Venetian cognoscenti, Arcangela was determined to have her voice heard by a wider audience, and her words in defense of women taken seriously by the reading public, in sum, to have her work put to press.

Arcangela Tarabotti had the heart of a writer, simply expressed in her own words: "Ion scrivo per applause ne' per premio, ma per aderire al mio proprio genio e gusto"[361] (I do not write for applause, nor for prizes, but rather to hold fast to my own natural talent and pleasure). In this respect, Arcangela was no different from any other writer, the outcome of putting to press one's work a natural goal of the communicative process. What renders Tarabotti exceptional, however, is her tenacity in keeping to the quest for publication, confronted by the built-in barriers that would have broken the will of the less resolute.

Establishing a far-flung network of elite contacts, relying on an internal and external system of material and cultural exchange, Tarabotti, from behind the grille, succeeded in gaining her desired entrance into the literary community of post-Tridentine Venice, publishing five works in her lifetime.

Through *Lettere*, Arcangela defends her authenticity in retaliation against critics, former supporters who, after publication of her *Antisatira* responding to Francesco Buoninsegni's misogynist Menippean satire, openly questioned the legitimacy of her authorship. Tarabotti's letter volume not only makes public the nun's talent and temperament, but also brings to light sophisticated strategies of self-representation, as the author carefully chronicles the trajectory of her literary career. Revealed in *Lettere* are the dynamics of Tarabotti's expedient network of contacts, cultivated by the aggressive nun, taking full advantage of the epistolary genre to showcase her relationships with the most prominent and powerful.

Although half of Arcangela's collected letters contain clear or oblique references to her literary works, we find scant mention of her family; except for her brother-in-law Giacomo Pighetti, whose influence and connections as an Incogniti member served the nun well and to whom seven letters are addressed, there is but one mention of her mother (mentioning her death).[362], [363] The opening line of one tension-filled letter to two of her sisters begins with words of rancor: "Lo scrivere a chi non si degna di respondere e' pazzia" (Writing to someone who will not deign to reply is crazy).[364] In this brief letter, Arcangela implores her sisters to recognize the affection she has for them. In the second letter, we find out that her sisters did eventually write, a letter that "consoled" Arcangela when she "least expected it." Tarabotti is not one to forget nor let others forget. In the next line, her gentle gratitude turns to sarcasm: she is pleased that in her sister's letter she did not find "altro che tratti di complimento e d'amore senza pontigli come sete sempre aveszze di fare" (anything other than compliments and love, without the usual barbs you always include). Tarabotti continues, reminding her sisters that they were all born from the same womb, and provides reassurance that she has no such thoughts like those of the *primi gemelli* (the first twins), sardonically referring to Cain and Abel.[365]

Enclosed nuns typically stayed close to their families, yet her correspondence gives no indication that this was the case for Arcangela. Instead, we learn that she built up around her an impressive group of powerful and prestigious acquaintances with whom she communicated and from whom she sought advice, support, encouragement, and favors. Her involvement with an outside network of associations shows itself in such letters as the one to the Illustrissima Signora Malipiero, sister of Regina Donà, in which Arcangela pleads the case of a young man called to serve in the military. Through the noblewoman's connections, Tarabotti hopes to have the man avoid going to war, justifying her plea stating that he is married with children, suffers from dizzy spells, and has a heart condition; sending him to war would be to condemn him to death, and neither he nor his wife has any male relatives that could take over the household in this event.[366] The request suggests a cordial and close relationship that would enable the nun to ask for such a favor, a relationship that we see with other women addressees[367] as well as with male recipients.

Writing to the anonymous Illustrissimo Signor N., Arcangela's connections to the lay society beyond the walls of Sant'Anna become apparent. She conveys information to her friend about a "Signor M." and certain ladies in need of protection from him and the "calciate di colui" (the kicks of this man),[368] advising that the *gentildonne* (respectable ladies) need husbands to protect them. It appears that Signor M. expects more inheritance than given to him by his father, a sum that would hinder marriage possibilities for the young ladies bereft of sufficient dowries. Tarabotti asks the addressee to look into this situation in her pleas to protect the young women, who without inheritance could be forced into the convent—undowered, unable to marry.[369]

Along with her extensive outreach beyond cloistered borders, Tarabotti's life in what she often referred to as her "prison" consisted of typical material and spiritual exchanges that nuns engaged in to maintain affective rapport with family and friends in the few ways open to them. In addition to parlatorio socializing (taking part in neighborhood gossip and learning of parish events, city receptions, and current news), nuns, whether offering their prayers or exchanging their handiwork, kept in contact with the outer world. Arcangela, although spending much of her time reading and writing, pursued convent activities, establishing relationships and capitalizing on the available structures to fill her life, and fulfill the desire to gain her coveted place in the Venetian literary world.

Acting as an intermediary between her lace-making *consorelle* and those who would purchase the precious handwork,[370] Suor Arcangela reinforced her connections to prominent women. In a letter to the Illustrissima Signora Isabetta Piccolomini Scarpi,[371] Arcangela consigns a *punt'in aria* lace collar to the recipient who represents the Marchese di Galeranda and her request for the lace-work. Held in high esteem, the coveted *punt'in aria* lace for which Venice was famous had become the fashion in Italy and France. This intricate pattern, literally "stitch in the air," was produced exclusively by women in charitable institutions and convents, the prized lace becoming a commodity of exchange.[372] Lacework produced in Sant'Anna Convent offered Tarabotti the opportunity to interface with eminent women, high-placed female friends who supported and respected the literary nun.

The premium lace is the subject of several letters to distinguished women. Tarabotti apologizes to Madama d'Amo, wife of Jean Hameaux, ambassador to France,[373] for the delay in consigning her lace order and provides a sample of the commissioned work, begging her pardon: "Se da me sola dipendesse il servire Vostra Eccellenza Illustrissima, anteponerei sempre I Suoi commandi alla mia istessa vita" (If this depended on only me, I would put all your commands before my own life). Tarabotti negotiates the final price for the lace, with work to commence immediately upon Madama d'Amo's approval of the sample, Tarabotti herself guaranteeing to see that "quelle poi che lavorano meglio," (those nuns who do the best work) make the larger pieces. In subsequent correspondence (Tarabotti does not date her letters)[374] the nun, again acting as agent and broker, lets Madama d'Amo know that the lace makers will not accept less than two *scudi* from anyone, no matter who she was, for their work, nor would the *maestre* (supervisors of the lacework) accept anything less than *ducati tre l'uno*, referring to three ducats per piece of lace. The amount Tarabotti was quoting for this intricate lacework, based on the average income in 1600 Venice of thirty-seven ducats, was substantial.

Arcangela occupied time in her "inferno" participating in customary convent activities, capitalizing on these typical occupations to forge and nurture expedient relationships in her pursuit of recognition and publication. Along with lace making, one of the most significant functions of female monasteries was to educate young girls whose families temporarily placed them as boarders in care of the nuns for a period of years, often until marriageable age. In the confines of the convent, young girls received a primary education as well as religious and moral instruction. Known as *serbanza*, this practice, most girls entering between the ages of seven and nine years old, forged strong bonds between the nuns and their *educanda* as well as between the nuns and the young girl's family who entrusted them with their daughter's preparation and education.

Most likely through her well-connected brother-in-law Giacomo Pighetti, Suor Arcangela came into contact with Nicolas Bretel de Gremonville, who replaced Hameaux as the ambassador of France in Venice,[375] and his wife who entrusted their two daughters to the care and tutelage of Tarabotti as *putte a spese,* as they were called in Venice.[376] Arcangela was honored to have the ambassador's daughters as her pupils, a charge she took seriously and one that enabled her to foster close ties with the eminent Frenchman and his family.[377] Not only did the Bretels consign the education of their daughters to Tarabotti; but upon the birth of their son and heir, the ambassador, in his own hand, wrote immediately to the nun, giving her the good news and requesting that she ask his daughter, perhaps the older of the two (referred to by Tarabotti as *mamosella di Ravano*),[378] how she will like having a little brother.[379] Tarabotti relates to the ambassador that the girl, who had entered the convent when her mother was pregnant, was in fact very jealous for the love of her father, alarming news to give to the proud parent of a hoped-for heir.[380]

The letter that Tarabotti writes back to the ambassador alternates between advising him of the child's jealousy and congratulating him on the birth of his son. Tarabotti, sensitive to the girl's plight—and involuntarily complicit to it—relates that the little girl "cries and grieves over the news, with happiness for her parents," and urges the ambassador to "love and pity her."[381] In typical Tarabottian style, forthright candidness attenuated with encomiastic laudation, the nun immediately follows her outspoken request with an eloquent sonnet[382] praising the birth of the noble heir, referring to the child as "Alcide"[383] who, "born in the Venice of lions, will be a strong fighter against the infidels." It appears that the ambassador paid homage to La Serenissima, naming his heir Marco.

With devotion, Arcangela cared for and nurtured the Gremonville girls, exchanging seven letters to the ambassador and three to his wife, Anne-Francoise de Lomenie (Madame Anna di Gremonville), professing in one letter that she treats the girls with love as if they were born of her own womb, serving them with the attention and respect that their birthright demands.[384] Indeed, even before the Gremonville heir was born, Tarabotti had written to the pregnant Anne-Francoise—in one breath expressing best wishes and hopes that Anne give birth to a male heir, and in the next breath telling about her daughter's jealousy that apparently had been brewing for a time in the young girl; Tarabotti related that the child fears losing her mother's affection and that the little girl is beginning to hate her still-to-be-born sibling.[385]

The ambassador and his family left Venice in 1645, taking with them their daughters who eventually were placed in convents with nothing the nun could do to prevent the sanctioned practice except continue an unwavering drive to have the world read her intrepid condemnation of forced monachization in *Tirannia paterna*. To that end, Arcangela's relationship with the Gremonville family endured after their departure from Venice, with Tarabotti's campaign to publish her "firstborn" persisting in hope that France, "dove godendosi libertà"[386] (where they enjoy freedom of conscience), would be more open to the polemic work.

Strengthening rapport with those who could support and promote her literary endeavors, Suor Arcangela capitalized on another customary practice of Venetian nuns, participating in arranging patrician marriages. Of the many rituals, the ceremonies related to marriage—whether spiritual or temporal—were the conventions that most tied female monasteries to the city's patriciate and *cittadini* castes. Typically, upper-class girls spent their formative years under the tutelage of nuns, side by side with young novices, most of whom were coerced into cloistered life. The future brides of Christ and the future worldly brides inhabited the same communal space, both sets of girls awaiting their fate. The synergy between aristocratic family decisions and female monasteries formed an enduring symbiotic partnership: with noble clans entrusting their daughters' upbringing and often their entire lives to the convent, indurate bonds were formed. When the *educande* left to marry, they honored the close ties and associations of their youth by visiting the convent as brides-to-be to receive good wishes and gifts from the novices and nuns with whom they shared their early years.[387]

As marriage was at the center, forming the foundation of Venetian longevity, it is no surprise that the rituals surrounding the event would involve not only the family, but the entire community. From the onset, the convent occupied an essential role, beginning with the formality of signing the contract, the initial event that included the important dowry arrangements, usually taking place in the *parlatorio*.[388] Housed in the local nunneries were the sisters, aunts, and other female relatives of the temporal bride, relatives that she visited with the complete wedding party after an elaborate celebration—the public and private, the sacred and secular converging in the convent.

By the early seventeenth century, these customs were still in practice, notwithstanding mandates issued by Patriarch Trevisan a century prior, prohibiting brides or her relatives to enter the gate of the convent to either see the nuns or touch their hands.[389] If Arcangela Tarabotti's reaction to seeing the bedecked bride and being brought leftover delicacies is an indication of how other young nuns might have felt, we can understand Patriarch Trevisan's orders. In *L'inferno monacale*, Suor Arcangela describes the luxurious dress of "real brides," contrasting the costly extravagance of colored silk ordered from as far away as Syria to the "unlucky" sister's garb that covered her in rough cloth of black or brown.[390] From every point of view, Arcangela decried the selective preference for the "lucky" sister—"born of the same womb" as the one condemned to claustration.

In her tirades against patriarchal dominance over women's lives, Tarabotti focuses on the evils of men. The title of a text referred to but either lost or never written suggests Tarabotti had posited arguments against "unhappy marriages"—*Purgatorio delle malmaritate* (Purgatory of the unhappily married).[391] Whether the book included preferences for celibacy as well as condemnation of coerced unions, Tarabotti had in mind to complete her Dantesque trilogy with this tome. Nevertheless, Suor Arcangela dedicated her time and effort to finding husbands for marriageable girls. The convent as the nexus for marital rituals involved the nun in the matchmaking process, her advising, counseling, and concern made public in over a dozen letters. Assisting aristocratic families in finding suitable husbands for their daughters, Tarabotti partook in the process whereby she not only encouraged successful unions, but also promoted her expedient relationships, associations that clearly publicized her connections to the most prominent families of Venice. She congratulates Giovanni Dandolo[392] upon his marriage to Orsa Gabriel in 1644,[393] complimenting the nobleman on the match that will bring forth children with the breeding of the "compitissimi cavaglieri e di nobilissima dame" (most accomplished gentleman and most noble lady). Interestingly, Tarabotti, while publicizing her intimacy with the most eminent, also seems to be tacitly approving of the glory and necessity of patrician endogamous unions that produce offspring of noble breeding.

It is tempting to label as contradictory Tarabotti's condemnation of men and her participation in the matchmaking process that ensured continuity of the ruling patrician patriarch class. Yet, for as much as we can look at Arcangela as a protofeminist, we do not want to anachronistically dislocate the seventeenth-century nun, living in Venice where careful selection of wives for patricians was an absolute necessity; prospective brides from the *cittadini* class or from the aristocracy of the Venetian-controlled territories could not marry a patrician man without the approval of the Avogadori di Comun, a process that would ensure future sons from the alliance legitimate right to sit in the Great Council.[394] Nor should we gloss over Arcangela's constricted state that necessitated artful perspicacity to circumvent societal and ecclesiastical blockades. Reared to respect the religious and cultural institutions that sustained Venice, Arcangela, for all her outspoken condemnation of the deplorable societal practice of forced monachization, teetered on the tightrope of pleasing and respecting the aristocrats (patrons and supporters) without whom her literary aspirations could not reach fruition.

With concern about the merits of the prospective bridegroom for a patrician girl, Arcangela replies to a note received the evening before from "Signor N."[395] She advises this friend to be very careful about the prospective husband's lineage (*parentado*), to make sure there is not even a shadow of doubt about him as a worthy prospect, protecting the interests of the lady in question. It seems that the letter recipient is in a position to investigate the background and parentage of the man in question. Opportunely, along with this marriage advice, Suor Arcangela includes a request to have her manuscript,[396] in possession of the addressee, returned to her because since this work is "her daughter and virgin" (*Mia figlia e vergine*), she would not want her (the book) to encounter in his hands the disgrace and misfortune that others have.[397] The personification of and allusion to her books as her "offspring" is a recurrent motif, emblematic of the nun's devotion to her literary production—this motherly devotion shedding light on the fierce fight that Arcangela waged to protect and publish her life's output.

Arcangela's concerns about marriageable men for elite daughters align with Venetian cultural guidelines. In this threatening fluid society driven by a burgeoning wealthy merchant class, the interests of the Republic required statutory as well as cultural separation of patricians from the underclasses. Marriage alliance was the significant path to upward mobility for nonaristocratic caste members who through advantageous marriages of daughters and sisters could permeate the supposed hermetically sealed Venetian aristocracy. Tarabotti is as much a part of her Venice as she is a vociferous critic of La Serenissima's injustices against women, her participation in fostering marriage alliances grounded in the cultural considerations of her day. She makes it clear, for example, that the prospective bride in one matchmaking process "is the daughter of the most excellent ambassador of his Caesarean majesty," referring to the ambassador of the Holy Roman Empire in Venice. In another missive, the nun acknowledges her part in investigating "the age, profession and expectations of the bridegroom,"[398] considerations that were foremost in the process of elite marriage arrangements.

Although Tarabotti's matchmaking takes into consideration the social and economic status of the prospects, she also encourages alliances that could result in happiness for the couple. In a letter to "Signora N.," the nun acknowledges that a certain groom is young and that the young lady in question "awaits him with bated breath."[399] To another anonymous recipient, Suor Arcangela writes about marriage arrangements they seem to be working on together: "the young girl absolutely does not want the 'N' because—all joking apart—her mother has information that he has practically nothing, and she also says that forty years is too old for a young lady."[400]

Tarabotti advises that another young man would be more to her liking, "a handsome young fellow, lively and affectionate who is hard working rather than the silly old widower." Again, with typical Tarabottian practicality, in the same correspondence, the ambitious nun discusses her work, referring to an unacceptable copyist.[401] In fact, half of the letters in the volume mention one or more of her own works, with still others containing oblique connections to the nun's literary production.

The nun describes the perfect wife in her defense of "Lady N."[402] whose marriage arrangements concern Tarabotti: "She is a strong woman…who will be active in governing the household and contemplative in her awareness of her husband's desires to always fulfill them." She will gladly oversee his finances, not to dissipate his money but to have it grow. In sum, this fellow will be able to truly say *mulieris bona beatus vir*[403] "in spite of those men who always complain about their wives."[404]

22

Arcangela's Salon: Working the Parlatorio

F irmly confined to the convent in these Tridentine times, Arcangela took full advantage of the social space of the *parlatorio*, hardly the sedate and solemn sphere authorities would have preferred. To the contrary, seventeenth-century Venetian *parlatorios* were civic centers that attracted a well-heeled crowd, functioning as social hubs where marriage negotiations took place, bridal parties visited enclosed relatives, and music, dance, and dramatic performances were presented. This osmotic link, the junction between convent confinement and secular social spaces, offered Arcangela the possibility of mastering at least a portion of her circumscribed condition.

Tarabotti embraced and exploited this marginal space, evinced by her letters in which she refers to personal encounters in the *parlatorio*. In one instance, the nun takes the reins in organizing a concert at the convent, writing to an unidentified "The Most Illustrious Countess S." Tarabotti invites the countess, who was also a singer, to perform at Sant'Anna "lunedi prossimo" (next Monday). The missive chronicles Tarabotti's enterprising spirit as she organizes *parlatorio* entertainment; the subtext of her letter, however, shows the nun, who never misses an opportunity to keep her literary self in full view, twice alluding to her published *Paradiso monacale*: "Music is a part of the glories of *Paradise*," she claims, inviting the countess and her husband not to deny the glory of music to her "convent Paradise."[405] Whether paradise or inferno, as Tarabotti alternately characterizes the convent—ever mindful of the letter addressee—the confined nun communicated with her numerous contacts who often visited in the *parlatorio* where Arcangela could discuss public affairs, exchange manuscripts, receive prohibited books,[406] and meet with literati, establishing social networks, threads of contacts reinforced and further enhanced through her letters exchanges, of allies and patrons essential to the nun's publication goal.

Entertainment in the convent, celebration on feast days, for instance, attracted a distinguished crowd. In one case, Arcangela apparently had misunderstood a situation that involved the Illustrissima ed Eccellentissima Signora Madama Gilda, wife of a renowned war hero, who had requested seats for the feast of Sant'Anna.[407] Arcangela apologizes, explaining that had she known of the lady's request, she would have "flown to heaven" to furnish chairs appropriate for her rank, referring to the noblewoman's request for seats at the event.[408]

Indeed, the *parlatorio* became a sort of salon for Suor Tarabotti. Among a formidable array of notable visitors was Arcangela's brother-in-law Giacomo Pighetti, married to the nun's youngest sister, Lorenzina. Impressed with her courageous writing, Pighetti, an early supporter, lent her books, looked at manuscripts, and eventually introduced the nun to Giovan Francesco Loredan, eminent noble and founder of the Accademia degli Incogniti of which Pighetti was a member. The elite freethinking literary group—anticlerical, patriotic, and libertine—was intrigued by the outspoken Benedictine nun. It was Loredan, controlling the Venetian press in mid-Seicento Venice, who would eventually circulate and facilitate the publication of Tarabotti's manuscripts, *Paradiso monacale* the first to press in 1643.

Paradiso, penned after Tarabotti's failed attempts to have her previously written works, *Tirannia paterna* and *L'inferno monacale*,[2] published, touted the convent as "paradise" for those with religious calling. On the other hand, *Tirannia* and *Inferno*, written prior to *Paradiso,* were sulfurous indictments of the patriarchal powers—social, economic, and political forces—behind the practice of "imprisoning innocents," as Tarabotti often characterized forced *clausura*. A determined Tarabotti, although aware that even in the culturally liberal Venice of mid-Seicento these iconoclastic texts could never pass ecclesiastical and state scrutiny, persisted throughout her life to have her profane, and most eloquent work, *Tirannia*, published, an event that took place in Holland two years after the nun's death in 1652.

Arcangela, from her subaltern state, in order to distinguish herself as a formidable woman of letters, would continually be at the mercy of the mighty to legitimize her intellectual worth and concretize her writerly identity. Often, the catalysts of the nun's expedient associations originated from within Sant'Anna Convent itself. Through Tarabotti's *consorella* Betta Polani,[409] Arcangela established a relationship with Betta's influential uncle, Giovanni Polani, a prominent patrician and visitor to the *parlatorio*, frequently acting as intermediary between Tarabotti and those who could help her publish. In fact, it was Giovanni Polani, whom Arcangela implored in her indefatigable quest to see her works in print, to pass on a copy of *Paradiso* to Loredan:[410]

> Supplico per tanto la di Lei impareggiablile gentilezza far capitare l'annessa al illlustrissimo ed Eccellentissimo Loredano, insieme con quell'opera ch'egli s'e compiacciuto d'imparadisare con la sua celebratissima penna.[411] (I beg you in your unequalled kindness to give this enclosed letter to the illustrious and most excellent Loredano, together with the work that he kindly 'imparadised' with his most celebrated pen.)

This sort of value chain was one of the few strategic avenues open to a woman with literary ambition, especially one constricted and confined by walls, dictums, and religious rigors.

Her time "at the *finestrina*" appears to have been pleasurable as Zanette comments regarding Arcangela's penchant for socialization.[412] The biographer also notes that most of Tarabotti's visitors from 1640 until her death in 1652 were women (friends and supporters) who likely offered their stories for the material in *Antisatira* and (the lost) *Purgatorio delle mal maritate*,[413] confiding in the nun at the *finestrina* of the *parlatorio*. Visits from such illustrious members of Venetian society as the wife of Giovan Francesco Loredan were immortalized in Tarabotti's letters: to Loredan, referring to herself as an "archangel," full of pride," Tarabotti expresses how delighted she was upon the visit of his Illustrissima ed Eccellentissima spouse, Laura Valier.[414]

Loredan himself visited the nun in the *parlatorio*. Tarabotti, on one occasion, had asked the nobleman to procure a scandalous text for her. Arriving at the convent two days after Loredan's visit was the infamous—and prohibited *Anima di F. Pallavicino*[415] hidden in a copy of her *L'inferno monacale* just as Tarabotti had requested, and then, several days later, returned in the exact same way, the nun in violation of conventual codes, fearing discovery.[416]

Attesting to the autodidact nun exchanged books passed to her through the *ruota* of the *parlatorio*. Giovanni Polani was perhaps the one contact who delivered to Suor Arcangela all the books she was so avid to read.[417] Tarabotti's writings are enlightened by copious study of such authors as Boccaccio, Petrarch, Ariosto, and Dante, works not available in the Sant'Anna Convent library. The *parlatorio*, with its *ruota*, was the seat of book exchanges, texts by no means allowed in these Tridentine times.

Polani, a frequent *parlatorio* visitor, was often the go-between to deliver manuscripts or letters to influential associates. In one of the earliest letters of the collection, [418]Tarabotti tells of her *inferno di tristezza* (inferno of sadness) endured upon seeing the numerous printing errors found in the copy of *Paradiso monacale*, errors that make her look like a laughing stock, as if, "like a monkey" she wanted to imitate learned men without knowing what they were saying.[419] She asks Polani to please understand and help to oversee the printing process.

Expanding her network, Tarabotti established a noteworthy connection with the French contingent in Venice. From 1642 until their departure from Venice in 1645, the French ambassador Hameaux and his family visited and corresponded with Suor Arcangela. Through the ambassador's wife, Anne Hameaux (Italianized by Tarabotti as Madama d'Amo), the nun came to meet Anne's niece, Margherita de Fiubet, with whom the nun engaged in *cara, spiritosa* (dear and lively) conversation at the grille. Tarabotti refers to these visits affectionately as *un dono di Paradiso* (a gift from Paradise).[420] She admires Margherita's rare beauty at such a tender age, "like a celestial Venus," noting the blue gown the lady wore when she last saw her. The nun also praises Margherita's "intellect, nobility and decorum of wealth."[421] In emotional tones, Tarabotti writes to Margherita upon the lady's voyage to Rome, conveying "un doloroso sentiment del mio cuore"[422] (a painful feeling in my heart) and wishing her a pleasant pilgrimage to Santa Casa and Rome to see the new pope, Innocence X,[423] wishing her a speedy return to Venice.

Before the Hameaux family departed Venice in 1645,[424] the young noble lady had died, Arcangela expressing her deep grief in a letter of condolence to Madam Hameaux.[425] The relationship between Margherita and Arcangela appears to be one of sincere affection; possibly the niece of Madama d'Amo could also have acted as a go-between for the nun who had asked the ambassador's wife to procure indulgences for her from the new pope. Addressing Margherita, Tarabotti had requested that she relate apologies to the ambassadress for perhaps asking too much of a favor.

Whether consulting with lady friends with whom Tarabotti collaborated to arrange marriages, or meeting with prominent literary figures, these encounters rarely exclude from conversation the overarching goal of the iron-willed nun to have her work see the light of day. Exceptions are few; notwithstanding the expedient association with Betta Polani's uncle Giovanni Polani, some of the most heartfelt and endearing letters are addressed to Betta Polani, Tarabotti's former *consorella* with whom she had established a close friendship that continued after Betta was taken out of the convent by her uncle who had arranged for her marriage. In these emotional missives, we find Tarabotti reluctant to mention her work at all. Rather, the two correspondents seem to have had a unique friendship, Tarabotti often lamenting about her own health and advising about Betta's well-being.

23

"Socrates used to do it": The Art of Self-Promotion

The blending of praise and humility, requisite in a missive from "low to high," is a winning strategy that Arcangela perfects through effective pairing of cheeky charm with customary courtesies as she procures favors, lauds her supporters, and admonishes her detractors, often with mock modesty that belies her obvious intelligence and literary ability as well as her prodigious learning.

The nun launches the good fight during her protracted campaign to publish.[426] She defends her authorial identity, armed with only her "poor intellect" and "black pen." Working within parameters of Early Modern epistolary manner, Tarabotti posts eloquent letters imbued with self-deprecating humility, implying that she little values her prodigious talent. It hardly seems congruous, then, that the writing nun would spend her energy and a good part of her life battling to see her words in print. We can argue that she certainly did know the value of her texts, confident of their press-worthiness. Additionally, we note the nun's overt pride in her "offspring" and motherly devotion to them. Confidence in knowing her work must be printed belies the deferential semiotics.

Tarabotti offers two of her manuscripts to a Paolo Donado,[427] (not precisely identified), apologizing for her "imperfect words" placed before the recipient's eyes, admitting her "shortcomings," and characterizing her writing as "rough lines." She begs compassion for the weakness of her "sterile and uncultured mind." References to her "sterile mind" appear frequently, but even in consideration of Baroque sociopragmatic polite excess, Tarabotti's grandiloquent mock modesty suggests a well-oiled approach to glean the patronage and goodwill of the addressee. She exercises a cultural civility expected of her as a seventeenth-century woman religious, tempering her requests with humility that might not have been as opaque as we would expect. Indeed, Arcangela adheres to the ritualistic epistolary practices of devaluing oneself and exalting the recipient in asymmetrical correspondence. In many ways, the contemporary social deixis and formulaic deference serve Arcangela well, for she is compelled to seek favors and request cooperation from those in positions of power.

Employing irony and humility in a letter to Giacomo Pighetti, her well-connected brother-in-law, she asks him not to circulate her *Antisatira* manuscript, while clearly in other correspondence we see her desire to have the work known and put to press:

> Sia come si voglia, dichiaro I miei scritti non solo indegni delle stampe, ma anche immeritevoli d'esser mirati da altri che dai miei cari congionti.[428] (Be what it may, I declare my writings not only unworthy of publication, but also undeserving to be looked at by anyone else except my dear relatives.)

Pighetti did not take Tarabotti at her word, or perhaps ignored her veiled wishes, and did in fact show the text to Angelico Aprosio, igniting a heated squabble between the Augustinian friar and the Benedictine nun, a conflict that we look at in the next chapter.

Cicero's lessons were not lost on Arcangela as she evidences her rhetorical dexterity in the collected letters. Informed by Early Modern epistolary manners, the nun, writing to societal superiors, strategizes to gain the respect and goodwill of her recipients, cleverly working within the parameters of established correspondence norms. What highlights Tarabotti's formal letters is her ability to shower praise while promoting her own cause and asserting her literary identity.

Time and again in Tarabotti's letter collection, we see her rhetorical pendulum swinging from self-deprecation to earnest entreaties to have her "sterile mind" [s] "rough words" read by the world. Reaching out beyond Venice to have *Tirannia* published, Arcangela writes to the "Altezza Serenissma di Vittoria Medici dalla Rovere, Granduchessa di Toscana"[429] (Her Serene Highness Vittoria Medici dalla Rovere, Grand Duchess of Tuscany), one of a series of notes and letters addressed to the noble Florentine woman. Tarabotti solicits the duchess's patronage to help her obtain the right to publish the scathing polemic *Tirannia paterna* in Florence or perhaps Rome. Playing to the noblewoman's devout faith, Arcangela highlights her own situation, using the fact that she is a nun to her benefit, her *poverta' religiousa* (religious poverty), to apologize for her lack of rhetorical ornament.

It was not unusual for nuns to communicate with high-placed women, and especially the grand duchess would have been a recipient of nuns' letters requesting donations.[430] What sets Tarabotti apart is that she pleads not for blessed beneficence, but instead for her own writing to be published, a supplication that required acute rhetorical skills. Moreover, cultivating close associations with the powerful would protect Tarabotti, as we learn when *Antisatira* came under attack. Having dedicated this work to the grand duchess and having gained her patronage, Tarabotti feels protected against detractors who rail against *Antisatira*:

> Sappia dunque che con tutto che da molti mi fosse rifferitio che v'era chi impiegava la penna contro di me, difficilmente m'inducevo a crederlo, presuppondendo per certissimo d'esser piu' che sicura da' colpi dell'altrui malignita' mentre vivo sotto lo scudo della protezione." dell'altezza Serenissima della gran duchessa di Toscana, di cui, non ch'alto, il nome di Vittoria mi promette in ogni occorrenza un trionfo.[431] (Know, therefore, that with everything people are telling me about those who

were using their pens against me, it is hard for me
to believe, knowing for certain that I am more
than safe from the blows of those malicious persons while I live beneath the protective shield of
Her Most Serene Highness, the grand duchess of
Tuscany, whose name alone, Vittoria, promises to
me in any circumstance a triumph.)[432]

Arcangela's attempts to have the duchess clear the path to
Tirannia paterna's publication met with no success. The first letters were cordial, the duchess glad to have a book dedication; but as
time went on, perhaps the noblewoman, who was in correspondence
with many other nuns, came to understand that this particular nun,
enclosed in the modest Venetian convent of Sant'Anna di Castello,
was quite unorthodox.[433]

Tarabotti's ornate, often obsequious wording, in her formal letters especially, reflects Early Modern epistolary manners, strategies
reliant upon a five-part letter structure standardized in the late eleventh century, going back to antiquity: ars dictaminis, having its roots
in Italy, provided for the epistle to convey the intended meaning of
the sender through the classically stylized forms of salutation, the
greeting that identifies the recipient's social status; securing the goodwill (*Captatio Benevolentia*), usually including a proverb or quotation
from Scripture; narration, statement of purpose; petition, the argument deduced from previously stated premises; and conclusion.[434]
Working within established correspondence norms, Arcangela conveys her self-worth and defends her literary persona. Even at her most
self-effacing, Tarabotti's grandiloquent manner in letters to recipients
of superior status promotes her cause and establishes her identity.

Most of the missives in the collection fall into the "low to high"
realm, the nun of lower social, political, and economic status than
her recipients. Indeed, Arcangela Tarabotti, lacking formal education, devoid of hereditary lineage, was situated inferiorly to most
recipients. Arcangela presents fourteen letters written to doges or
future doges, an impressive correspondence for the incarcerated nun
of *cittadini* class, and testimony to the writer's talents as well as her
self-marketing skills.

From Aristotle to Nietzsche,[435] the "virtue" of gift giving has been discussed in terms of the giver's moral strength and the recipient's indebtedness. Capitalizing on the tactic of gift giving, Tarabotti sends her *Tirannia paterna* as a "gift" to the highest power elites of Venice, an act that can only elicit a reply of gratitude (debt?) from the recipient. This double-edged offering succeeds in putting the nun's work in front of La Serenissima's most noble powers: Tarabotti proudly broadcasts as the first missive of her letter book correspondence addressed to "The Most Serene Prince of Venice Francesco Erizzo."[436] She presents the doge with her *Paradiso monacale*, a present offered in gratitude for the doge having read her manuscripts, works she depicts as products of her *povero ingegno* (poor intellect), all the while showcasing impressive literary skills, adroitly manipulating figures and tropes in humble self-promotion. Elegantly referencing the ancients who marked favorable times in "white chalk" (*bianca pietra*), the nun claims she is moved to do the same now, blessed by her lucky stars that the doge has cast his eyes upon her work.

> A Lei si dovrebbono in dono nobilissimi e ricchissimi scettri, regni, e amplissime monachie, non in chiostri oscuri, carratteri mal formati e fogli leggeiri.[437] (You merit noble and rich scepters, realms and huge kingdoms, not in black ink, poorly formed letters, and flimsy pages.)[438]

Although she places *Paradiso* beneath his high worth, Arcangela does so with imaginative metaphor that showcases her literary finesse—couched in humble self-promotion. The backhanded "gift" succeeds in putting *Paradiso* in front of the supreme Venetian while positioning the nun on high moral ground as gift giver, the recipient now in a form of debt at least requiring acknowledgment and thanks. When Doge Erizzo was succeeded by Francesco Molino in 1646, Tarabotti wrote an encomiastic letter to the successive doge, joining in the acclaim of the entire senate, rejoicing that *la regina dell'Adria* (the queen of Adria) "has crowned the temples and the ducal diadem for the consolation of our city and the glory of the Venetian Empire."[439]

To Doge Molino, she also sends a copy of *Paradiso monacale*, twice naming her brother-in-law Giacomo Pighetti, a name-dropping that serves Tarabotti well, as she mentions that Pighetti has spoken with reverence to her about the doge. She does not fail to include that Pighetti, who apparently was a good friend of the doge's deceased brother, remembers his lost friend, "never without tears."[440]

When Tarabotti presents a copy of *Antisatira* to the "Illustrious Signora N.,"[441] sister of an unnamed count—both of whom remain anonymous—she asks pardon for her "boldness," a frequent request, thereby proffering herself as an apologetic gift giver to minimize the imposition. The "boldness apology" goes a long way to satisfy the face-wants of addressees[442] who may also look upon the nun's gustiness as admirable. Nonetheless, as epistolary politic behavior demands in asymmetric relations, Arcangela dutifully separates herself in rank and position from the recipient, commenting tactfully that persons of the noblewoman's stature are in the habit of frequently receiving gifts from servants, Arcangela positioning herself as one.

Encoding her social identity, requisite in seventeenth-century epistolary exchange, by placing herself as "servant" to the recipient, Tarabotti highlights her helpless position as she asks for an egocentric favor. Bestowing upon the anonymous sister of a count, "Illustrissima Signor N.,"[443] a copy of *Antisatira*, the nun positions herself as a servant giving to one of such high and noble rank who is used to receiving and is always appreciative of gifts[444]—the nun fulfilling her intentions to put the text into the hands of those who could be of service to her.

Alluding to her literary production as "questo picciol aborto del mio sterilissimo ingegno" (this small miscarriage of my sterile intellect) and including the boldness apology, Arcangela puts forth the ostensive reason for having written *Antisatira*: at the behest of others "per ubbidir ai commandi di chi devo sono caduta nell'errore di componerlo e di publicarlo per mezzo delle stampe" (to obey the commands of those I must, I have fallen into the error of composing and having it printed).[445] In a letter to the Grand Duchess of Tuscany,[446] to whom *Antisatira* is dedicated, Tarabotti reiterates the same rationale: she has followed the orders of "molte nobilissime dame" (many noble gentle ladies) to whom she is "obliged to obey like a vassal" ("alle quali sono tenuta obedire come vassalla").[447]

Asking for favors was the only course open to a determined Tarabotti. When possible, the nun offers her own "gift" in exchange, often promising her prayers for the health and well-being of the recipient. Concomitant with prayers, the nun often presents her literary works. She compliments Signor Enrico Cornaro[448] on his "sweetest nature" and seeks from him a book of poems. In return, she gifts him with her *Lagrime...per la morte dell'illustrissima signora Regina Donati* (*Tears upon the Death of the Most Illustrious Signora Regina Donati*).[449] Tarabotti persuades the letter recipient with her rhetorical skills combining obligatory exordium and honorifics with poetic hyperbole designed to render her reader compliant. She never loses her bearing, cleaved to the course of literary recognition and publication.

24

No One's Fool: Arcangela's Ire

*I*n *Lettere*, Arcangela Tarabotti presents a self-portrait illustrating her worth, controlling the platform as both subject and author. She surrounds herself with the most prominent members of Venetian society and looks directly at them with a bold yet humble aspect, portraying a constructed image of feisty temperament and noteworthy talent as she straddles the public-private arenas.

From the time Suor Arcangela realized her intellectual capacities and began putting pen to paper,[450] her life was marked by stalwart combat to publish and ceaseless struggle to assert and defend her literary integrity. Four supporters, through whom she succeeded in having *Paradiso monacale* and *Antisatira* put to press, were also to be her most fervent detractors: Angelico Aprosio, Girolamo Brusoni, Giacomo Pighetti, and Giovan Francesco Loredan all at one point turned against Tarabotti, at times even stooping to make sport of the susceptible nun. As well, Renata di Claramonte, Marchese di Galeranda,[451] whom Tarabotti turned to in the uphill battle to have her "firstborn," as the nun referred to *Tirannia paterna*, breathe public air, would show herself to be unreliable, possibly double-crossing, overtly provoking the ire of Arcangela, who by this time[452] was determined to shape her authorial persona and practice her true vocation.

Having been deprived of liberty and choice as a child, plucked from the outside world and inserted into, in her own words, "a living hell,"[453] Suor Arcangela would not now have her agency extricated and would do battle, armed with figures and tropes, with those attempting to interfere with or impede what had become Arcangela Tarabotti's raison d'être. The resolute nun would protect and defend her irreverent *Tirannia,* which pulsates with the palpable furor of Tarabotti's stinging prose, while laying bare the open wounds of young Elena Tarabotti's forced confinement "to a perpetual labyrinth of the cloister"[454] in an "L'inferno monacale." To those who would defame her intellect and ability, she dispatched eloquent missives laced with obligatory respect, full of invective.

The Marchese di Galeranda, Renata di Claramonte, for one, learned that Suor Arcangela would not be duped. The nun had entrusted the marchioness, whom she had met through the French diplomatic core residing in Venice, with a copy of *Tirannia paterna,* as well as the manuscript of *Inferno monacale,* hoping to finally see *Tirannia* published in the more accepting and anticlerical environment of Paris. In five missives addressed to the French noblewoman, Tarabotti chronicles the convoluted events of the saga, beginning with a short letter, containing a metaphor confirming the nun's maternal pride in her first two written tomes. She refers to *Tirannia* as the girl (the title is feminine in Italian) and *Inferno* (the title is masculine in Italian) as the boy.

> Due parti del mio sterilissimo ingegno vengono a servire Vostra Eccellenza, ma con stravaganti condizione. La femina, che dovrebbe star retirata e lontana dalla pratiche perche in questa patria sarebbe mal veduta, voglio che diventi donna publica nella Francia. Il maschio dovra' star nascosto sino alli occhi del Cielo, in conformita' della di Lei irrevocabile parola.[455] (Two offspring of my most sterile intellect come to serve Your Excellency, but with exceptional conditions. The girl, who must remain withdrawn and far from worldly practices because in this city she would be badly viewed, is to become a public woman in France. The boy should stay hidden even from the eyes of heaven, as in keeping with your irrevocable word.)

Not having heard from the marchioness in over a year, Arcangela's ensuing letters become steadily more acidic, reprimanding the noblewoman for not having written, demanding news about the entrusted manuscripts; and finally, openly cross, the exasperated author shows her grit: having heard that the marchioness's secretary, Colisson, had intentions of publishing the book himself, Tarabotti pens an ireful missive to the "Illustrissima ed Eccellentissima Signora Renata di Claramonte":

> Finally, after so long you have inquired if I am dead or alive. Thank God I am very much alive and ready to fight against anyone who attempts to trick me so that instead of being defrauded, the trickster himself will be defrauded.[456]

Menacingly, Tarabotti promises that if Colisson publishes her book, whether in French or English, under another name other than her own, he would be robbing "a poor little woman of her glory and would bear the brunt of the hate and blame of all the world."[457] Diplomatically excusing the marchioness of complicity, Tarabotti sardonically lauds the noblewoman, asserting that "una dama di tanto merito" (a woman of your high worth would never lower herself to take part in such a ruse, so I will therefore go ahead full force against the person I mentioned above).[458] The incensed nun would not allow her issue to be kidnapped and, in no uncertain terms, realizing that the marchesa cannot be trusted, insists that she promptly return the manuscript.[459]

The drama contains several subplots involving Tarabotti's part in having a lace collar made for the marchioness and the nun's wrath at finally receiving several printed pages of *Tirannia*, full of errors that the fuming nun declares would embarrass her and defile her work. Neither text would be published in the nun's lifetime.

Constantly being put on the defensive, and rising to the task, Arcangela successfully safeguards her literary standing by successfully suppressing the publication of Angelico Aprosio's *La maschera scoperta*, which would have libeled the nun by revealing her name as the author of *Antisatira* and accusing her of not having written her books, citing the stylistic differences between *Paradiso monacale* published the year before *Antisatira* in 1643. Aprosio (1607–1681),[460] an itinerant friar, author, and Incogniti member, at first supported the nun, then turned on her with his proposed publication while denying his nefarious intentions. Defending her motives for trying to suppress his text, and responding to Aprosio's protests of innocence, Tarabotti sends the would-be vilifier a letter[461] with proof of his intent:

> Just to let your Reverend Lordship know it is not true that you do not intend to print your *Maschera* with my name clearly apparent. And I, with just cause, have moved to have it cancelled, am sending you the frontispiece copied from the original written in your own hand. If you can deny this and that you have not read the work to many gentlemen with my expressed name, many times over, I will have to say that you have an intellect more than divine, while even God with all of his omnipotence cannot make things that happened not happen: "Quod factum est fieri non potest."—What has been done cannot be redone because what exist cannot be re-made.[462]

Tarabotti lets Aprosio know that she intends for him to remove her name from his "comedy" so that it does not end in a "tragedy" for someone. Arcangela was not firing blanks when she threatened Aprosio, letting him know that it was not a good idea to publish his invectives against her, declaring open war, her clear intentions stated, knowing she is on the side of justice. Losing her patience, she declares,

> Perche' il quinto element di cui sono formata e' el sincerita', risolvo di far finalmente intendere a Vostra Paternita', che io sempre sprezzai l'insolenze frateshe, e che derido quei cani che latrano

alla luna. Puo' desistere dallo scrivermi, poiche' per l'avvenire le sue lettere non saranno lette da me, e le daro' quel recapito che meritano, si com'anche delle sue composizioni, o stampate o manuscritte, faro' quella stima ch'hanno fatto tutti i letterati d'Italia, delle publicate da lei contro il P.N.[463] (Because the fifth element of which I am formed is sincerity, I resolve to finally clarify to Your Reverence, that I have always disdained friarly insolence, and that I despise those dogs who howl at the moon. You can stop writing to me since in the future, I will not read your letters and will give them the reception they deserve, as well I will do the same to your compositions, or publications or manuscripts, I will give them the esteem that all of the literary men of Italy have given to your publications against P.N.)[464]

Another initial proponent, Girolamo Brusoni (1614–1686), a contentious erstwhile monk and libertine writer, member of the Accademia degli Incogniti,[465] at first supported Tarabotti, sharing the nun's outrage with enforced *clausura*, he too having been involuntarily placed in a monastic institution. It seems the tension between the two might have been literary rivalry on the part of the apostate friar, for it was the publication of *Antisatira* that inspired Brusoni to threaten with a response; his ad hominem attacks belie a misogynistic bent, verbal assaults that might have been what enraged Arcangela the least—but we cannot know this.

We do, however, know that these incursions upon her very person evoked bilious retorts: Brusoni mocked her in writing and to her face for her lameness, eliciting from Suor Arcangela, the tender definition of her "deformity" inherited from her father, "quell difetto col quale forse il mio genitore ha volute contrasegnarmi per sua figliuola" (that defect that perhaps with which my father had wanted to mark me as his daughter). Brusoni attacked the nun (and even repeated the insult years after Suor Arcangela's death), as "crippled in body and mind."[466] In a repartee that cannot help but evoke empathy for Suor Arcangela, she asserts that,

> Ad ogni modo mi glorio d'esser zoppa perche' così' certo saro' delli invitati a quella gran cena che voi altri, dritti del corpo ma zoppi dell'anima e stropiati nell'operazione, dal Padre di Famiglia sete stati esclusi per sempre. A Dio. (I glory in the fact that I am lame, because of it, I am sure I will be invited to the great supper that you others, with straight bodies but lame of soul and crippled ways, have been excluded forever by our Family Father. Adieu.)[467]

Arcangela continues her letter to the friar, recalling his previous praise and support. She casts doubt on his honesty and questions his motives, expressing surprise irritation with his invectives. Tarabotti is taken aback by Brusoni's unexpected ambush: "Io son pur quella Angelica tanto da Vostra Signoria gia' tempo lodata, e ora I miei scritti sono cosi' spezzabili" (I am still that same Angelica[468] who Your Lordship once praised so highly, and now you find my writings so despicable). Arcangela is disheartened as she ingenuously comments that Brusoni had considered *Tirannia paterna* "una meraviglia" (a marvel), and now claims her words are heretical and unworthy: "Chi puo' tacere a tali sentimenti ha gran prudenza. Io mi confesso inabile a restistere" (Whoever can keep silent in the face of such sentiments has great prudence. I must confess I am unable to resist).[469]

Arcangela also had to defend herself against noxious rumors, apparently spread by Brusoni, and had to protect her integrity against charges of plagiarism. Her former supporter, now traducer, had cited the very nuns of Sant'Anna, Suor Arcangela's *consorelle*, as those who spread the rumor that she was not the author of her works. Tarabotti replies,

> Se il credere che le mie monache avessero disseminate quella zizania che Vostr Signoria m'accennna fosse punto de fede, morirei certamente eretica e

piu' tosto crederci di veder il diavolo a farsi la croce che supponere una tal improprietade.[470] (If believing that my nuns had disseminated that rumor Your Lordship mentions to me, it would be a point of faith, and I would certainly die a heretic and believe I have seen the devil make the sign of the cross, rather than believe such an impropriety.)

In this same letter, she tells her turncoat friend that she will return all his letters as soon as she has the confirmation that he will do the same and return her letters. Protecting her "offspring," and her literary worth, Arcangela, irate with Brusoni, accuses him of plagiarizing her work: "I am astonished that Your Lordship claims to have mentioned in your work the topic of forced nuns, [you] having seen my work. You were obligated to not speak of something so discussed by me."[471] She tells Brusoni that eminent gentlemen had already read her work (*Tirannia paterna*)[472] before he had set eyes on it, confident that her authorship will be proven. However, the battle takes a toll on Suor Arcangela: she ends this letter telling Brusoni that although she has purged herself (of her anger and disappointment), instead of feeling relieved, she is "aggravata in maniera che sto peggio che mai" (aggravated to such an extent that I am worse than ever). She concludes, telling Brusoni, "The expertise of the physicians of our time know how to handle these miracles. Patience. A Dio."

It was one thing to have the iconoclastic nun's manuscripts circulated (*L'inferno monacale* and *Tirannia paterna*) and to publish the mild *Paradiso monacale*, but apparently, the response to *Antisatira*'s defense of women's vanity was a bridge too far for literary men. Tarabotti provided a logical retort to the woman's vanity argument, offering examples of men's own vanity, which in reference to clothing, at this time, was a strong argument.

Another close associate, Arcangela's brother-in-law Giacomo Pighetti, after his initial support, going so far as to pen an introductory encomium to *Paradiso monacale*, would come to deeply disappoint the nun. Apparently working both sides of the fence, Pighetti is accused by an irate and deluded Tarabotti of having promoted and encouraged Aprosio's attacks on her literary merit in his *La maschera scoperta*,[473] which questions her authorship. Pighetti's denials to his sister-in-law's certainty (evidence in hand, she claims) suggest that he settled on the side of Loredan, with whom he had strong ties. She addresses him in no uncertain terms, "My Dear Brother-in-law, your prudence understands better than I do that there is nothing that can remain hidden circulating on the tongues of so many." She has evidence, which she cannot now reveal; and she knows well that Aprosio, Pighetti's good friend, would never have written such an invective against his sister-in-law without approval from her brother-in-law first.[474]

In this, one of the lengthiest letters of the collection, Arcangela's disappointment and distress are apparent: She acknowledges that her grief is not at all because she has been attacked, since one who writes expects this. However, she continues, "Ma ben mi traffigge l'anima il sentire ch'il merito d'una mia sorelle, da me singolarmente amato e riverito per le sue somme virtu', ne sia stao il promotore" (But what really pierces my soul is to hear that my sister's husband, whom I have singularly loved and revered for his supreme virtues, was the one who promoted this).[475]

Tarabotti also defends herself against accusations of being ambitious: "Non e' stata ambizione che mi abbia persuasa al metter alle stampe questa mia operetta," and points out to Pighetti "that one would have to be crazy to rely on the praise of men, who if one minute they exalt you, in the next moment they besmirch and mistreat you."[476] Also in this poignant letter, we find Tarabotti getting to the core of her argument—mistreatment of women, declaring that she knows well "che la virtu' e' sprezzata e abborrita nelle donne" (that virtue is despised and deplored in women).[477]

The ending to this letter encapsulates the emotional toll of Tarabotti's uphill battle for literary legitimacy:

> Lei s'assicuri ch'io non mai sono concorsa ad offenderLa ne' a pregiudicarLe, ma ben ho sempre stimata la Sua penna e amata la Sua persona con affetto fraterno, se bene mal corrisposta, e Le baccio affettuosamente le mani.[478] (I can assure you

that I have never tried to offend you nor put you in jeopardy, but instead have always esteemed your pen and loved your person with sisterly affection, even if it was not returned, and affectionately, I kiss your hands.)

Although disappointed and crestfallen, Arcangela does not hesitate to set straight her erstwhile supporters. She is not above reprimanding the powerful patrician Giovan Francesco Loredan who seems to have played a silly trick on her and to have significantly misjudged the astute nun; she raises her literary sword, upbraiding him for visiting her with the sole purpose to ask for a book (Pallavicino's *Giuseppe* [*Joseph*], a book that would not be in her possession) rather than visit her out of friendship. He denied having done this, insisting he would never have looked for such a book so intolerant of women in a convent full of one hundred nuns. This incident appears to have been a puerile joke played on the nun, a joke that she discovers, and in a forthright letter to the powerful nobleman of the hour, launches a tactful self-assertion letting him know that she is on to his ruse. Apparently, Loredan smoothed over this incident as did Arcangela, testimony to the nun's force of character; most cordial exchanges followed this incident, including Loredan's visits to the *parlatorio*, presenting his wife to Suor Arcangela. The nun would go on to dedicate *Lettere* to Loredan whose coat of arms appears on the title page.

In another missive, Arcangela showers Loredan with effusive praise, thanking him for having written the presentation letter of *Paradiso monacale*, which she "read and re-read," referring to his "celebratissmia penna" (most celebrated pen) and calling him "un miracolo di natura" (a miracle of nature), claiming that "like bees, readers will be drawn to his divine style and suck his words like honey." She thanks him for the great honor he has conferred upon her, apologizes for her "debolezze" (weak words) and promises to pray for "Sua Divina Maestà" (His Divine Majesty) and for his house, pledging herself to him, "always."[479]

Tarabotti's twelve letters to Loredan reveal a complex and volatile professional rapport, the pendulum swaying from the nun's laudatory respect to her scolding sarcasm. Their mercurial exchanges range from Tarabotti thanking Loredan for his gift of "sweet sugar" that he had given her, addressing the nobleman as "mio principe" (my prince). Whether the gift was edible or whether Arcangela was metaphorical, perhaps referring to a book, is not clear.[480] Loredan, however, although the force behind the nun's publications, was not consistent in his support; and Tarabotti was not reticent in expressing her dismay: with playful sarcasm, censuring the patrician for his inconsistency, she gibes, "Non sono pero' tenute alla parola le deita', e perche' incomprensibili sono I lor giudizi non se no devono doler I mortali" (However, deities are not held to their word, and since their judgments are not comprehensible, mortals should not complain).[481]

25

The Deathbed Letter: Books Not Burned

T wo years before her physical death, and over three decades after her interment in the Convent of Sant'Anna di Castello, Arcangela Tarabotti, in 1650, sent to her closest friend, Betta Polani, a small chest accompanied by a letter:[482]

> Because the pilgrimage of my life has arrived at it ultimate destination in this world, to you who have been absolute mistress of the dearest part of myself, I am sending my writings, my most precious possessions and what I most regret leaving behind. I would say they should be burned, but in here I have no one I can trust to do this. The Compilations of a Loving Soul, The Road to Heaven, and The Convent Light, may be printed, if that is to your liking. The rest should be tossed into the sea of oblivion, I beg you in Visceribus Christi.[483] Pray for this soul, for I, will certainly do likewise from there. Love me even after my death, and adieu forever.

Arcangela refers to three works of solemn content (judging from the titles), all three according to Tarabotti worthy of publication, and all three lost to us. Although she claims the content of the chest should have been burned, in fact, they were not. That she could trust no one in the convent to do away with the books seems a rather weak rationale, especially considering that her writings were her dearest possessions, her "offspring"—her life's work.

Despite intimations of death, Suor Arcangela would live to write and publish one more work,[484] and to see this deathbed letter published in *Lettere familiari e di complimento*. As noted by her biographer, although Tarabotti was a Benedictine nun, what she valued most in her life was her writing,[485] reaffirming that Arcangela had realized her true vocation.

As far as the nun being moribund as she penned the letter and sent it to Polani along with her "dearest possessions," there can be little doubt that Tarabotti was in a fragile state. Indeed, she had suffered bouts of ill-health her entire life, adding to a motive that would have further solidified her father's decision to monachanize his daughter. In fact, in twenty-nine of the two hundred and fifty-six missives in *Lettere*, Arcangela directly refers to her health that often rendered her weak and bedridden.

Tarabotti's literary battles are mirrored in her physical struggles, not only with poor health, but with medical doctors as well. She tells of agitation resulting as much from her illness as from the physicians who "torment" her "incessantly with little pity" and how she has been "abbandonata da' medici" (abandoned by the doctors).[486] In a letter to the Duke of Parma,[487] Ferdinando Farnese, Tarabotti explains that she herself, out of all the infirm people, more than any other, harbors an antipathy toward doctors and medicine. Apparently, the duke had advised her to keep to a good regimen and moderate ways, advice that the nun claims, unfortunately, does not help to keep her healthy. She complains of a "continuo strettura di petto" (a continual tightness in the chest)

> Che mi consuma posso dir sino le ossa e mi toglie quasi affatto il respire, m'assalisce nell'autunno e primavera con veemenza tale che sovente mi reduce in stato di render improvisamente l'anima al Creatore. (that I can say consumes me to my very bones and almost completely takes my breath away, attacking me in the autumn and spring with

a vehemence that often reduces me to all of sudden render my soul to the Creator.

To Signor Cavallier Francesco Polani, Incogniti member and medical doctor who had sent her a letter and a book,[488] she replies,

> Mi capitorono in tempo che, languente nel letto, disperata di salute, sperava di terminare il pelegrinaggio di questo mondo. Era moribonda, tormentata da un inesorabile stretta di petto che di quando in quando mi fa odiare la vita e temere la morte."[489] (They arrived at a time when, languishing in bed, despairing of my health, I was hoping to end my pilgrimage in this life. I was moribund, tormented by an inexorable tightness in the chest that from time to time makes me hate life and fear death.)

Arcangela tells Polani she is still very weak from her illness. Yet despite her infirmity, she does include a written tribute to Polani's friend, perhaps requested by the addressee. Tarabotti refers to the "tightness" in her chest in ten letters, with language that reveals how this constriction delimited her:

> Sto malissimo della mia stretta di petto.[490] (I am very sick from my tightness in the chest.)

> Fui assalita da una fierissima strettura di petto, la quale mi privo ad un istesso tempo del respiro, e puossi dir, della vita.[491] (I was attacked by a most fierce constriction in my chest, which took away my breath and at the same time, one could say, my life.)

> Ma una continua strettura di petto, che mi consuma, posso dir, sino le viscere e mi toglie quasi a fatto il respiro, m'assalisse con veemenza tale che, facendmi penar il corpo, mi fa gettar la penna di lontano.[492] (But a continuous tightness in my chest that consumes me, I can say, to my very core and almost takes my breath away, attacking me with

vehemence such that my whole body suffers, making me throw my pen away.)

Often, Tarabotti excuses herself and her writing, laying blame on her illness with which she had to cope while composing the missive. To an anonymous recipient who had advised her of a mistake she had made in a previous letter, the nun admonishes,

> Dovera' Ella compatir a quell male che, levandomi tutte le memorie, rende doglioso e tormentato questo infelice individuo.[493] (You should have compassion for that illness that robs this unhappy person of memory, leaving me miserable and tormented.)

Although her letters are not dated, one surmises from the consistent mention of her bad health in her own and others' letters that Arcangela dealt with frequent periods of debilitating illness. Exactly what this malady was is never specified, but Zanette eliminates tuberculosis and consumption since the nun does not mention coughing seizures.[494] She does tell of seasonal, fall and spring, exacerbation that might suggest asthma, although this too would incorporate coughing. Cures for whatever it was exactly that caused such severe suffering for Arcangela were "primitive and common":[495] bloodletting, barley juice, fruit juices, and infusions of linen seeds with milk.[496]

The illness that weakened her, at times bringing Suor Arcangela to the door of death, did not, however, dull her spirit. Following the recount of her near-death encounter in the letter to the Duke of Parma, one of the lengthier missives in the volume, Tarabotti goes on to discuss the battle she is waging against attackers of *Antisatira*. With spunky retaliation, she quotes Scripture (Matthew 7:15)[497] and then asks the addressee,

> E chi potra' negar che siano lupi se vedando una innocente pecorella se le aventano contro per levarle la vita coll'ingoiarle quell poco di applause che le viene dall'ingenuita'altrui? (And who can

deny that they are wolves who when they see an innocent little lamb, they advance against it to take away her life and swallow up the little applause she has received from the ingenuousness of others?)

Besieged by periods of intense malady, Arcangela recovers sufficiently to keep up her life's work. With a letter addressed to a prominent member of the publishing community,[498] Tarabotti sends a copy of *Che le donne siano della specie degli uomini*,[499] apologizing for her "unconcise style" that she claims is her own "natural defect." With continued bowing for her "confused work," since she has "nessun altr'ordine di retorica" (no other rhetorical guidelines) than her "poco giudizio" (poor judgment), Tarabotti adds to these apologies, letting her reader know that not only her own "ignoranza" but also her sickness is to blame for "sentences" that may be "unbalanced or have "missing parts." She relates that her ill-health has lasted "incessantly now for fifteen days" and has "oppressed" her so that she was not able "to write or read with diligence anything of value."[500]

One cannot overlook the lacrimoso refrain of infirmity resounding throughout the letter volume. And although Zanette believes Tarabotti to have been a valetudinarian, I would argue that for as much as Suor Arcangela embodied determination and persistence, she also possessed an ingenuous strain of veracity that compelled her to honesty about herself and her health. Perhaps it was this forthrightness that endeared the nun to many of those with whom she exchanged letters.

Some of the sincerest exchanges in the letter book were with Arcangela's one-time *consorella* with whom she had established a close friendship that continued even after Betta Polani had left Sant'Anna. The twelve letters addressed to her friend reveal a reciprocal devotion. The only mention of Arcangela's mother comes in a letter addressed to Betta, telling her friend of the death of "chi a me diede la vita" (the one who gave me life)—a loss of "everything good."[501]

Often, Tarabotti asks her friend's pardon and apologizes for not having written sooner. She thanks Betta for her "gentilissime line" (kind words), but the "male" (illness) had prevented her from replying. She avows that her affection toward her friend "sara; sempre piu' fermo che rupe al vento o scogl'in mar sonante" (will always be more solid than a cliff in the wind or rocks in the roaring sea).[502] Tarabotti had received *preggiati carratteri* (precious words) from Betta but, again, could not pen a timely reply, "tormentata da quell' ostinatissimo male che non mi lascia godere ne' pur un poco di bene" (tormented by that obstinate illness that does not let me, not even for a little bit, enjoy some well-being), Tarabotti limiting this correspondence to a few lines only. In another missive, she writes "with the first breath God has granted me" after a long period of illness during which Betta had come to Sant'Anna, but bedridden Arcangela could not see her.

Tarabotti and Polani exchanged advice pertaining to recovering or staying well, reminiscent of two old friends confessing their concerns about their own and each other's health. Arcangela worries about her friend's "obstinate sickness"[503] and has asked everyone about medical advice that can help cure her, noting that "perche' questo mondo e' fornito di musici, medici, e matti, sento gran diversita' d'opinioni" (since this world is full of musicians, medical doctors, and madness, I hear a good deal of diverse opinions). The nun's humorous bent shines through, perhaps attempting to cheer up her friend, as she tells her that some recommendations have been to live moderately, some to take medicine, others suggesting a live lizard, and "everyone agreeing that a good husband is the cure." Then, in a more serious tone, Arcangela advises Betta to be careful about the air outside that is now full of "pestilence, so foggy and misty."[504] This heartwarming letter is the only one of the published missives to Polani that addresses her as "Illustrissima Mia Cara e Unica Signora Betta Polani" (The Most Illustrious and My Dear and Only Lady).

With Betta's departure from the convent in 1647 after many years, and the death of Regina Donà on March 31, 1645, the little girl with whom Tarabotti had taken the veil in 1620, Arcangela lost her only convent friends[505] with whom she shared loving relationships, both of whom would look after her when she was bedridden and care for her as would family.

Although Arcangela's letters refer to her own illness and often to that of her addressee, we find no mention in Tarabotti's extant works of the horrific event assailing Venice in 1630. At this time, the twenty-six-year-old nun had already written her first book, *Tirannia paterna*, and probably completed the second one (her *figliuolo cattivo*, bad child) *L'inferno monacale*,[506] when the Plague (*peste*) ravished Venice. Recorded deaths rose to forty-six thousand, roughly one-third of the population of La Serenissima wiped out in sixteen months.[507] More women than men succumbed to the disease, the mean age, twenty-four.[508] This ferocious epidemic initiated a wave of penitential rituals, including votive offerings to God and the Virgin Mary. Authorities asked all religious institutions to pray in continuation and ordered the architect Baldassare Longhena to build a temple dedicated to the Virgin, protector of health.[509] Venice had seen numerous rounds of this pandemic, but the 1630 outbreak was by far the worst, contributing, according to historians, to the major decline in trade and power and ultimate weakening of the Republic left with a decimated number of troops to fight for open trade routes, eventually contributing to vulnerability that led to her downfall.

To the extent that convents and churches were involved in the quest to seek from God a stop to the scourge, and to the extent of the cataclysmic effects on the city's population, Suor Arcangela Tarabotti's silence about this event is puzzling. Although only one nun in Sant'Anna succumbed to the *peste*, two hundred deaths in one day were recorded in the parish of San Pietro where the convent was located.[510] Certainly, Arcangela would have prayed for the dead and implored the Almighty to put a stop to the siege. We know she continued her work dedicated to exposing the abuses of office and family, the despoiling of the city perhaps not taking precedence over the infectious epidemic of forced monachization.

While there is nothing confessional or overtly autobiographical in her work, behind Arcangela's words, we cannot help but see the psychological torture this discarded daughter must have endured. The furor she must have felt, unloved and abandoned to the convent, permeates her language. In *Tirannia paterna*, a text of about one hundred and fifty pages, we find the root word and derivatives of *castig-*

are (to punish) twenty-six times, *crudelta* (cruelty) forty-seven times, *colpa* (blame) fifty-eight times, and *femina* (female/woman) one hundred and thirty-one times. The relationship between Arcangela's discourse and content should not be overlooked. Written out of anger and rebellion, her work echoes of a free spirit mewed up, never completely having come to terms with her captivity. The strong autobiographical strain, especially throughout her early works, throbs with the steady pulse of Arcangela Tarabotti's determination and vulnerability, her dolente heartbeat permeating every word, all the while avoiding what might have been a confessional account of an unhappy nun. Instead, Arcangela demonstrates acute political awareness, analyzing and courageously writing about the forces at play that relegate women to confinement and deprive them of free will.

Arcangela Tarabotti fought back with her unchaste words and succeeded in turning her soul-wrenching, abandonment and confinement into a self-realization, fulfilling what had become her real vocation, tapping into her inherent talents, channeling her anger, defining its source, and then broadening what could have been a personal story into a treatise defending the rights of all women.

Index

Bibliography

Accampo, Elinor. "G. Robina Quale, A History of Marriage Systems." Westport, CT: Greenwood Press, 1988, 400 *International Journal of Comparative Sociology* 32, nos. 3–4 (1991): 353–4. Print.

Akkerman, Tjitske, and Siep Stuurman, eds. *Perspectives on Feminist Political Thought in European History: From the Middle Ages to the Present.* London: Routledge, 2013. Web. 7/2/2016 1:56:15 PM.

Alberi, Eugenio. *Le Relazioni degli Ambasciatori Veneti al senato durante il secolo decimosesto,* Firenze, 1861, *Le Relazioni Degli Ambasciatori Veneti al Senato Durante il Secolo Decimosesto,* vol. 4 (Classic reprint in Italian, paperback—November 29, 2016).

Alberti, Leon Battista, Ruggiero Romano, and Alberto Tenenti. 1969. I libri della famiglia. Torino: G. Einaudi.

Alfrey, Penelope. Review of *The Dress of the Venetians, 1495–1525,* by Stella Mary Newton. *Renaissance Studies* 6, no. 1 (1992): 68. Print.

Allen, Prudence. *The Concept of Woman.* Grand Rapids, MI : W. B. Eerdmans Pub. Co., 1997, 1985. Print. Isotta Nogarola, Opera, 1, 42–44 in The Concept of Woman: The Early Humanist Reformation, 1250–1500, part 2, Prudence Allen.

Aretino, Pietro. *Selected Letters [of] Aretino.* 317 vols. Penguin Classics, 1976. Print.

———. *The Secret Life of Wives.* London: Hesperus, 2006. Print.

Aristotle. "Physics 1.9. 192a20–24," in *The Complete Works of Aristotle,* ed. Jonathan Barnes, Rv. Oxford trans., 2 vols. (Princeton, 1984), 1 *Nichomachean Ethics* by Aristotle, Public Domain English Translation by W. D. Ross.

Barton, David, and Nigel Hall. *Letter Writing as a Social Practice*. 9 vols. John Benjamins Publishing, 2000. Print.

Benjamins Current Topics: Understanding Historical (Im)Politeness: Relational Linguistic Practice Over Time and Across Cultures. Philadelphia, NL : John Benjamins Publishing Company, 2012. Web.

Bennett, Judith M., and Ruth Mazo Karras. *The Oxford Handbook of Women and Gender in Medieval Europe*. 1st ed. Oxford; New York: Oxford University Press, 2013. Print.

Benson, Pamela Joseph, and Victoria Kirkham. *Strong Voices, Weak History: Early Women Writers & Canons in England, France, & Italy*. Ann Arbor: University of Michigan Press, 2005. Print.

Berger, Adolf. Philadelphia: American Philosophical Society, 1991 (c1953). Reprint; originally published 1953.

Bernstein, Basil B. *Class, Codes and Control*. 4 vols. London: Routledge and K. Paul, 1971, 1990. Print. Primary Socialization, Language and Education.

Betten, Francis S. *Forbidden Books*. St. Louis, MO 1909. B. Herder.

Bhasin, Christine Scippa. *Prostitutes, Nuns, Actresses: Breaking the Convent Wall in Seventeenth-Century Venice*. Print.

Biga, Emilia. "The Mask Uncovered." Una Polemica Antifemminista Del '600: La Maschera Scoperta Di Angelico Aprosio. (Ventimiglia: Civica biblioteca Aprosiana, 1989.)

Black, Christopher F. *Church, Religion, and Society in Early Modern Italy*. Houndmills, Basingstoke, Hampshire; New York: Palgrave Macmillan, 2004. Print. European Studies Series.

_____. *Early Modern Italy: A Social History*. Florence, KY: Routledge, 2000. Web.

Blackburn, Robin. *The Making of New World Slavery: From the Baroque to the Modern, 1492–1800*. London; New York: Verso, 1997. Print.

Boccaccio, Giovanni Boccaccio, *De mulieribus claris* (Famous Women). I Tatti Renaissance Library 1. Translated by Virginia Brown (Cambridge, Massachusetts: Harvard University Press).

Botero, Giovanni. "Contents." Toc. In Botero: *The Reason of State*, edited by Robert Bireley, v–x. Cambridge Texts in the History of Political Thought (Cambridge: Cambridge University Press), 2017.

Boholm, Åsa. *The Doge of Venice: The Symbolism of State Power in the Renaissance*. Gothenburg, Sweden: Institute for Advanced Studies in Social Anthropology, University of Gothenburg, 1990. Print.

Bono, Salvatore. "S. Bono, Europa e Islàm Nel Mediterraneo (XVI Sec.—1830)." In *Capri e l'Islàm. Studi Su Capri, Il Mediterraneo, l'Oriente, a Cura Di E. Serrao e G.C. Lacerenza*. Capri, 2000, 125–150. Print.

Bouwsma, William J. *A Usable Past: Essays in European Cultural History*. Berkeley: University of California Press, 1990. Print.

Bouwsma, William J., and American Council of Learned Societies. *Venice and the Defense of Republican Liberty*. Berkeley: University of California Press, 1968. Print.

Brady, Thomas Jr., ed. *Handbook of European History 1400–1600, Volume 1: Structures and Assertions*. 1 vol. Brill, 1994. Print.

Brinton, Selwyn. "The Renaissance in Italian Art, Part 6 By Selwyn Brinton." Print.

Bromley, James M. *Intimacy and Sexuality in the Age of Shakespeare*. Cambridge; New York: Cambridge University Press, 2012. Print.

Brown, Horatio F. *Venice: An Historical Sketch of the Republic / by Horatio F. ... Brown, Horatio F. (Horatio Forbes), 1854–1926*. Print.

Brown, Clifford M. *Isabella d'Este in the Ducal Palace in Mantua: An Overview of Her Rooms in the Castello Di San Giorgio and the Corte Vecchia*. 116 vols. Rome: Bulzoni, 2005. Print. Biblioteca del Cinquecento.

Brown, Gillian, and George Yule. *Discourse Analysis*. Cambridge; New York: Cambridge University Press, 1983. Print. Cambridge Textbooks in Linguistics.

Brown, Judith C., and Robert C. Davis. *Gender and Society in Renaissance Italy*. London; New York: Longman, 1998. Print. Women and Men in History.

Brown, Patricia Fortini. *Art and Life in Renaissance Venice*. Print.

Brown, Penelope, and Stephen C. Levinson. *Politeness: Some Universals in Language Usage*. 4 vols. Cambridge; 1997. Art and life in Renaissance. New York: Prentice Hall. New York: Cambridge University Press, 1987. Print. Studies in Interactional Sociolinguistics.

Brundin, Abigail, and Matthew Treherne, Abigail Sarah Brundin, and Matthew Treherne, eds. *Forms of Faith in Sixteenth-Ccentury Italy, eds*. Forms of Faith in Sixteenth-Century Italy. Catholic Christendom, 1300–1700. (Aldershot: Ashgate Publishing).

Brulotte, Gaétan. "Pallavicino, Ferrante." *Encyclopedia of Erotic Literature*. 2006. Print.

Bunt, Cyril G. E. *Venetian Fabrics*. 2 vols. Leigh-on-Sea: F. Lewis, 1959. Print. World's Heritage of Woven Fabrics

Buonarroti, Michelangelo, et al. *Michelangelo and Raphael: With Botticelli, Perugino, Signorelli, Ghirlandaio and Rosselli in the Vatican: All the Sistine Chapel, the Stanzas, and the Loggias*. Special Edition for the Museums and Papal Galleries. Italy: Monumenti, Musei e Gallerie Pontificie, 1982. Print.

Burckhardt, Jacob. *Italian Renaissance Painting According to Genres*. Los Angeles, CA: Getty Research Institute, 2005. Print. Texts & Documents.

Calimani, Riccardo. *The Ghetto of Venice*. New York: M. Evans, 1987. Print.

———. *The Venetian Ghetto: The History of a Persecuted Community*. Riccardo Calimani, translated by Katherine Silberblatt Wolfthal (New York: M. Evans, c1987).

Campagnol, Isabella. *Forbidden Fashions: Invisible Luxuries in Early Venetian Convents*. Lubbock, TX: Texas Tech University Press, 2014. Print. Costume Society of America Series.

Campbell, Julie, and Anne R. Larsen, eds. *Early Modern Women and Transnational Communities of Letters*. Print.

Campbell, Stephen J., and Michael Wayne Cole. *A New History of Italian Renaissance Art*. London: Thames & Hudson, 2012. Print.

Contarini, Gasparo. *The Commonwealth and Government of Venice*, trans. Lewes Lewkenor (1599), 1483–1542.

Cartwright, Julia. *Isabella d'Este, Marchioness of Mantua, 1474–1539: A Study of the Renaissance*. New York: E. P. Dutton and Company, 1926. Print.

Castelli, Elizabeth A., and Rosamond C. Rodman. *Women, Gender, Religion: A Reader*. 1st ed. New York: Palgrave, 2001. Print.

Casola, Viaggio a Gerusalemme di Pietro Casola, Edizioni dell'Orso (2001, Torino).

Cavell, Stanley. *Must We Mean What We Say?: A Book of Essays*. Updated. Cambridge; New York: Cambridge University Press, 2002. Print.

Cereta, Laura. *Collected Letters of a Renaissance Feminist*. Edited by Diana Maury Robin. Chicago: University of Chicago Press, 1997. Web. 2/12/2012 8:25:01 PM.

———. *The Other Voice in Early Modern Europe: Collected Letters of a Renaissance Feminist*. Edited by Diana Robin. Chicago: University of Chicago Press, 2007. Web. 11/26/2016 4:33:45 PM.

Cherewatuk, Wiethaus, ed. *Dear Sister: Medieval Women and the Epistolary Genre*. Philadelphia: University of Pennsylvania Press, 1993. Print.

Chojnacka, Monica. *Working Women of Early Modern Venice*. 2001. Print.

Chojnacki, Stanley. *Women and Men in Renaissance Venice: Twelve Essays on Patrician Society*. Baltimore: Johns Hopkins University Press, 2000. Print.

———. *In Search of the Venetian Patriciate: Families and Factions in the Fourteenth Century in Renaissance Venice*, J.R. Hale. Faber and Faber, 1974.

Clement, Clara Erskine. *The Queen of the Adriatic*. Venice: Dana Estes and Co., 1834–1916. Web.

Clissold, Stephen. *The Barbary Slaves*. Totowa, NJ: Rowman and Littlefield, 1977. Print.

Clough, Cecil H., and Paul Oskar Kristeller. *Cultural Aspects of the Italian Renaissance: Essays in Honour of Paul Oskar Kristeller*. Manchester: Manchester University Press, 1976. Print.

Cohen, Thomas V. *Love and Death in Renaissance Italy*. Chicago: University of Chicago Press, 2010. Web.

Conybeare, Catherine. "Laurie J. Churchill, Phyllis R. Brown, and Jane E. Jeffrey, Eds., *Women Writing Latin, from Roman Antiquity to Early Modern Europe, 1: Women Writing Latin in Roman Antiquity, Late Antiquity, and the Early Christian Era; 2: Medieval Women Writing Latin; 3: Early Modern Women Writing Latin.* (Women Writers of the World.) New York and London: Routledge, 2002. 1: Pp. x, 186. 2: Pp. x, 323. 3: Pp. x, 298." *Speculum* 80, no. 2 (2005): 540–2. Web.

Cornelius, Ian. "The Rhetoric of Advancement: *Ars Dictaminis, Cursus*, and Clerical Careerism in Late Medieval England." *New Medieval Literatures* 12 (2010): 287–328. Print.

Coryat, Thomas. Coryat's Crudities. Thomas Coryat/Internet Archive, Center for Reformation and Renaissance, Victoria University.

Couchman, Jane, and Ann Crabb. *Women's Letters Across Europe, 1400–1700: Form and Persuasion.* Aldershot, England; Burlington, VT: Ashgate, 2005. Print. Women and Gender in the Early Modern World.

Cowan, Alexander. *Historical Urban Studies Series: Marriage, Manners and Mobility in Early Modern Venice.* Abingdon: Ashgate, 2013. Web.

_____. *Women Marriage and Social Distinction in Early Modern Venice.* Abingdon: Ashgate Publishing Group, 2007. Web.

Cox, Virginia. *The Prodigious Muse Women's Writing in Counter-Reformation Italy.* 2011. Print. *The Worth of Women: Wherein Is Clearly Revealed Their Nobility and Their Superiority to Men the Other Voic in Early Modern Europe*, Moderata Fonte: Translated by Virginia Cox Publisher University of Chicago Press, 2007.

Cross, F. "Contarini, Gasparo." *The Oxford Dictionary of the Christian Church.* 2005. Print.

Culpeper, Jonathan, and Dániel Z. Kádár. *Historical (Im) Politeness.* 65 vols. Bern; New York: Peter Lang, 2010. Print. Linguistic Insights.

Dallavalle, Lisa. "The Moretti Family: Late Marriage, Bachelorhood and Domestic Authority in Seventeenth-Century Venice." *Gender & History* 27, no. 3 (2015): 684–702. Print.

Davis, C. James. *A Venetian Family and Its Fortune;* 1500â€"1900: *The Donà and the Conservation of Their Wealth* by James C. Davis. Philadelphia: American Philosophical Society, 1975.

De Rycker, Kate. "Translating the Ragionamento: Reframing Pietro Aretino as the Castigator of Courtesans." *Literature Compass* 12, no. 6 (2015): 299–309. Print.

Degl'Innocenti, Luca, Brian Richardson, and Chiara Sbordoni. *Interactions between Orality and Writing in Early Modern Italian Culture.* Farnham, Surrey: Ashgate Publishing Limited, 2016. Print.

Dell'aquila, Giulia. *Le Ragioni Della Pseudonimia: Il Caso Angelico Aprosio.* Print.

Disputatio: An International Transdisciplinary Journal of the Late Middle Ages. Evanston, IL: Northwestern University Press, 1996. Print.

Dixon, Suzanne. "Infirmitas Sexus: Womanly Weakness in Roman Law." *Tijdschrift Voor Rechtsgeschiedenis* 52, no. 4 (1984): 343–371. DOI: 10.1163/157181984X00178. Print.

Dogli, Maria Luisa. *L'arte Delle Lettere: Idea e Pratica Della Scritura Epistolare Tra Il Quattro e Seicento.* Bologna: Il Mulino, 2000. Print.

Doglioni, Giovanni Niccolo. "Vita Della Signora Modesta Pozzo De'Zorzi Nominata Moderata Fonte." *Moderata Fonte, Il merito delle donne, ed. Adriana Chemello* (1988): 3–10. Print.

Dreher, Diane. *Domination and Defiance: Fathers and Daughters in Shakespeare.* Lexington: University Press of Kentucky, 1986. Print.

Dunhill, Anne. *The Nobility and Excellence of Women, and the Defects and Vices of Men.* University of Chicago Press, 1999.

Drescher, Seymour. *Abolition: A History of Slavery and Antislavery.* Cambridge; New York: Cambridge University Press, 2009. Print.

Earle, T. F., and K. J. P. Lowe. *Black Africans in Renaissance Europe.* Cambridge; New York: Cambridge University Press, 2005. Print.

Eden, Kathy. *The Renaissance Rediscovery of Intimacy.* Chicago: University of Chicago Press, 2012. Print.

Ell, Stephen R. "Three Days in October of 1630: Detailed Examination of Mortality during an Early Modern Plague Epidemic in Venice." *Reviews of Infectious Diseases* 11, no. 1 (1989): 128–39. Web. 12/15/2016 5:04:59 PM.

Epstein, Donald B. "The Jews of Early Modern Venice: Davis, Robert C. Benjamin C. I. Ravid, Eds.: Baltimore: Johns Hopkins University Press, 314 Pp., Publication Date: Winter 2002." *History: Reviews of New Books* 30, no. 2 (2002): 70. Web. 12/9/2016 2:03:47 PM.

Evangelisti, Silvia. "Monastic Poverty and Material Culture in Early Modern Italian Convents." *The Historical Journal* 47 (2004): 1–20. Print.

————. *Nuns: A History of Convent Life 1450–1700*. Oxford: Oxford University Press, 2007. Web. 12/30/2016 2:07:30 PM.

Fairclough, Norman, and Isabela Fairclough. *Political Discourse Analysis*. New York: Routledge, 2012. Print.

Faroqhi, Suraiya and Halil Inalcik, eds. *The Ottoman Empire and Its Heritage Politics, Society and Economy*. Print.

Fasoli, Gina, and Francesca Bocchi. *La Citta` Medievale Italiana*. 4 vols. Firenze: Sansoni, 1973. Print.

Fay, Mary. "Slavery in the Ottoman Empire and Its Demise." *International Journal of Middle East Studies* 30, no. 4 (1998): 574. Print.

Fedele, Cassandra. *The Other Voice in Early Modern Europe: Letters and Orations*. Chicago: University of Chicago Press, 2007. Web. 9/26/2016 5:04:10 PM.

Feldman, Martha, and Bonnie Gordon, eds. *Courtesan's Arts: Cross-Cultural Perspectives*. Cary, NC: Oxford University Press, 2006. Web.

Feminist Encyclopedia of French Literature. Westport: Greenwood Press, 1999. Web.

Ferraro, Joanne Marie. *Marriage Wars in Late Renaissance Venice*. Cary, NC: Oxford University Press, 2001. Web.

————. *Venice: History of the Floating City*. Print.

Findlen, Paula, Michelle Fontaine, and Duane J. Osheim, eds. *Beyond Florence: The Contours of Medieval and Early Modern Italy*. Palo Alto: Stanford University Press, 2003. Web.

Fink, Z. S. "2. Venice and the Defense of Republican Liberty: Renaissance Values in the Age of the Counter Reformation. by William J. Bouwsma. Berkeley and Los Ang." *Historical Journal* 13, no. 1 (1970): 173–6. Print.

Firpo, M. "Rethinking Paolo Sarpi." *Studi Storici* 47, no. 4 (2006): 993–1001. Print.

Fonte, Moderata. *Il Merito Delle Donne... Ove Chiaramente Si Scuopre Quanto Siano Elle Degne e Più Perfette De Gli Huomini*, 1988. Print.

Fabio and Agostino Zopini Fratelli, *Le oration volgari di Luigi Groto cieco di Hadria da lui medesimo...*, Fabio & Agostino Zopini Fratelli, 1586.

Frick, Carole Collier. "Gendered Space in Renaissance Florence: Theorizing Public and Private in the 'Rag Trade.'" *Fashion Theory* 9, no. 2 (2005): 125, 146. Print.

Gabba, Emilio. "Walter Burkert e La Religione Greca in Italia." *Quaderni Urbinati di Cultura Classica* 80, no. 2 (2005): 105–7. Print.

Gibbins, Keith. "Meaning of Garments: Relation between Impression of an Outfit and the Message Carried by Its Component Garments." *Perceptual and Motor Skills* 51, no. 1 (1980): 287. Print.

Glixon, Beth L. "Private Lives of Public Women: Prima Donnas in Mid-Seventeenth-Century Venice." *Music & Letters* 76, no. 4 (1995): 509–31. Print.

Goffman, Erving. *Asylums: Essays on the Social Situation of Mental Patients and Other Inmates*. Chicago: Aldine Pub. Co., 1968, 1961. Print.

Gouwens, Kenneth. *The Italian Renaissance: The Essential Sources*. Malden, MA: Blackwell Pub., 2004. Print.

Grassby, Richard. *The Business Community of Seventeenth-Century England*. Cambridge; New York: Cambridge University Press, 1995. Print.

Guicciardini, Luigi, and James H. McGregor. *The Sack of Rome*. New York: Italica Press, 1993. Print.

Gupta, Atul, Sudhanshu Hate, and Andrew Siemer. *ASP.NET 4 Social Networking*. Olton, Birmingham: Packt Publishing, 2011. Web.

Guzzetti, Linda. "Dowries in Fourteenth-Century Venice." *Renaissance Studies* 16, no. 4 (2002): 430, 473. Print.

Hale, J. R. *Renaissance Venice*. Faber and Faber, 1973, 1974.

Hale, J. R, et al. *War, Culture, and Society in Renaissance Venice: Essays in Honour of John Hale*. London; Rio Grande, Ohio: Hambledon Press, 1993. Print.

Hartt, Frederick, and David G. Wilkins. *History of Italian Renaissance Art: Painting, Sculpture, Architecture*. 6th ed. Upper Saddle River, NJ: Pearson Prentice Hall, 2006, 2007. Print.

Hay, Denys. *Renaissance Essays*. London; Ronceverte, WV: Hambledon Press, 1988, 1951. Print. History Series.

Heller, Wendy, and American Council of Learned Societies. *Emblems of Eloquence*. Berkeley: University of California Press, 2003. Print.

Hills, Helen. *Invisible City: The Architecture of Devotion in Seventeenth-Century Neapolitan Convents*. Oxford; New York: Oxford University Press, 2004. Print.

Holderness, Graham. "Anglo-Italian Renaissance Studies: Shakespeare and Venice." Print.

Hunt, Alan. "Sumptuary Laws." In *Europe, 1450 to 1789: Encyclopedia of the Early Modern World*, edited by Jonathan Dewald, 546–548. 5 vols. New York: Charles Scribner's Sons, 2004. Print.

Hunt, Jocelyn. *Renaissance*. Florence, KY: Routledge, 1999. Web.

Intersections: Women Writing Back / Writing Women Back: Transnational Perspectives from the Late Middle Ages to the Dawn of the Modern Era. Boston, NL : Brill, 2010. Web Series: Intersections, Volume 16. Editors: Anke Gilleir, Alicia Montoya, and Suzan van Dijk.

Jackson, Emily. *A History of Hand-made Lace: Dealing with the Origin of Lace, the Growth of the Great Lace Centres, the Mode of Manufacture, the Methods of Distinguishing and the Care of Various Kinds of Lace*. London: L. Upcott Gill, 1900, pp. 153–157.

Jedin, Hubert, and American Council of Learned Societies. *A History of the Council of Trent*. London: T. Nelson, 1957, 1961. Print.

———. *A History of the Council of Trent*. London: T. Nelson, 1957. Web. 12/9/2016 2:31:24 PM.

Jenkins, Allan K., and Patrick Preston. *Biblical Scholarship and the Church A Sixteenth-Century Crisis of Authority*. Ashgate, 2007.

Johnston, David. *Key Themes in Ancient History: Roman Law in Context*. Cambridge: Cambridge University Press, 1999. Web.

Johnstone, Barbara. *Discourse Analysis*. 2nd ed. 3 vols. Malden, MA: Blackwell, 2008. Print. Introducing Linguistics.

Jordan, Constance. "More from 'the Other Voice' in Early Modern Europe." *Renaissance Quarterly* 55, no. 1 (2002): 258–71. Print.

———. *Renaissance Feminism: Literary Texts and Political Models*. Ithaca, NY: Cornell University Press, 1990. Print.

Kane, J. "Letter from Laura Cereta: Brescia, 1488 (Poetry)." *Feminist Studies* 20, no. 3 (1994): 564. http://login.ezproxy1.Lib.Asu. edu/login?url=http://search.proquest.com.ezproxy1.lib.asu. edu/docview/1295936319?accountid=4485. Print.

Kenney, Theresa M., ed. *Women Are Not Human: An Anonymous Treatise and Responses*. Translated by Theresa M. Kenney. The Crossroad Publishing Company, 1998. Print.

Keenan, Charles. "Paolo Sarpi. A Servant of God and State. By Jaska Kainulainen. (Studies in Medieval and Reformation Traditions, 180.) Pp. Ix 292. Leiden-Boston: Brill, 2014. €114. 978 90 04 26114 3; 1573 4188." The Journal of Ecclesiastical History 66, no. 4 (2015): 885–87. doi:10.1017/S0022046915001177.

Kidwell, C. *Pietro Bembo: Lover, Linguist, Cardinal*. Montreal: McGill-Queen's University Press, 2004. Web.

Killerby, Catherine Kovesi. *Sumptuary Law in Italy 1200–1500*. Oxford: Clarendon Press, 2002. Print. Oxford Historical Monographs.

King, Margaret Leah. "Thwarted Ambitions: Six Learned Women of the Italian Renaissance." *Soundings: An Interdisciplinary Journal* 59, no. 3 (1976): 280–304. Print. *Beyond Their Sex: Learned Women of the European Past*. New York: New York University Press, 1980.

————. *Venetian Humanism in an Age of Patrician Dominance.* Princeton, NJ: Princeton University Press, 1986. Print.

Kirkham, Victoria, and MyiLibrary. *Boccaccio: A Critical Guide to the Complete Works.* Chicago: University of Chicago Press, 2014. Print.

Kuehn, Thomas, and American Council of Learned Societies. *Law, Family & Women.* Chicago: University of Chicago Press, 1991. Print. Thomas Kuehn, "Daughters, Mothers, Wives, and Widows," in *Time, Space, and Women's Lives in Early Modern Europe*, edited by Anne Jacobson Schutte, Thomas Kuehn, and Silvana Seidel Menchi. Kirksville, Missouri: 2002 Turman State University Press, Kirksville, Missouri, USA.

Kuhns, Elizabeth. *The Habit: A History of the Clothing of Catholic Nuns.* 1st ed. New York: Doubleday, 2003. Web. 12/8/2016 4:51:54 PM.

Landucci, Luca. *A Florentine Diary from 1450 to 1516.* New York: Arno Press, 1969, 1927. Print.

Lowe, K. J. P. *Nuns' Chronicles and Convent Culture in Renaissance and Counter-Reformation Italy.* Goldsmiths, University of London, December 2003. Print.

Lurie, Alison. *The Language of Clothes.* 1st ed. New York: Random House, 1981. Print.

Mackenney, Richard. "Continuity and Change in the 'Scuole Piccole' of Venice, c. 1250-c. 1600." *Renaissance Studies* 8, no. 4 (1994): 388. Print.

Maclean, Ian. *The Renaissance Notion of Woman: A Study in the Fortunes of Scholasticism and Medical Science in European Intellectual Life.* Paperback ed. Cambridge; New York: Cambridge University Press, 1983. Print. Cambridge Monographs on the History of Medicine.

Madden, Thomas F. *Venice: Islands of Honor and Profit: A New History.* New York: Viking, 2012. Print.

Malpezzi Price, Paola. "Moderata Fonte (1555–1592)." *Italian Women Writers: A Bio-Bibliographical Sourcebook* (1994): 128–37. Print.

Manca, Joseph. *Subject Matter in Italian Renaissance Art: A Study of Early Sources.* 460 vols. Tempe, AZ: Arizona Center for Medieval and Renaissance Studies, 2015. Print. Medieval and Renaissance Texts and Studies.

Mancini, Girolamo. *Vita Di Leon Battista Alberti, Di Girolamo Mancini.* 1882. Print.

Martin, John Jeffries, and Dennis Romano, eds. *Venice Reconsidered: The History and Civilization of an Italian City-State, 1297–1797.* Baltimore, MD: Johns Hopkins University Press, 2000. Web.

George R. Marek, *The Bed and the Throne.* New York: Harper & Row Publishers, New York, 1976.

Massimo Baldini, *Semiotica della moda, Armando,* 2005. Roma: Luiss University Press, 2005.

McConnell-Ginet, Sally, Ruth Borker, and Nelly Furman. *Women and Language in Literature and Society.* New York: Praeger, 1980. Print.

McCutcheon, Shawn. "History of the Floating City." *Urban History Review* 42, no. 2 (2014): 63. Web. 12/20/2016 8:07:55 PM.

Medioli, Francesca. "Arcangela Tarabotti's Reliability about Herself: Publication and Self-Representation (Together with a Small Collection of Previously Unpublished Letters). Source: Italianist. 2003, Vol. 23 Issue 1, p54–101. 48p. Document Type: Article." *Italianist* 23, no. 1 (2003): 54–48. Print.

Medioli, Francesca. "Arcangela Tarabotti: Una Famiglia Non Detta e Un Segreto Indicibile In Famiglia," Archivo Veneto, Milano-Venezia-Verona. Venezia, 2013.

———. "Arcangela Tarabotti's Reliability about Herself," Archivo di Stato Venezia, Notarile, Testamente, Marcellini, 620, note. 233, 6 December 6, 1647; The Italianist, 23. Tarabotti Fra Omissioni E Femminismo: Il Mistero Della Sua Formazione di Francesca Medioli.

Menchi, Silvana Seidel. "Italy" in *The Reformation in National Context,* eds. Scribner, Poorter, and Teich, ed. Cambridge University Press, 1994.

Meyer, Edith Patterson. *First Lady of the Renaissance: A Biography of Isabella d'Este.* 1st ed. Boston: Little, Brown, 1970. Print.

Lo spazio del chiostro: clausura costrizione e protezione nel 17: Francesca Medioli, Publisher: [S.l.]: [s.n.], 1999. Edition/ Format: Article: Italian Publication: Tempi e spazi di vita femminile tra medioevo ed età moderna / a cura di Silvana Seidel Menchi, Anne Jacobson Schutte, and Thomas Kuehn.

Miato, Monica1948. *L'Accademia Degli Incogniti Di Giovan Francesco Loredan Venezia (1630–1661)*. Edited by Firenze Leo S. Olschki. 1948. Print.

More, Alison. *Representing Medieval Genders and Sexualities in Europe: Construction, Transformation, and Subversion, 600–1530*. Edited by Elizabeth L'Estrange. Farnham: Routledge, 2016. Web.

Molmenti, Pompeo. Istituto Italiano d'Arti Grafiche; Bergamo, 1927–1929.

———. *Venice: Its Individual Growth from the Earliest Beginnings* to Molmenti, The Fall of the Republic (Six volumes, complete) Chicago, Illinois (USA): A.C. McClurg, 1906–8. London. Published between 1906 and 1908.

———. *La Storia di Venezia Nella Vita Privata,* Torino, 1880 BiblioLife Reproduction Series.

Muir, Edward. *Culture Wars of the Late Renaissance: Skeptics, Libertines, and Opera*. Cambridge: Harvard University Press, 2007. Web.

Murphy, Caroline P. *The Pope's Daughter*. New York: Oxford University Press, 2005. Print.

Musacchio, Jacqueline M. Art, *Marriage, and Family in the Florentine Renaissance Palace* (New Haven: Yale University Press, 2008).

Najemy, John M. *Italy in the Age of the Renaissance: 1300–1550*. Oxford: Oxford University Press, 2004. Web.

Newton, Stella Mary. *The Dress of the Venetians 1495–1525*. 1988. Print.

Neale, J. E. *Queen Elizabeth I*. J. E. Neale, J.E.: Academy Chicago Publishers, 1992.

Novati, Francesco, Egidio Gorra, Vittorio Cian, Giulio Bertoni, and Carlo Calcaterra, eds. *Giornale Storico Della Letteratura Italiana*. Veena Talwar Oldenburg. *Dowry Murder: The Imperial Origins of a Cultural Crime*. 600dpi TIFF G4 page images E-Distribution Information MPublishing, University of Michigan Library,

Ann Arbor, Michigan. Source version *Dowry Murder: The Imperial Origins of a Cultural Crime*/Veena Talwar Oldenburg. Oldenburg, Veena Talwar Oxford: Oxford University Press, 2002. 42: 279. Print.

Ogg, Frederic Austin, ed. *A Sourcebook of Medieval History*. New York: American Book Company, 1907.

Oldenburg, Veena Talwar, and American Council of Learned Societies. *Dowry Murder*. Oxford; New York: Oxford University Press, 2002. Print.

O'Neill, Michael, Mark Sandy, and Sarah Wootton. *Venice and the Cultural Imagination*. Pickering & Chatto Publishers, 2012. Print.

Origo, Iris. *The Merchant of Prato, Francesco Di Marco Datini*. London: J. Cape, 1957. Print.

Osteen, Mark, ed. *The Question of the Gift: Essays Across Disciplines*. Print.

Paulicelli, Eugenia. *Writing Fashion in Early Modern Italy: From Sprezzatura to Satire*. Paulicelli, Eugenia. Farnham: Ashgate, 2014.

Pallavicino, Ferrante. *The Celestial Divorce*. London: J. Brown, 1718. Print.

_____. *The Whore's Rhetorick, Calculated to the Meridian of London and Conformed to the Rules of Art, in Two Dialogues*. New York: I. Obolensky, 1961. Print.

Paltridge, Brian. *Discourse Analysis: An Introduction*. London; New York: Continuum, 2006. Print. Continuum Discourse Series.

Panizza, Letizia, ed. *Arcangela Tarabotti Che Le Donne Siano Della Spezie Degli Uomini*. Institute of Romance Studies, 1651 [1994]. Print.

Panizza, Letizia, and Sharon Wood. *A History of Women's Writing in Italy*. Cambridge; New York: Cambridge University Press, 2000. Print.

Panizza, Letizia, and University of Oxford. *Women in Italian Renaissance Culture and Society*. Oxford: University of Oxford, 2000. Print. Legenda/European Humanities Research Centre.

Partner, Peter. *Renaissance Rome, 1500–1559: A Portrait of a Society.* Berkeley: University of California Press, 1979; 1976. Print.

Patricia, Allerston. "Clothing and Early Modern Venetian Society," p. 367. *Continuity and Change*, 15, no. 3.

Patterson, Orlando. *Slavery and Social Death: A Comparative Study.* 1982. Print.

Petrucci, Armando. *Scrivere Lettere Una Storia Plurimillenaria.* Roma-Bari: Editori Laterza, 2008. Print.

Petrarca, Francesco. *Petrarch's Letters to Classical Authors.* Translator: Mario Cosenza. January 3, 2015 (e-book #47859) English character set encoding: UTF-8 *** Start of this project Gutenberg e-book Petrarch's letters.

————. *Petrarch: The First Modern Scholar and Man of Letters.* New York: G. P. Putnam, 1898. Scanned by Jason Boley and Jacob Miller in August 1995.

Phelan, Carolyn. "Venice and Its Merchant Empire." *The Booklist* (Chicago, IL, 1969) 98, no. 12 (2002): 1011. Print.

Poster, Carol. and Linda C. Mitchell. *Letter-Writing Manuals and Instruction from Antiquity to the Present: Historical and Bibliographic Studies.* Columbia, South Carolina: University of South Carolina Press, 2007.

Pullan, Brian S. *The Jews of Europe and the Inquisition of Venice, 1550–1670.* Oxford: Basil Blackwell, 1983. Web. 12/21/2016 4:21:09 PM; 12/21/2016 4:21:09 PM.

Putnam, George Haven. *Books and Their Makers During the Middle Ages*, G.P. Putnam's Sons. New York, London: G. P. Putnam's Sons, 1896.

Queller, Donald. "Father of the Bride: Fathers, Daughters, and Dowries in Late Medieval and Early Renaissance Venice." *Renaissance Quarterly* 46, no. 4 (1993): 685. Print.

Rapp, Richard T. *Industry and Economic Decline in Seventeenth-Century Venice.* 69 vols. Cambridge: Harvard University Press, 1976. Web. 12/20/2016 7:53:46 PM.

Ray, Meredith. "Letters and Lace." In *Early Modern Women and Transnational Communities of Letters.* Print.

_____. *Writing Gender in Women's Letter Collections of the Italian Renaissance.* Toronto: University of Toronto Press, 2009. Print. Toronto Italian Studies.

Ray, Meredith, and Lynn Westwater, eds. *Arcangela Taraboti Lettere familiari e di complimento.* Rosenberg & Sellier, 1650 [2005]. Print.

Riha, Daniel, and Anna Maj, eds. *Emerging Practices in Cyberculture and Social Networking.* Amsterdam: Editions Rodopi, 2010. Web.

Robin, Diana Maury, ed. *Women and Society, p. 81 Laura Cereta Collected Letters of a Renaissance Feminist.* Transcribed, translated, and edited by the University of Chicago. Chicago and London. Print.

Romano, Dennis. Review of *Venice: History of the Floating City*, by Joanne M. Ferraro, and *Venice: A New History*, by Thomas F. Madden. *Journal of Interdisciplinary History* 44, no. 2 (2013): 261–3. Web. 12/15/2016 5:54:16 PM.

Rosand, David. *The Invention of Painting in America.* New York; Chichester: Columbia University Press, 2004. Print. University Seminars/Leonard Hastings Schoff Memorial Lectures.

_____. *Myths of Venice: The Figuration of a State.* University of North Carolina Press; Aug 1, 2005.

Rosenthal, Margaret F. "Venetian Women and Their Discontents." In *Sexuality and Gender in Early Modern Europe*, edited by James Grantham Turner (1993): 197–32. Print.

Ross, Sarah Gwyneth. *The Birth of Feminism: Woman as Intellect in Renaissance Italy and England.* Cambridge: Harvard University Press, 2010. Web.

Rubin, Patricia Lee, et al. *Renaissance Florence: The Art of the 1470s.* London: National Gallery Publications Limited, 1999. Print.

Rubin, Patricia Lee. *Images and Identity in Fifteenth-Century Florence.* New Haven: Yale University Press, 2007. Print.

Ruggiero, Guido. *Binding Passions: Tales of Magic, Marriage, and Power at the End of the Renaissance.* Cary, NC: Oxford University Press, 1993. Web.

Ruggles, D. *Women and Slavery in the Late Ottoman Empire.* *International Journal of Turkish Studies* 18, no. 1/2 (2012), 165. Print. *Dowry Murder: The Imperial Origins of a Cultural Crime* / Veena Talwar Oldenburg. 600dpi TIFF G4 page images E-Distribution Information Publishing, University of Michigan Library, Ann Arbor, Michigan. Source version: *Dowry Murder: The Imperial Origins of a Cultural Crime* / Veena Talwar Oldenburg. Oldenburg, Veena Talwar Oxford: Oxford University Press, 2002.

Salsini, Laura A. *Addressing the Letter: Italian Women Writers' Epistolary Fiction.* Toronto; Buffalo: University of Toronto Press, 2010. Print.

Salzman, Todd A. *Method and Catholic Moral Theology: The Ongoing Reconstruction.* Omaha, NE: Oxford University Press, 1999. Print.

Sansovino, Francesco. *Venetia Citta Nobilissima.* Venice: Steffano Curti, 1663. Print.

Sansovino, Francesco, and Giustiniano Martinioni. *Venetia Citta Nobilissima (Venice, 1663).* Farnborough: Gregg, 1968, 1663. Print.

Sanudo, Marin. *I Diarii Di Marino Sanuto: (MCCCCXCVI-MDXXXIII) Dall' Autografo Marciano Ital. Cl. VII Codd. F.* Visentini, 1903. Print.

Sanudo, Martin. "Praise of the City of Venice," 1493. Martin Sanudo, Laus Urbis Venetae, BVC ms Cicogna 969, ff. 8v-19r (Sandudo ed. Fulin, 1880), pp. 28–66 in *Renaissance Society of America,* ed. Chambers.

Sanudo, Marin, et al. "How to (and How Not to) Get Married in Sixteenth-Century Venice (Selections from the Diaries of Marin Sanudo)." *Renaissance Quarterly* 52, no. 1 (1999): 43–72. Print.

Sarpi, Paolo. Treatise on the Interdict, Paolo Sarpi, Trattato Dell' Interdetto Della Santità Di Papa Paolo V.

Schutte, Anne Jacobson. *Aspiring Saints: Pretense of Holiness, Inquisition, and Gender in the Republic of Venice, 1618–1750.* Baltimore, MD; London: Johns Hopkins University Press, 2001. Print.

_____. *By Force and Fear: Taking and Breaking Monastic Vows in Early Modern Europe*. Ithaca, NY: Cornell University Press, 2011. Web.

Schutte, Anne Jacobson, Thomas Kuehn, and Silvana Seidel Menchi. *Time, Space, and Women's Lives in Early Modern Europe*. 57 vols. Kirksville, MO: Truman State University Press, 2001. Print. Sixteenth-Century Essays & Studies.

Scribner, Robert W., Roy Porter, and Mikuláš Teich. *The Reformation in National Context*. Cambridge; New York: Cambridge University Press, 1994. Print.

Sherman, Nancy. *Aristotle's Ethics: Critical Essays*. Lanham, MD: Rowman & Littlefield, 1999. Print. Critical Essays on the Classics.

_____. *Fabric of Character: Aristotle's Theory of Virtue*. Oxford: Clarendon Press, 1989. Web.

Shulvass, Moses A. *The Jews in the World of the Renaissance*. Leiden: Brill, 1973. Print.

Singh, Jyotsna G. "Cesare Vecellio, Venetian Writer and Art-Book Cosmopolitan." Oxford: Wiley-Blackwell, 305–322. Web.

Simmel, Georg. "Fashion," *International Quarterly*, 10, no. 1. October 1904, pp. 130–-155, reprinted in *American Journal of Sociology*, 62, no. 6, May 1957.

Sluhovsky, Moshe. "Authority and Power in Early Modern Italy: Recent Italian Historiography; Fonti Ecclesiastiche Per La Storia Sociale e Religiosa d'Europa: XV-XVIII Se." *The Historical Journal* 47, no. 2 (2004): 501. Print.

Smith, Patrick J. *The Tenth Muse: A Historical Study of the Opera Libretto*. 1st ed. New York: A. A. Knopf, 1970. Web. 12/8/2016 10:51:05 AM.

Dowry Murder: The Imperial Origins of a Cultural Crime / Veena Talwar Oldenburg. 600dpi TIFF G4 page images E-Distribution Information Publishing, University of Michigan Library, Ann Arbor, Michigan. *Dowry Murder: The Imperial Origins of a Cultural Crime* / Veena Talwar Oldenburg. Oxford: Oxford University Press, 2002.

Sperling, Jutta Gisela. *Convents and the Body Politic in Late Renaissance Venice*. University of Chicago Press, 1999. Print.

———. "Dowry or Inheritance? Kinship, Property, and Women's Agency in Lisbon, Venice, and Florence (1572)." *Journal of Early Modern History* 11, no. 3 (2007): 197, 238. Print.

Stanton, Domna C. *The Dynamics of Gender in Early Modern France: Women Writ, Women Writing (Women and Gender in the Early Modern World)*. Farnham: Routledge, 2016. Web. 7/2/2016 1:54:55 PM.

Stemp, Richard. *The Secret Language of the Renaissance: Decoding the Hidden Symbolism of Italian Art*. London: Duncan Baird, 2006. Print.

Stinger, Charles L. *The Renaissance in Rome*. Bloomington: Indiana University Press, 1985. Print.

Strocchia, Sharon T. *Nuns and Nunneries in Renaissance Florence*. Baltimore, MD: Johns Hopkins University Press, 2009. Web.

Strozzi, Alessandra. Selected Letters of Alessandra Strozzi, Bilingual edition. Biblioteca Italiana. Reprint Publisher University of California Press, 1997.

Swanton, Christine. *New Directions in Ethics: The Virtue Ethics of Hume and Nietzsche*. Somerset: Wiley, 2015. Web. 11/17/2016 1:38:02 PM.

Tamassia, Nino. *La Famiglia italiana: nei secoli decimoquinto e decimosesto, Multigrafica Editirice*, 1971. The University of Virginia, 1971.

Tarabotti, Arcangela. *L'inferno monacale Di Arcangela Tarabotti*. Torino: Rosenberg & Sellier, 1990. Print. Tarabotti, Arcangela Tarabotti. La semplicita' ingannata (1654). Leida: Gio. Sambix; Elzevir, Daniel, and

———. *Paradiso monacale*. 1663 [1643]. Print. Digitalized December 16, 2009, Original from Bavarian State Library.

Tarabotti, Arcangela, et al. *Letters Familiar and Formal*. 20 vols. Toronto: Iter Inc., 2012. Print. The Other Voice in Early Modern Europe: The Toronto Series.

———. *Lettere familiari e di complimento*. 2005 Torino editors Meredith Ray and Lynn Westwater, Resenberg & Seller.

_____. *Arcangela Tarabotti Che Le Donne Siano Della Spezie Degli Uomini.* Institute of Romance Studies, 1651 [1994]. Print. Ed. Panizza, Letizia

_____. *Satira e Antisatira.* Author: Francesco Buoninsegni. Publisher: CreateSpace Independent Publishing Platform, 2012. ISBN: 1480139904, 9781480139909. Length: 60 pages.

Tenenti, Alberto. *Piracy and the Decline of Venice, 1580–1615.* Berkeley: University of California Press, 1967. Print.

Weaver, Elissa B. *Arcangela Tarabotti: A Literary Nun in Baroque Venice Longo.* Editore: Ravenna, 2006.

_____. Francesco Buoninsegni, *Contro'l lusso donnesco: satira Menippea,* in *Satira e Aantisatira.* Buoninsegni, Francesco e Tarabotti, Arcangela; Traduttore: Curatore: Elissa Weaver.

Whaley, Leigh Ann. *Women's History as Scientists: A Guide to the Debates.* Women's History as Scientists: A Guide to the Debates Contemporary Issues in Science Series Controversies in science. Author: Leigh Ann Whaley. Edition illustrated. Publisher: ABC-CLIO, 2003.

Westwater, Lynn Lara. "A Rediscovered Friendship in the Republic of Letters: The Unpublished Correspondence of Arcangela Tarabotti and Ismaël Boulliau." *Renaissance Quarterly* 65, no. 1 (2012): 67–134. Print.

Wilckens, Leonie. Review of *The Dress of the Venetians, 1495–1525,* by Stella Mary Newton. *Zeitschrift für Kunstgeschichte* 52, no. 4 (1989): 573. Print.

Yriarte, Charles. *Venice: Its History, Art, Industries and Modern Life.* Print.

Zanette, Emilio. *Suor Arcangela Monaca Del Seicento Veneziano.* Venice/Rome: Istituto di Soria della Societa' e dello Stato, Venice 1960. Print. San Giorgio Maggiore, Venezia.

Zilfi, Madeline C. *Women and Slavery in the Late Ottoman Empire.* Cambridge University Press, October 25, 2012. Print.

Endnotes

1   Martin Sanudo, "Praise of the City of Venice, 1493," Laus Urbis Venetae, BVC ms Cicogna 969, ff. 8v-19r (Sandudo ed. Fulin, 1880), 28–66, in *Renaissance Society of America*, ed. Chambers and Pullan, 4–21.

2   Thomas Coryat, *Coryat's Crudities*, Internet Archive, Center for Reformation and Renaissance, Victoria University. Thomas Coryat visited Venice in 1609.

3   Chambers and Pullan, eds. *Venice: A Documentary History, 1450–1630* (University of Toronto Press, 1992), 31.

4   From a report by Don Alonso della Cuerva, Marquess of Bedmar (Raulich, 1898, 9–19) in Chambers and Pullan.

5   Edward Muir, *Civil Ritual in Renaissance Venice* (Princeton, 1981), 72.

6   The Feast of the Annunciation marks the day that the archangel Gabriel visited the Virgin Mary to inform her she would be the mother of Jesus Christ, the Son of God. The Feast of the Ascension (La Sensa) is the oldest of the Venetian ritual ceremonies, thought to date back to Doge Pietro II Orseolo and his expedition to Dalmatia in the year 1000, establishing Venetian control of the Adriatic. Candlemas celebrates Mary's divine motherhood and her purification after giving birth to Jesus. From Edward Muir's *Civic Ritual in Renaissance Venice*, Edward Muir, (Princeton University Press, 1981), pp. 15–40:

7   "Candlemas, also called Presentation Of The Lord, or Presentation Of Christ In The Temple, or Hypapante, in the Christian church, festival on February 2, commemorates the occasion when the Virgin Mary, in obedience to Jewish law, went to the Temple in Jerusalem both to be purified 40 days after the birth of her son and to present Jesus to God as her firstborn (Luke 2:22–38). The festival was formerly known in the Roman Catholic church as the Purification of the Blessed Virgin Mary and is now known as the Presentation of the Lord. In the Anglican church, it is called the Presentation of Christ in the Temple. In the Greek Church, it is called Hypapante (Meeting), in reference to Jesus' meeting in the Temple with the aged Simeon.

     The earliest reference to the festival is from Jerusalem, where in the late 4th century the Western pilgrim Etheria attended its celebration on February 14, 40 days after Epiphany (then celebrated as Christ's birthday), and wrote of it in the Peregrinatio Etheriae. It soon spread to other Eastern cities, and in 542 Justinian I decreed that its date should be moved back to February 2 (40 days after Christmas). By the middle of the 5th century the custom of observing the festival with lighted candles had been introduced, and the name Candlemas developed from this custom. In the Western church, Pope Sergius I (687–701) instituted the festival in Rome. In the East, it is primarily a festival of Christ; in the West, it was primarily a celebration of the Virgin Mary until the calendar reform of 1969." Britannica, T. Editors of Encyclopaedia. "Candlemas." Encyclopedia Britannica, June 19, 2019.

8 *Patriarchino* is the liturgy that Venice adopted, unique to the Republic. The doge would give his blessing and could initiate changes, rendering the religious rite informed by political considerations, thus aligning political expedience with public worship, eventually morphing into a liturgy of state. For further information, see Muir, *Civil Ritual in Renaissance Venice.*

9 Roman law defined the male head of household as authority over his family. In Chapter 9, I contextualize the legal and cultural concepts.

10 Tradition has it that in the thirteenth century, the church and monastery are attributed to the doge Sebastiano Ziani who was persuaded by Cardinal Ugolino, bishop of Ostia, to erect a church named Santa Maria Nuova in Gerusalemme in memory of the same one that had been in Jerusalem taken by the Saracens. The doge took the occasion to begin work on the church and attached to it a monastery that remained under the jurisdiction of the doges of Venice. Work may have begun as early as 1199 (from "Delle Inscrizioni veneziane raccolte ed illustrate da Emmanuele Antonio Cigogna, dittadino Veneto," Volume 5, Venice MDCCCXLIL, 1).

11 Jutta Gisella Sperling, *Convents and the Body Politic in Late Renaissance Venice*, 84. Sperling refers to a "Marian" Venus. As Luigi Groto phrased it, Venice was a "new Venus born naked in the midst of the sea," yet she was a virgin city "without walls."

12 Venus Anadyomene is from the Greek. Venus rising from the sea is a depiction of Aphrodite and can be seen in the iconic 1520 Titian painting and Botticelli's *The Birth of Venus*, 1486.

13 David Rosand, *Myths of Venice: The Figuration of a State* (University of North Carolina Press, 2005), 177–96.

14 Fabio and Agostino Zopini Fratelli, *Le oration volgari di Luigi Groto cieco di Hadria da lui medesimo…*, 1586, 108.

15 Silvio Tramontin, *Realita' e Leggende in Muir*, 80-81.

16 This term refers to the transfer of Saint Mark's bones from Alexandria to Venice.

17 See Muir, 80–82, for further details relating to the transfer story.

18 The relics of Saint Mark were reaffirmed in the Translatio document that has unclear origins, dating back to the eleventh century.

19 "I Santi patroni," 82–83, "Una Voce Venetia," Coordinamento di Una Voce delle Venezie (CUVVE); Tramontin, "Realita' e leggenda," 36–44, 53–54; idem, "San Marco," 47–52; Niero, "I Santi patroni," 82–83; Gina Fasoli, "Nascita di un mito," in Muir, 84, note 53.

[20] The Interdict of 1482 involved Venetian expansion on the mainland, terra firma, and her commercial interests driving Pope Sixtus IV (Francesco Della Rovere) to send his troops to ally with Venice. Eventually, fear of Venetian dominance caused the pope to declare war upon his former ally and to place Venice under interdict in 1482 until Venice withdrew from Ferrara, all ending with peace in 1484. For further information about the Interdict of 1483, see, for example, *War, Culture, and Society in Renaissance Venice: Essays in Honour of John Hale*, Hale, Chamber, eds., 70–72.

[21] For further information about the Interdict of 1606, see, for example, "The Venetian Interdict and the Problem of Order" in *A Usable Past*, by William Bouwsma (University of California Press, 1923), 97–111. (Histoire—Philosophie—Religion, published by the Academy's Institute of Philosophy and Sociology as volume 12 of the Archiwum Historii Filozofii i Mysli Spolecznej [Warsaw, 1966], 127–140.)

[22] Silvana Seidel Menchi, "Italy" in *The Reformation in National Context*, eds. Scribner, Poorter, and Teich (Cambridge University Press, 1994); C. F. Black, *Church, Religion and Society in Early Modern Italy*, 4.

[23] Alberi, Eugenio, *Le Relazioni degli Ambasciatori Veneti al senato durante il secolo decimosesto, Firenze, 1861, Le Relazioni Degli Ambasciatori Veneti al Senato Durante IL Secolo Decimosesto*, vol. 4 (Classic reprint in Italian, paperback—November 29, 2016).

[24] Sarpi, Istoria dell' Interdetto, 5, in Bouwsma, 353. http://www.bibliotecaitaliana.it/indice/visualizza_testo/si227.

[25] Giovanni Botero, *The Reason of State*, trans. P. J. and D.P. Waley, 1606 (New Haven: Yale University Press, 1956) in Bouwsma, 354.

[26] Bouwsma, *A Usable Past*, 247.

[27] Sarpi, 53.

[28] Wotton, Sir Henry (1568–1639) in *Studies in Medieval and Reformation Traditions*, by Jaska Kainulainen, vol. 180; Paolo Sarpi, *A Servant of God and State* (Leiden: Brill, 2014). ProQuest ebrary. Web. 11 February 2016. Also, see "Venice and Rome" in *The Addresses and Dispatches of Sir Henry Wotton: First English Embassy to Venice, 1604–1610*.

[29] For further information, see William J. Bouwsma, *Venice and the Defense of Republican Liberty* (Berkeley: University of California Press, 1968), 115.

[30] Riccardo Calimani, *The Venetian Ghetto: The History of a Persecuted Community*, trans. Katherine Silberblatt Wolfthal (New York: M. Evans, 1987), chapter 11.

[31] Giovanni Botero, *The Reason of State, Book 1*, http://www.nlnrac.org/critics/machiavelli/primary-source-documents/the-reason-of-state.

[32] Marin Sanudo, *Venice, Città Excelentissima: Selections from the Renaissance Diaries of Marin Sanudo*, ed. Patricia H. Labalme, Laura Sanguineti White, trans. Linda L. Carroll (2008), 16.

[33] For further information, see *The History of the Decline and Fall of the Roman Empire* by Edward Gibbons; *The Decline of Spain in the Seventeenth Century/The*

Rise and Decline of Nations: Economic Growth, Stagflation, and Social Rigidities by Mancur Olson; *The Economic Decline of Empires* by J. V. Vives (1970).

34 The Teatro di San Cassiano opened, in 1637, is located in the Cassiano district near the Rialto.

35 Commencing with Giorgione (c. 1477–1510) and Giovanni Bellini (c. 1430–1416)—including Titian (1489–1576), Tintoretto (1518–1594), Veronese (1528–1588), and Bassano (1510–1592)—the Venetian School of painting incorporated new techniques of oil painting, premised on prior artistic styles to create a uniquely Venetian art. For further information, see, for example, *History of Italian Renaissance Art* by Frederick Hartt and David G. Wilkins (Prentice Hall, 2011).

36 For further reading, see, for example, *The History of the Decline and Fall of the Roman Empire* by Edward Gibbons; *The Decline of Spain in the Seventeenth Century* by Christopher Storrs (University of Dundee); *The Rise and Decline of Nations: Economic Growth, Stagflation, and Social Rigidities* by Mancur Olson (Yale University, 1982).

37 Venice lost most of its mainland territory in a humiliating defeat a century ago (League of Cambrai/Agnadello, 1509). There existed a maritime rivalry between the Dutch and the Venetians over what Venice considered its *golfo* (the northern Adriatic, the Gulf of Venice, considered *nostro mare* [our sea] by Venetians). For further information, see, for example, Paolo Sarpi, *His Networks, Venice, and the Coming of the Thirty Years' War*, Tarpley, Webster G. (Ann Arbor, MI, 2009).

38 Chambers and Pullan, 168.

39 Ibid.

40 Ibid.

41 Molmenti, *History of Venice in Private Life*, 48.

42 See Richard Tilden Rapp, *Industry and Economic Decline in Seventeenth-Century Venice* (Harvard University Press, 1976).

43 From *Richard III*, Shakespeare, act 3, scene 2.

44 Pompeo Molmenti, *Venice: Its Individual Growth from the Earliest Beginnings*, vol. 5, 24–25.

45 See Stanley Chojnacki, *In Search of the Venetian Patriciate: Families and Factions in the Fourteenth Century in Renaissance Venice* (Faber and Faber, 1974).

46 See Stanley Chojnacki, *Women and Men in Renaissance Venice*, (Johns Hopkins University Press, 2000), 115–20, for historical perspectives.

47 *Serrata*, Italian for "closure," signified the restriction of seats on the Great Council only to adult males who could trace their nobility back to the thirteenth century, limiting the Venetian oligarchy to a closed number of patricians.

48 The Great Council consisted of up to two thousand aristocrats who elected a senate of two hundred to three hundred that chose the Council of Ten. For further reading, see, for example, *Venice Reconsidered: The History and Civilization of an Italian City-State, 1297–1797*, eds. John Martin and Dennis Romano (Baltimore and London: Johns Hopkins University Press, 2000).

49 Marin Sanudo, "ASVE, CD, C, 2,14v-17v," in *Patrician Purity and the Female Person in Early Renaissance Venice* by Stanley Chojnacki and *The Registration of Noble Births, 1506*, ASV compilazioned delle Leggi, b. 294.

50 *The Registration of Noble Births, 1506*, from a decree of the Council of Ten, August 31, 1506: ASV Compilazione delle Leggi, b. 284; p. 244 in Pullan.

51 Gasparo Contarini, *The Commonwealth and Government of Venice*, trans. Lewes Lewkenor (1599), 1483–1542.

52 Ibid. This work was first published in Latin between 1523 and 1531.

53 Elizabeth Norton, *Jane Seymour: Henry VIII's True Love* (Amberley Publishing, 2009), 123.

54 J. E. Neale, *Queen Elizabeth I* (Academy Chicago Publishers, 1992), 59–60.

55 William J. Bouwsma, *Venice and the Defense of Republican Liberty* (University of California Press, 1968), 62–65.

56 Marin Sanudo, "Laus Urbis Venetae: BCV ms. Cigogna 969, Praise of the City of Venice, 1493," in *Venice: A Documentary History, 1450–1630*, eds. Chambers, Fletcher, and Pullan (Oxford: 1992), 16.

57 Ibid.

58 Kathryn Hinds, *Venice and Its Merchant Empire*, 48.

59 Contarini, *De magistratibus et republica venetorum*, p. 131. In English, p. 41 in Muir's *Civic Ritual in Renaissance Venice*.

60 Memmo, Giovanni Maria, Dialogo, p. 6. "In non giudico che la felicita di una Repulblica consista nella grandezza dello imperio &dello stato, ma nel vivere quieto in unione," in *Studies in Medieval and Reformation Traditions*, vol. 180, ed. Jaska Kainulainen; Paolo Sarpi, *A Servant of God and State.* (Leiden, NLD: Brill, 2014). ProQuest ebrary. Web. February 11, 2016.

61 Contarini, in Muir, 131.

62 Chojinacki, *Women and Men in Renaissance Venice*, 206.

63 For more information about dowries in the New World, see, for example, Muriel Nazzari, *Disappearance of the Dowry, Women, Families, and Social Change in Sao Paulo, Brazil, 1600–1900* (Stanford University Press, 1991).

64 For more information, see, for example, Jack Goody and Stanley Jeyaraja Tambiah, *Bridewealth and Dowry*, no. 7. CUP Archive, 1973; Jane Lambiri-Dimaki, *Dowry in Modern Greece: An Institution at the Crossroads between Persistence and Decline*; *The Marriage Bargain: Women and Dowries in European History* (1985), 165–78.

65 Chojinacki, 132–152.

66 The Council of Trent, Session XXIV, November, 1563: "The perpetual and indissoluble bond of matrimony was expressed by the first parent of the human race, when, under the influence of the divine Spirit, he said: 'This now is bone of my bones and flesh of my flesh. Wherefore a man shall leave father and mother and shall cleave to his wife, and they shall be two in one flesh.'"

[67] Lisa Dallavalle, "The Moretti Family: Late Marriage, Bachelorhood and Domestic Authority In Seventeenth-Century Venice," *Gender & History* 27, no. 3 (2015): 684–702.

[68] Jutta Gisela Sperling, *Convents and the Body Politic in Late Renaissance Venice* (University of Chicago Press, 1999), 25.

[69] Most likely the unusual eschewing of primogeniture derived from ancient customs that the early Venetians inherited and continued to practice. James C. Davis, *A Venetian Family and Its Fortunes* (1975), 85.

[70] Ibid, 93.

[71] Will of Leonardo, son of Giambattista, 1609, ASVTN 1256.III.60 in James Davis, *A Venetian Family and Its Fortune.*

[72] Franco Niccolai, quoted in *Law, Family & Women: Toward a Legal Anthropology of Renaissance Italy* by Thomas Kuehn (1991), 239.

[73] "Volumen statutorum, Correttion del Trevisan, cap. 11, 197v," in *Dowries*, eds. Donald E. Queller and Thomas F. Madden, *Renaissance Quarterly* 46, no. 4: 685–11.

[74] At midcentury, there were about 2,500 women in Venetian convents (see Francesca Medioli, "Monache e monacazioni nel Seicento," one of three essays in Gabriella Zarri, Francesca Medioli, and Paola Vismara Chiappa, "De monialibus [secoli XVI–XVIII]," Rivista di storia e letteratura religiosa 33, note 3 [1997], 676–78). Jutta Sperling estimates the number of nuns in Venice at 2,905 in 1642, with about 69 percent of these coming from patrician families, families of a higher social status than Tarabotti's; according to Sperling, in 1642, more than 80 percent of patrician girls were nuns; *Convents and the Body Politic in Late Renaissance Venice* (Chicago: University of Chicago Press, 1999), 28, table 2.

[75] Zanette, 36.

[76] Ibid.

[77] Una Barzelletta di Benedetto da Cingoli for the wedding of Pascucci-Caterbini. This "joke" taken from a rare document printed in Rome in 1503 is from the rhymes of B. da Cingoli, Giornale storico della letteratura italiana, Volumes 41–42; Torino, 1903.

[78] Sperling, 35.

[79] Giovanni Botero *The Reason of State, 1540–1617,* trans. P. J. and D. P. Waley (New Haven: Yale University Press, 1956), 267–8.

[80] Basillius Bessarion was a Roman Catholic cardinal, the patriarch of Constantinople. For further information, see, for example, Bianca Concetta, *Da Bisanzio a Roma: Studi sul cardinale Bessarione*, Rome: Roma nel Rinascimento, 1999; John Monfasani, Byzantine Scholars in Renaissance Italy: Cardinal Bessarion and Other Émigrés: Selected Essays, vol. 485 (Variorum Publishing, 1995); Alex G. Keller, "1. A Byzantine Admirer of 'Western' Progress: Cardinal Bessarion," *Cambridge Historical Journal* 11, no. 03 (1955): 343–348.

[81] These small portable editions were referred to as "octavos." Manutius's edition of Virgil's opera in 1501 was the first octavo volume that he produced.

[82] George Haven Putnam, *Books and Their Makers during the Middle Ages* (New York; London: G. P. Putnam's Sons, 1896), 437.

[83] For more information about the literary and political climate of the time, see, for example, Mario Infelise, "Books and Politics in Arcangela Tarabotti's Venice," in Weaver, *Arcangela Tarabotti*, 56.

[84] Miato, Monica. 1998. *L'Accademia Degli Incogniti Di Giovan Francesco Loredan*: Venezia (1630–1661) Firenze: Olschki.

[85] Cremonini successfully defended himself from the Inquisition and prevented the Jesuits from teaching philosophy at Padua.

[86] For further information about Cesare Cremonini (1550–1631), professor of philosophy at the University of Ferrara and University of Padua (under Venetian rule) and influential to a generation of scholars, see page 254 of Bouwsma, *Venice and the Defense of Republican Liberty*; Charles B. Schmitt, "Aristotelianism in the Veneto and the Origins of Modern Science: Some Considerations on the Problems of Continuity" in *The Aristotelian Tradition and Renaissance Universities* (London: Variorum Reprints, 1984).

[87] For more information and a complete bibliography of Pallavicino, see Laura Coci, "Bibliografia di Ferrante Pallavicino," *Studi secenteschi*, 24 (1983): 221–306. Biblioteca dell, "Archivum Romanicum," series 1, vol. 174.

[88] Eugenia Paulicelli, *Writing Fashion in Early Modern Italy: From Sprezzatura to Satire* (Farnham: Ashgate, 2014), 183.

[89] For detailed information about Loredan and L'Accademia degli Incogniti, see Monica Miato, *Accademia Degli Incogniti Di Giovan Francesco Loredan Fenezia* (1630–1661); Leo S. Olschki Editore, 1948; Pompeo Gherardo Molmenti, *La storia di Venezia nella vita privata dalle origini alla caduta...*, Capitolo XII, 486–487.

[90] To protect the faith and morals of Roman Catholics, books thought to contain heretical and immoral content were banned. For further reading, see Francis S. Betten, *The Roman Index of Forbidden Books* (United States, 1909).

[91] Giovanni Franceso Loredano, Bizzarrie academiche. Parte prima. Venice: Guerigli, 1654. Bizzarrie academiche. Parte seconda. Venice: Guerigli, 1654.

[92] _____. *Bizzarrie Accademiche di Gio*: Francesco Loredano Nobile Veneto; 1:61: "Il veleno uscito dagli occhi di bella donna avrà tolta la vita all'amante, e non vorremo dunque che sia nero il volto dell'amante ucciso dal veleno? Non vorremo dunque, ch'appariscano nel volto gl'indici della sua morte?"

[93] Francesco Buoninsegni's "Contro il lusso donnesco," a quasi-satiric moral treatise, disparages female fashion excess and the foolish women who waste money on the luxuries of ornament and attire. Suor Arcangela replies with *Antisatira* in 1644, a clever, vituperous reply to the author's misogynist contentions.

[94] È nata nobile, di dignissimi parenti; ma non avendo dote uguale alla nascita, bisogna o che degradi dalla sua condizione o che avventuri agl'incommodi della povertà. Cited in Luciano Menetto / Gianni Zennaro, Storia del malcostume a Venezia nei secoli XVI e XVII (Piovan, 1987), 104.

95 Zanette, 2–30; Francesca Medioli, "Arcangela Tarabotti: Una Famiglia Non Detta e Un Segreto Indicibile In Famiglia," Archivo Veneto, Milano-Venezia-Verona (Venezia, 2013), 125. Medioli finds the sum of 3,500 ducati paid as dowry.

96 "La fisionomia della Famiglia resto' fissata nel suo aspetto prevalentaemente muliebre e di conseguenza alquanto malinconico"; Zanette, 4; see Medioli, "Una Famiglia Non Detta…," 110, for complete archival records of the children born into the Tarabotti family.

97 Zanette suggests that possibly the experience with their first daughter might have influenced the family to not monachanize another.

98 Letter 53.

99 Medioli, "Una Famiglia Non Detta…," 109.

100 Zanette, 9.

101 Sanudo, *Venice, Cita' Excelentissima*, ed. Labalme and White, 287.

102 Sansovio, "Venetia città nobilissima et singolare, 1663," in *Private Lives in Renaissance Venice: Art, Architecture, and the Family*, ed. Patricia Fortini Brown (New Haven and London: Yale University Press, 2004), 3.

103 Chambers and Pullan, *Venice: A Documentary History, 1450–1630*, 26.

104 Medioli, "Famiglia Non Detta": "Entrambe dunque non erano più giovanissime, almeno per l'epoca, quando l'età media per sposarsi fra le patrizie veneziane nel Seicento si aggirava sui 19 anni, anche se poi il 42,2% si sposava fra i 15 e i 19 anni e il 39,6% fra i 20 e i 24. Ed entrambe con due partiti non precisamente ideali, per quanto appartenenti alla nuova classe emergente delle libere profession," 116.

105 Marin Sanudo, *Praise of the City of Venice*, Laus Urbis Venetae in Pullan, 18.

106 Ibid.

107 Zanette 3, 5.

108 Ibid., 3: "Ma erano dei rami di terzo e quaro ordine, che non riuscirono a dare un impronta qualsiasi all zona: le superbe moli patrizie, che furono stile e spendore di Venezia, vi mancavano del tutto."

109 Ibid, 11.

110 Ibid, 12.

111 Rodolfo Gallo, La familgia di Jacopo Tintoretto, Venejia, Ferrara, 1941, in Zanette, 13.

112 Molmenti, 85; He names the sisters as Alturia and Perina Robusti.

113 There is a discrepancy: Tarabotti herself tells that she was eleven years old (*Lettere*, 141) However, the date of 1615 has been contested by Zanette and by Medioli, as no trace of periodical conventual payments can be found until August 10.

114 Zanette, 22.

115 Valdeberto di Luzeuil in Regole Monastiche femminili (2003), 168, in Gabriella Zarri, Novizie Ed Educande Nei Monasteri Italiani Post-Tridentini VS 18 (2011), 7–23.

116 *Inferno*, 11.

[117] (p. 27). Zanette reveals that this first payment was actually for two daughters, most likely Camilla, the second-born female. However, Camilla never became an *educanda*, all future records showing payments for one child only

[118] Zanette, 28.

[119] Zanette, 28; Arcangela herself tells us that she entered the convent when she was eleven years old in 1615. However, this date has been contested by Zanette and by Medioli, as no trace of periodical convent payments can be found until August 1617.

[120] Francesca Medioli, "Arcangela Tarabotti's Reliability about Herself," Archivo di Stato Venezia, Notarile, Testamente, Marcellini, 620, note 233, December 6, 1647; *Italianist*, 23.

[121] New religious orders such as the Capuchins and Discalced Carmelites began to grow in the sixteenth century. For further information about the diffusion of these religious orders throughout Europe, see, for example, *Handbook of European History, 1400–1600: Late Middle Ages, Renaissance, and Reformation*, vol. 2, eds. Thomas A. Grady, Heiko Oberman, and James D. Tracy (Leiden: I. J. Brill, 1995), 284–298.

[122] Weaver, 41.

[123] *Tirannia paterna*, 66: "Non danno per ispose à Giesù le più belle, e virtuose; mà le più sozze, e defformi, e se nella lor famiglia si rittrovano zoppe gobbe, sciancate, ò scempie, quasi ch'il diffetto della natura, sia diffetto d'esse, vengono condennate à starsi prigione tutte il tempo della lor vita."

[124] A. P. V Priuli, Visite die Monasteri 1592–1596 in Zanette, Note, 32.

[125] Zanette, 36; Gian Francesco Morosini, Patriarch of Venice from 1644 to 1678.

[126] *Inferno*, 12: "Molti havrano da pentirsi d'haver in questo modo chiusi gl'occhi sopra questi interessi per la sola Raggion di stato…che riempie gli oridi sepolchri de'chiostri di misere ed innocenti donne!"

[127] *Inferno*, 36.

[128] *L'inferno monacale*, 3: "Concedete a qual si sia natione della vostra bella metropoli libertà non circonscritta, di modo che ne godono tutt'i crocifissori dell' Figliolo della vostra Santissima Protettrice. Nella primiera edificatione della vostra città in queste lagune penetrò questa fama fin ne gli abissi, di dove trasse la Tirannia Paterna che, celatasi sotto la maestà delle vesti de' vostri senatori, ha finalmente piantata sua sede nel Palaggio Ducale e domina la città tutta, seguendo per l'ordinario I vassali l'orme de' prencipi, come fa l'ombra e 'l corpo. riuscitta tanto accetta ed è statta tanto volentieri abbracciata e seguita, questo mostro d'Inferno della Tirania patterna da' vostri nobilissimi signori, che non mi resta d'onde temere che questa mia, lineata dalla rozza penna che già mai habbia vergati fogli, non sia per riuscirvi grata… Vi dedico dunque e consacro questo mio primo parto come capriccio d'inteletto feminile."

[129] Ibid. "Mi protesto che i miei detti non sono intentionati a biasmar la religione né a ragionar se non contro quei padri e parenti che con violenza imbavarano le figliole. Ell'è una grand'ingratitudine che quella patria che è protetta par-

cialmente dalla Vergine, che per mezzo d'una donna ottene già vittoria contro gl'impiti ribelli di Baiamonte Tiepolo, più di qual si vogl'altro dominio del mondo avvilisca, inganni e privi di libertà con forza le sue vergini e donne. Non vo' mendicar scuse e colori per insinuarvi la mia sincerità: che ad ogni modo non resta che perdere a chi ha perduto la libertà."

[130] *Semplicità*, 130.

[131] The work was considered too polemic to be published and only saw light of day two years after Tarabotti's death, in 1654, with a less provocative title, *Semplicità ingannata*.

[132] *Semplicità*, Libro 2, 112.

[133] Adolf Berger, *Encyclopedic Dictionary of Roman Law, 1882, 1881*, American Philosophical Society (1968), 620–621.

[134] Chojnacki, *Women and Men in Renaissance Venice*, 169.

[135] De re uxoria, 63; Kohl's translation, 194, in Chojnakci, *Women and Men in Renaissance Venice*.

[136] Nino Tamassia, *La Famiglia italiana: nei secoli decimoquinto e decimosesto, Multigrafica Editirice* (University of Virginia, 1971), 203.

[137] Chojnacki, 153–168.

[138] *Semplicità*, 115: "Vuoi, che promettano d'abassar il capo ad ogn' insulto, e che ricevuta una guanciata, prontamente espongano la gota non offesa ad esser percossa, mentre tù non puoi soffrire, nè pure una bieca guattatura."

[139] Letter 53.

[140] *Semplicità*, 116: "Ma ti basta di cacciartele di casa col minor pregiudicio della tua borsa, senza sminuire quelle somme di denari, che ti fanno impazzire."

[141] *Semplicità*, Libro 2: "Com' è possibile, ò ingannatori, che chiudiate in seno un cuore cosi crudele, che soffra di tormentar il corpo delle vostre figliuole, che pur son vostre viscere, con perdita forse della lor anima, la cui natura è tanto nobile, che per salvarne una sola se bisognasse, Christo di nuovo discenderebbe dal cielo in terra, e tornerebbe à patir morte di croce;. Pur saria meglio, che 'l giorno della nascita di queste semplici, ch'ingannate, e imprigionate frà claustri, fosse lor occidente."

[142] *Semplicità*, 29: "ruffiani dell' infernal mostro" (Satan's pimps).

[143] Ibid., 133: "Padri e parenti di figlie tali, non vi scusi il dire non m'erano noti simili particolari, & altro non pretesi, che di volerle gloriosamente vergini, levandole da'i travagli humani, poichè l'esser secoli de secoli, che 'l mondo tutto pratica…, più che non sono chiari i raggi del Sole…"

[144] Ibid., 112: "Le madri, anche esse per compiacer al marito, concorrono con ogni studio e sforzo in stiracchiare le spese e pesano il tutto alla sottile sopra la statera dell'ingiustitia per potter poscia più prodigamente scialaqur il benefficio delle destinate a nozze mondane."

[145] Letter 32.

[146] *Inferno*, 18.

[147] Ibid., 131.

[148] Ibid., 132.

[149] Ibid., 134.

[150] ASV, PSM, B. 263, 1555, Giovanni Lateran in *Virgins of Venice*, Mary Laven (Penguin Books, 2004), 38–39.

[151] ASV, PSM, B. 265, 1614, S. Zaccaria in *Virgins of Venice*, Mary Laven (Penguin Books, 2004), 186–189.

[152] Busenello (1598–1659) was a Venetian poet, librettist, and lawyer, educated by Paolo Sarpi and Cesare Cremonini. For further reading, see, for example, Patrick J. Smith, *The Tenth Muse: A Historical Study of the Opera Libretto* (New York, 1970).

[153] Boccaccio, *Decamarone*, Terza Giornata, "Novella prima; Masetto da Lamporecchio si fa mutolo e diviene ortolano di uno monistero di donne, le quali tutte concorrono a giacersi con lui."

[154] *Inferno*, 20.

[155] Ibid., 19.

[156] Ibid., 19–20: "Le più immonde schifeze, fugite dalle più vili serve nelle case private, ad essa son risservate per esercitio. L'abassamento di capo, anco verso cui non conviene, l'assistenza e prontezza nell'obedienza e l'assiduità nel coro continua, se da queste tali non sono pontualmente osservate, si sentono con rimproveri cruciare con non dissimili voci da quelle che, come esse, furono sposate a Cristo con violenza: «Sei novizza: a te, a te s'appartengono i dissagi».

"Tu, come ultima entrata in monastero, devi suplir per l'altre, ché così habbiam fatto ancora noi a' nostri tempi." "Non è decente che tu prettenda di voler star al paragone con le professe e sacratte…"

[157] Ibid., 22: "Che tormentan la borsa al tenacissimo vecchio."

[158] *Inferno*, 19, Libro Secondo, "Inganno è un de' più horridi mostri che concorrano ad infettar la quiete e felicità de' miseri mortali, cagionando loro gl'infortunij, sotto falso pretesto e finta apparenza di bene servire, aportar mali tanto più tormentosi quanto meno aspettati" and p. 12, "Tenerelle d'età, non han cognitione bastevole per ellegersi più una vitta che un'altra; anzi, s'affrettano a imbavararle prima che s'accorgano d'essere imprigionate. O che inganno!"

[159] Letter 22: To Eustochium; St. Jerome, On Marriage and Virginity.

[160] *Inferno*, Libro Primo, 5.

[161] Ibid., 10, 15; Dante, 26, 33, 36, 39.

[162] Zanette, 93.

[163] *Inferno*, 11.

[164] Zanette, 85, 88.

[165] *Inferno*, 17.

[166] Ibid., 12.

[167] *Inferno*, 14: "Gli ori, le gemme son chiamati ad arricchire la costei belezza e se la consegna insino un maestro perito che l'insegni I modei del carrolare…" (my translation).

[168] Francesco Guicciardini, quoted in Jacqueline Marie Musacchio, *Art, Marriage, and Family in the Florentine Renaissance Palace* (New Haven: Yale University Press, 2008), 11.

[169] *Inferno monacale*, 33.

[170] Ibid.

[171] Council of Trent, chapter 17, 249.

[172] *Inferno*, 34–37.

[173] Zanette, 85–86.

[174] Ibid.

[175] *Semplicità*, 55, 56: "Ne' sacri Canoni si legge, che la donna non debba privarsi di quella chioma, che il Sign. le diede, dicono per segno della soggettion sua, anzi dich' io, perch' ella è libera, e non soggetta, essendo la chioma segno eccellente di libertà, e di superiorità insieme. Come dunque stà bene, ch' elle si suellino i proprii capelli, levandossi la vaghezza, & il maggior ornamento, ch' habbiano dalla natura? Commandava Iddio nel Levitico à sacerdoti, che in modo alcuno non si troncassero la chioma. Non obtundetis caput in rotundum, nec barbam radetis: per ciò à Nazareni fù confirmata la legge, De nutrienda coma. Sino à quei tempi era in gran stima l' andar co' capelli longhi, poiche la testa rasa era contrasegno di servitù: me ne sia testimonio Ezechiele, ch' asserisce, che Nabucdonosor usò per castigo di far tagliar la chioma al popolo di Dio. Nabucdonosor servire fecit servitute magnâ omne caput decalvatum, & omnis humerus depilatus: il principe de' filosofi dice. Comam esse libertatis argumentum. Perche dunque, ò ingiustissimi e ingannevoli, volete levar anche i contrasegni di libertà à chi è libero quanto voi?"

[176] *Semplicità*, 55.

[177] Elizabeth Kuhn, *The Habit: A History of the Clothing of Catholic Nuns* (New York: Doubleday, 2005), 116.

[178] ACPV Archivo Della Curia Patriarcale Di Venezia, visite passati, Vendramin 1609–1618 in *Virgins of Venice*, 4.

[179] Pompeo Molmenti, 270–1.

[180] *Inferno*, Dedication: "Alla Serenissima Republica Veneta."

[181] Zanette, 113.

[182] Ibid. ASV Manimorte, Note, 113.

[183] This "depression" was defined as a typical syndrome of nuns by Bernardino Ramazzini, a medical doctor of Modena in the eighteenth century. In Arcangela Tarabotti, *Lettere familiari e di complimento*, eds. Meredith Ray and Lynn Westwater (Rosenberg and Sellier, 2005), 10.

[184] *Inferno*, 104.

[185] Erving Goffman, *Asylums: Essay on the Social Situation of Mental Patients and Other inmates* (Garden City, NY: Doubleday and Co., 1961), xiii.

[186] *Semplicita' ingannata*, Libro 1, 2: "Chiudono con inganno forzatamente frà quattro mura d' un Monastero le semplici donne, facendole in perpetuo hab-

itatrici d' una prigione… anche più meritevoli d' esser compatite, servite, e sollevate, e non d' esser racchiuse in una carcere eterna."

[187] *Semplicità*, Libro Secondo, 186.

[188] Goffman, 114.

[189] *Semplicità*, 305.

[190] *Inferno*, 23.

[191] "Monache e donne nel Friuli de Cinquecento," in *Societa e cultura del Cinquecento* (Pordenone, 1984), 218, in *Letters*, Ray and Westwater.

[192] *Semplicità*, 106.

[193] Ibid., 113.

[194] Ibid., 13.

[195] Ibid., 16.

[196] Ibid., 7.

[197] *Tirannia*, 33.

[198] *Tirannia*, 102.

[199] Calimani, Ghetto Veneziano interdict; for further information about Sullam, see, for example, Howard Adelman, "The Literacy of Jewish Women in Early Modern Italy," in *Women's Education in Early Modern Europe: A History, 1500–1800*, ed. Barbara J. Whitehead (New York, 1999), 133–158, or "Jewish Women and Family Life, Inside and Outside the Ghetto," in *The Jews of Early Modern Venice*, eds. Robert C. Davis and Benjamin Ravid (Baltimore, 2001), 143–165.

[200] Giovan Franceso Loredan, in Leon Modena and Sarra Copia Sullam and l'Accademia degli Incogniti, Howard Adelman, Queen's U, RSA, Berlin, March 2015, 8 Wed March 25, 2463 (2415).

[201] For further reading, see, for example, *A History of the Council of Trent*, vols. 1 and 2, ed. Hubert Jedin, 1957–1961.

[202] Letter to Groslot, September 1, 1609, in Bouwsma, *Venice and Defense of Public Liberty*, 552, note 334.

[203] Girolomo Priuli, *I Diari*, vol. 4, 33–39, 115.

[204] Pietro Aretino, *Ragionamento e Dialogo, Edizione di riferimento: a cura di Giorgio Barberi Squarotti, Rizzoli* (Milano, 1988); For more information, see also Fiovanni Aquilecchia's "Aretino's Sei giornate: literary parody and social reality," in *Women in Italian Renaissance Culture and Society*, ed. Letizia Panizza (European Humanities Research Center, Oxford, 2000).

Aretino's work can be traced back to Lucian's *Dialogi meretrici* and mimics Boccaccio's ten days of *Decameron*. Aretino himself referred to his work as *dialoghi puttaneschi* (whorish dialogues) (letter 1, 280).

[205] APV. "Decretorum et mandatorium monialium'" 1591–9, fols.115r-6r in Christopher F. Black, *Church, Religion, and Society in Early Modern Italy*, 264, note 20.

[206] Elissa B. Weaver, ed. *Arcangela Tarabotti: A Literary Nun in Baroque Venice* (Longo Editore, 2006), 26–27.

207 Archivo della Curia Patriarcale, Vis. Past, Vendramin, 1609-18, S. Andrea, 1609 in *Virgins of Venice*, Mary Laven, 3, note 7.

208 Weaver, 27, note 24.

209 Laven, 6.

210 Weaver, 28.

211 Medioli, "Lo spazio del chiostro," 356.

212 Zanette, 292.

213 Casola, Viaggio a Gerusalemme di Pietro Casola, Edizioni dell'Orso (Torino, 2001), 93.

"E perché intendeva una grande fama de alcuni monasteri de done, io andai pure acompagnato a visitarne qualche uno, precipue el monastero de Santo Zacharia. Sono asai done de zovene e de vegie, se lassano volentera vedere; hano una bella giesia nova e de molte reliquie in lo altare. Credo sia la sua prima giesia, perché hano lì el suo coro. Se dice sono molto riche e non si fano molto cura de esser vedute. Un altro se chiama el monastero de le // [16] Vergene: sono asai done, sono riche e se dice chi lì non entrano se non done veneziane. Hano una bella giesia con lo suo coro, asai publico. Un altro monastero, chiamato a le Done Zelestre, andai per vederlo e trovai vano vestite de bianco."

214 *Semplicità*, 111.

215 See Goffman for sociocultural arrangements of the institutionalized, 189, 199. Partly in response to these processes of mortification, Goffman sees the inmates as developing what he calls secondary adjustments that, collectively, form the underlife of the institution. Thus, secondary adjustments are defined as "any habitual arrangement by which a member of an organization employs unauthorized means, or obtains unauthorized ends, or both, thus getting around the organization's assumptions as to what he should do and get and hence what he should be" (189). "These practices together comprise what can be called the underlife of the institution, being to a social establishment what an underworld is to a city" (199).

216 Georg Simmel, "Fashion," *International Quarterly* 10, no. 1 (October 1904): 130–155, reprinted in *American Journal of Sociology* 62, no. 6 (May 1957): 541–558.

217 Massimo Baldini, *Semiotica della moda,* Armando (Roma: Luiss University Press, 2005), 186–88.

218 Patricia Allerston, "Clothing and Early Modern Venetian Society," *Continuity and Change* 15, no. 3: 367–90.

219 *Coryat's Crudities*, 1. *Thomas Coryat on Venetian Orphans (1608)* (Glasgow: James MacLehose and Sons, 1905).

220 "Tutte le Monache debbono vestire con habiti honesti, et modesti tanto di sopra quanto di sotto talmente che non sia visto... ne' il petto, ne' altra parte scoperta..." Patriarch Lorenzo Priuli, visitation of Sant'Andrea de Zirada, April 9, 1592, Archivo Patriarchale di Venezia, visite Priuli (1592–96) in Jutta Gisela

Sperling, *Convents and the Body Politic in Late Renaissance Venice* (Chicago: University of Chicago Press, 1999), 322, note 31.

[221] The trousseaus of the brides of Christ contained an array of lavishly colored dresses. Isabella Campagnol, *Forbidden Fashions* (Texas Tech University Press, 2014), 131–152.

[222] Zanette, 180.

[223] *Coryat's Crudities*, Observations of Venice, 400.

[224] Ibid. "I saw a woman fall a very dangerous fall, as she was going down the staires of one of the little stony bridges with her high Chapineys alone by her selfe : but I did nothing pitty her, because shee wore such frivolous and (as I may truely terme them) ridiculous instruments, which were the occasion of her fall."

[225] Francesco Buoninsegni, *Contro'l lusso donnesco: Satira Menippea,* in *satira e antisatira* autore: Buoninsegni, Francesco e Tarabotti, Arcangela; Traduttore: Curatore: Elissa Weaver.

[226] In chapter 18, we look at "the woman question," a literary debate about the nature and status of women.

[227] Published in 1644.

[228] Zanette, 180.

[229] M. C. C. Grevenbroch, "Gli abiti de' Veneziani," vol. 1, 140, in Zanette, 180.

[230] Sperling, *Convents and the Body Politic in Late Renaissance Venice*, 123.

[231] Diana Robin, *Collected Letters of a Renaissance Feminist* (Chicago and London: University of Chicago Press, 1997), 79–80.

[232] Ibid., 231.

[233] Ibid., 231.

[234] Ibid., 231.

[235] Tarabotti, *Antisatira*, 41, in *Satira e antisatira*, Francesco Buoninsegni e Arcangela Tarabotti, curator: Elissa Weaver.

[236] Ibid.

[237] Ibid., 29.

[238] *Semplicità*, 64, Complete quote continues: "Mà voi animali perfetti ci superate ne gl' inganni, fallacie, e crudeltadi: è cosa da pazzo il lodar se stesso; mà io non posso adherire all' opinione di quei sublimi, e studiosi intelletti, che con gran energia di concetti privi di verità deludono, & oltraggiano à torto la semplicità, e bontà feminile."

[239] *Semplicità*, 64.

[240] Aristotle, "Physics 1.9. 192a20-24," in *The Complete Works of Aristotle*, ed. Jonathan Barnes, Rv. Oxford trans., 2 vols. (Princeton, 1984), 1, 328.

[241] See Aristotle, De Generatione Animalium, Book 1, Ch. 8; Book 2 for his theory on epigenesis.

[242] Ian Maclean, *The Renaissance Notion of Woman: A Study in the Fortunes of Scholasticism and Medical Science in European Intellectual Life*, 1st paperback ed. (Cambridge; New York: Cambridge University Press, 1983), 7–9. Web.

243 Thomas Kuehn, "Daughters, Mothers, Wives, and Widows," in *Time, Space, and Women's Lives in Early Modern Europe*, eds. Anne Jacobson Schutte, Thomas Kuehn, and Silvana Seidel Menchi (Kirksville, MO: Turman State University Press, 2002), 99–100.

244 Suzanne Dixon, "Infirmitas Sexus: Womanly Weakness in Roman Law," in *Tijdschrift voor rechtsgeschiedenis* 52, no. 4 (1984): 343.

245 John Andrew Couch, "Woman in Early Roman Law," *Harvard Law Review* 8, no. 1 (April 25, 1894): 39–50.

246 "Women and Criminal Law: The Notion of Diminished Responsibility" in *Prospero Farinaccio and Other Renaissance Jurists*; Marina Graziosi in *Time, Space, and Women's Lives in Early Modern Europe*.

247 André Tiraqueau (1488–1558). His work consists of over fifty folio pages of references, hundreds of authorities from the realms of medicine, ethics, and ancient law and literature.

248 Leigh Ann Whaley, *Women's History as Scientists: A Guide to the Debates*, 51.

249 Massimo Firpo, "Edizione critica Roma: Istituto storico italiano per l'eta' moderna e contemporanea, 1981–1995," in *Biblical Scholarship and the Church: A Sixteenth-Century Crisis of Authority*, eds. Allan K. Jenkins and Patrick Preston.

250 Maclean, 16, 2.7.5.

251 In the year 1215, Pope Innocent III issued a law commanding "that they shall be seized for trial and penalties, who engage in the translation of the sacred volumes, or who hold secret conventicles, or who assume the office of preaching without the authority of their superiors; against whom process shall be commenced, without any permission of appeal" (J. P. Callender, *Illustrations of Popery*, 1838, 387). Innocent "declared that as by the old law, the beast touching the holy mount was to be stoned to death, so simple and uneducated men were not to touch the Bible or venture to preach its doctrines" (Schaff, *History of the Christian Church*, VI, 723). Pope Innocent III stated in 1199, "To be reproved are those who translate into French the Gospels, the letters of Paul, the psalter, etc. They are moved by a certain love of Scripture in order to explain them clandestinely and to preach them to one another. The mysteries of the faith are not to explained rashly to anyone. Usually in fact, they cannot be understood by everyone but only by those who are qualified to understand them with informed intelligence. The depth of the divine Scriptures is such that not only the illiterate and uninitiated have difficulty understanding them, but also the educated and the gifted" (Denzinger-Schönmetzer, *Enchiridion Symbolorum*, 770–771). See also *Bridging the Gap—Lectio Divina, Religious Education, and the Have-Nots* by Father John Belmonte, SJ.

252 For example, Rule VI: "Books in the vernacular dealing with the controversies between Catholics and the heretics of our time are not to be generally permitted, but are to be handled in the same way as Bible translations," in *Die Indices Librorum Prohibitorum des sechzehnten Jahrhunderts* (Tübingen, 1886), 246f.

[253] *Forms of Faith in Sixteenth-Century Italy*, eds. Abigail Brundin and Matthew Treherne, 178–180.

[254] See Edwin Wilber Rice, *Our Sixty-Six Sacred Books*; also M'Crie, *Reformation in Italy* (1856), 56, 57.

[255] *Forms of Faith*, 179, note 33; Andrea del Col, "Il controllo della stampa a Venezia e I processi di Antonio Brucioli" (1548–1559), "Critica storica," 17 (1980), 457–510; Michael Douglas Scott, "Prohibition of Text and License of Images: Painters and the Vernacular Bible in Counter-Reformation Venice," in *Il Rinascimento italiano*, 234–8.

[256] Giovanni Boccaccio, *De mulieribus claris* [Famous Women], I Tatti Renaissance Library 1, trans. Virginia Brown (Cambridge, MA: Harvard University Press).

[257] *Semplicità*, 73: "Dio à pascersi di carogne, quando la candidissima colomba della donna fà sempre rittorno alle proprie case con la porpora di modestia su' l volto, e con la pace di Dio frà le labra. Ne giovi per diffesa à gl' huomini il ramentar le Semiramidi, le Cleopatre, le Lesbie, e le Messaline, alle quali però non mancarono qualità degne di memorie, e lodi eterne, perche (come si suol dire) ogni regola patisce eccettione, e l' Occeano non hà tanti flutti, nè tanto numero di stelle il cielo, quante donne vivono, e viveranno sempre con glorioso vanto di virtudi eccellenti, e di purissima castità; onde servono per essemplari all' altre in terra, e sù in cielo, accreceno gloria accidentale alla divinità."

[258] *Semplicità*, 73, Interestingly, Petrarch's commentary on one of the best known of Boccaccio's tales from *The Decameron* shed light on the complex attitudes toward women in a time of change.

"Degli uomini non avvien cosi: essi nascono buoni a mille cose, non pure a questa…ma la femine a niuna altra cosa che a fare questo e figliuoli ci nascono, e per questo son tenute care" (497). (With men it is different; they are born with a thousand other talents apart from this…but women exist for no other purpose than to do this and to bear children, which is why they are cherished and admired." Boccaccio, *The Decameron*, trans. G. H. McWilliam (Baltimore: Penguin, 1972), 472. All the translations from *The Decameron* follow this edition.

Boccaccio, affirms the effective enforcement of masculine will in stories such as that of Griselda.

[259] See Pietro Bembo, *The Prettiest Love Letters*, ed. Hugh Shankland (Collins Harvill, 1987).

[260] According to Cicero, Cornelia (mother of Gracchi and daughter of Scipio Africanus, conqueror of Hannibal at Zama) educated her sons after her husband's death. Cornelia's letters to her son Caius were among the first collected by the Romans. See Cheryl Glenn, *Rhetoric Retold* (Southern Illinois UP, 1997), 66–67.

[261] Petrarch is credited with having discovered Cicero's letters to Atticus, Quintus, and Brutus in 1345. Petrarch's own letters would become models for Renaissance epistolarians. See Francis Petrarch Familiar Letters from James Harvey Robinson, ed. and trans., *Petrarch: The First Modern Scholar and Man*

of Letters (New York: G. P. Putnam, 1898). Also, see, for example, Cecil H. Clough and Paul Oskar Kristeller, *Cultural Aspects of the Italian Renaissance: Essays in Honour of Paul Oskar Kristeller* (Manchester: Manchester University Press, 1976), 554.

262 For more information, see Jane Couchman and Ann M. Crabb, eds., *Women's Letters across Europe, 1400–1700: Form and Persuasion* (Aldershot and Burlington, VT: Ashgate Publishing, 2004), 1–18.

263 For a complete overview of the letter in its social context, see, for example, David Barton and Nigel Hall, eds., *Letter Writing as a Social Practice*, vol. 9 (John Benjamins Publishing, 2000). Also, Armando Petrucci's *Scrivere letter: una storia plurimillenaria*, 2008; Gius. Laterza & Figli offers a comprehensive history of letter writing, subtitled "Storia e Societa."

264 http://perseus.uchicago.edu/perseuscgi/citequery3. pl?dbname=PerseusLatinTexts&getid=1&query=Cic.%20Fam.%202.4.

265 Frederic Austin Ogg, ed., *A Sourcebook of Medieval History* (New York: American Book Company, 1907), 470–473.

266 Petrarch, Familiar Letters, "On the Scarcity of Copyists to Lapo da Castiglionchio," 275–278. From James Harvey Robinson, ed. and trans., *Petrarch: The First Modern Scholar and Man of Letters* (New York: G. P. Putnam, 1898). Scanned by Jason Boley and Jacob Miller in August 1995. Proofread by Monica Banas, Stephanie Hammett, and Heather Haralson in April 1996. Proofread and pages inserted by Jonathan Perry, March 2001.

267 *Petrarch's Letters to Classical Authors* by Francesco Petrarca and Mario Emilio Cosenza (University of Chicago Press, 1910).

268 Maria Luisa Doglio, *L'arte delle lettere: idea e pratica della scrittura epistolare tra Quattro e Seicento*, 8–10.

269 Cicero. Fam. 5.12: "I have often tried to say to you L. Lucceius, of whom we have heard before, as having some quarrel with Atticus. His work has not survived. No letter of the correspondence has brought more adimadversion on Cicero, and yet log-rolling and the appealing to friends on the press to review one's book are not wholly unknown even in our time. personally what I am about to write, but was prevented by a kind of almost clownish bashfulness. Now that I am not in your presence I shall speak out more boldly: a letter does not blush. I am inflamed with an inconceivably ardent desire, and one, as I think, of which I have no reason to be ashamed, that in a history written by you my name should be conspicuous and frequently mentioned with praise. to l. lucceus."

270 See Francesco Barbaro, *On Wifely Duties*, trans. Benjamin G. Kohl, cited in *The Earthly Republic: Italian Humanists on Government and Society*, eds. Benjamin G. Kohl and Ronald G. Witt (University of Pennsylvania Press, 1981, 1978), 189–230. Barbaro's advice to his friend Lorenzo de Medici upon Lorenzo's marriage was a treatise that reached circulation designed to focus on the importance of stable marriages, necessary to maintain aristocratic rule: "Isocrates warns men

to speak on those matters that they know well and about which they cannot, on account of their dignity, remain silent. We commend women to concede the former as the property of men, but they should consider the latter to be appropriate to themselves as well as to men. Loquacity cannot be sufficiently reproached in women, as many very learned and wise men have stated, nor can silence be sufficiently applauded. For this reason women were prohibited by the laws of the Romans from pleading either criminal or civil law cases."

[271] Petrucci, 60, cites Luisa Miglio, Governare l'alfabeto: Donne, scrittura e libri nel medioevo. Preface by Armando Petrucci, Scritture e Libri del Medioevo, 6.

[272] Panizza and Wood, *A History of Women's Writing in Italy*, 3.

[273] Petrucci, 66. Caterina Di Siena's missives constitute the first great collection of letters in the vernacular, dictated between 1365 and 1380.

[274] Panizza and Wood, *A History of Women's Writing in Italy*, 3.

[275] Petrucci, 60.

[276] Couchman and Ann M. Crabb, 30, note 22.

[277] *Selected Letters of Alessandra Strozzi*, trans. Heather Gregory, bilingual edition (University of California Press, 1997).

[278] For more information, see, for example, *The Bed and the Throne: The life of Isabella d'Este* (New York: Harper and Row, 1976); Maria Bellonci, *Private Renaissance* (New York: Morrow, 1989); Daniela Pizzagalli, *La Signora del Rinascimento. Vita e spendori di Isabella d Este alla corte di Mantova; Alessandro Luzio, Isabella d'Este e il Sacco di Roma; Milano Editrice L. F. Cogliati, 1908; Maria Bellonci, Tu Vipera Gentile, Modadori, 1972.*

[279] Deanna Shemek, "Isabella d'Este and the Properties of Persuasion," in *Women's Letters Across Europe, 1400–1700*, Couchman and Crabb, 123–126, and Letters of Isabella d'Este.

[280] George R. Marek, *The Bed and the Throne* (New York: Harper & Row Publishers, 1976), 193.

[281] Julia Mary Cartwright Ady, *Isabella D'Este, Marchioness of Mantua, 1474–1539* (London, 1907), 324.

[282] Laura Cereta, *Collected Letters of a Renaissance Feminist*, 26; Diana Robin, 2007.

[283] To Lucilia Vernacula, Vat. 67 (fols.52-53v), Ven. 56 (fols), Tom. 54 (22–25), in "Women and Society," 81, *Laura Cereta Collected Letters of a Renaissance Feminist*, transcribed, translated, and edited by Diana Robin (Chicago and London: University of Chicago).

[284] http://www.tertullian.org/fathers/juvenal_satires_06.htm, "The Ways of Women," trans. G. G. Ramsay.

[285] Isotta Nogarola, *Complete Writings: Letterbook, Dialogue on Adam and Eve, Orations*, ed. and trans. Margaret L. King and Diana Robin (Chicago: University of Chicago Press, 2004); Margaret L. King, "The Religious Retreat of Isotta Nogarola (1418–1466): Sexism and Its Consequences in the Fifteenth Century," *Signs* 3, no. 4 (Summer 1978): 807–822; Angela Nogarola (ca. 1400) and Isotta Nogarola (1418–1466), "Thieves of Language," in *Women Writing*

Latin: From Roman Antiquity to Early Modern Europe, v. 3, *Early Modern Women Writing Latin*, ed. Laurie J. Churchill, Phyllis R. Brown, and Jane E. Jeffrey (New York: Routledge), 11–30.

[286] Margaret L. King, "Book-Lined Cells: Women and Humanism in the Early Italian Renaissance," in *Beyond Their Sex: Learned Women of the European Past* (New York: New York University Press, 1980), 66–90; Diana Robin, "Cassandra Fedele (1465–1558)," in *Italian Women Writers: A Bio-Bibliographical Sourcebook*, ed. Rinaldina Russell (Westport, CT, and London: Greenwood Press, 1994), 119–27.

[287] Gideon Burton, "From Ars dictaminis to Ars conscribendis epistolis: Renaissance Letter-Writing Manuals in the Context of Humanism," in Carol Poster et al., eds., *Letter-Writing Manuals and Instruction from Antiquity to the Present: Historical and Bibliographic Studies* (Columbia, 2007), 88–101.

[288] P. Aretino, *Le Lettere, a cura di P. Procaccioli*, Salerno Editrice (Roma, 1997), 11. Also see Pietro Aretino, *Il Primo Libro delle Lettere a cura di Fausto Nicolini*, Bari (Gius. Laterza & Figli), 1913. Also, Pietro Aretino, *Selected letters [of] Aretino*, vol. 317 (Penguin Classics, 1976); *The Works of Aretino*, translated into English from the original Italian, with a critical and biographical essay by Samuel Putnam, illustrations by the Marquis de Bayros in two volumes (Chicago: Pascal Covici, 1926); vol. 2, 43–81; Edward Hutton, *Pietro Aretino, The Scourge of Princes* (Houghton Mifflin, 1922).

[289] P. Aretino, *Le Lettere, a cura di P. Procaccioli*, 200.

[290] See V. Colonna Visconti, Rime di Vittoria Colonna (Rome, 1840); Luzio, *Vittoria Colonna* (Mantua, 1884); Ferrero and Müller, *Carteggio di Vittoria Colonna, Marchesa di Pescara* (Florence, 1892); Reumont, trans. Müller and Ferrero, Vittoria Colonna, Vita, Fede, e Poesia nel secolo decimosesto (Turin, 1892); Tordi, *Vittoria Colonna in Orvieto* (Perugia, 1895); Jerrold, *Vittoria Colonna: With Some Account of Her Friends and Her Times* (London and New York, 1906).

[291] See Margaret F. Rosenthal, *The Honest Courtesan: Veronica Franco, Citizen and Writer in Sixteenth-century Venice* (University of Chicago Press, 1992).

[292] From Castiglione's idea of the perfect courtier: a natural grace exhibiting a superior detachment, "to avoid affection in every way possible…" See Baldassare Castiglione, *The Book of the Courtier* (London: Penguin, 1976), 66–68.

[293] Letter 99.

[294] Carlo Borromeo, *Regole appartenenti alle monache in Evangelisti, Silvia, Nuns: A History of Convent Life* (Oxford).

[295] "Her introduction to *L'inferno monacale* that Tarabotti dedicates 'Alla Serenissima Republica Veneta' (To the Most Serene Venetian Republic) closes with a proud non-apology, declaring that she will not seek excuses, nor will she try to convince readers of her sincerity, for in any case, there is nothing left to lose for one who has lost her liberty."

[296] www.sjsu.edu/…/Lecture_22%20Laura%20Cere…Cached Similar San Jose State University from Letter XVIII of Laura Cereta in Complete Letters; Laura Cereta, *Collected Letters of a Renaissance Feminist*, ed. and trans. Diana Robin (Chicago: University of Chicago Press, 1997).

[297] Simone de Beauvoir, *The Second Sex* [*Le Deuxieme Sexe*], trans. H. M. Parshley (New York: Knopf, 1953), Vintage Books paperback edition, 1989.

[298] Paul Schollmeier's *Aristotle and Women: Household and Political Roles* argues that while Aristotle claims men and women, by nature, have different psychologies, men superior to women, he does not exclude women participating in political rule, some women capable of holding office—a contention, I would argue, that represents a philosophical *querelle des femmes*.

[299] Rosalind Brown-Grant, *Christine de Pizan and the Moral Defense of Women Reading Beyond Gender* (Cambridge University Press, 1999), for the substance of Pizan's moral outrage, ed. and trans. David F. Hult (2010); *The Other Voice in Early Modern Europe.*

[300] *The Selected Writings of Christine de Pizan* translated by Renate Blumenfeld-Kosinski and Kevin Brownlee, ed. Renate Blumenfeld-Kosinski (Norton & Co., 1997), 119.

[301] "Cellui ou celle en qui plus a vertus est le plus hault, ne la haulteur ou abbaisement des gens ne gist mie es corps selon le sexe mais en la perfeccion des meurs et des vertus." Part 1, ch. 9, 24, Earl Jeffrey Richards, trans., *The Book of the City of Ladies* ([1982] 1983).

[302] Ibid., part 1, ch. 27, 63. "Si la coustume estoit de mettre les petites filles a l'escole, et que communement on les fist apprendre les sciences comme on fait aux filz, qu'elles apprendroient aussi parfaitement et entenderoient les subtilités de toutes les arz et sciences comme ils font."

[303] *The Concept of Woman: The Early Humanist Reformation, 1250–1500*, part 2; Isotta Nogarola, *Complete Writings: Letterbook, Dialogue on Adam and Eve, Orations*, ed. and trans. Margaret L. King and Diana Robin (Chicago: University of Chicago Press, 2004); By Prudence Allen.

[304] Isotta Nogarola, Opera, 1, 42–44 in *The Concept of Woman: The Early Humanist Reformation, 1250–1500*, part 2, Prudence Allen, 197–98.

[305] Margaret Leah King, "Thwarted Ambitions: Six Learned Women of the Italian Renaissance," *Soundings: An Interdisciplinary Journal* 59, no. 3 (Fall 1976): 280–304. The work of Margaret King has provided me with outstanding biographical information.

[306] See Laura Cereta, *Collected Letters of a Renaissance Feminist*, transcribed, translated, and edited by Diana Robin (Chicago and London: University of Chicago).

[307] Vat.77 (fols.65-67); Ven.67 (fols.126v-131v); Tom.65 (187–95); Rabil77. In *Collected Letters*, Robin notes the comical element to the name, suggesting it might be an invention of the author, "Bibulus" meaning drunkard.

[308] Boccaccio cites Queen Semiramis's incest with her son, for example.

[309] Letter, 75.

[310] Fedele died in 1558 at age ninety-three. Margaret L. King, "Book-Lined Cells: Women and Humanism," in *The Early Italian Renaissance*; chapter 4 in *Beyond Their Sex: Learned Women of the European Past*, ed. Patricia H. Labalme, (New York University Press, 1990).

[311] Ibid., 66–68.

[312] From Letter LXXXIV, to Magistro Stefano, member of the Servite Order, in *Letters and Orations*, by Cassandra Fedele, Diana Robin (University of Chicago Press), 118.

[313] Laurie J. Churchill, Phyllis R. Brown, and Jane E. Jeffrey, *Women Writing Latin: Early Modern Women Writing Latin*, 56.

[314] Letizia Panizza, "Reader over Arcangela's Shoulder," in *Arcangela Tarabotti: A Literary Nun in Baroque Venice*, 110, provides references to Tarabotti's writings that reveal her familiarity with these authors' works.

[315] Letter 7.

[316] In Dante's *Paradiso*, "Cantos, XXXI, XXXII, XXXIII" in the Tenth Heaven, Dante sees inside Rose Mary, Rachel, Sarah, Rebecca, Judith, and Ruth. The angels kneel before Mary; Dante looks up to the Virgin Mother.

[317] *Inferno*, 34.

[318] Ibid., 25.

[319] In *Semplicità*, Tarabotti pays homage to the *sesso feminile* (the female sex), mentioning not only the work of Marinella, but also of other women: "In contraposto una del divin sesso feminile, cioè Lucretia Marinelli, splendore della poësia, anima [pagina 165] delle scene caste e modeste, e norma vera di virtù grande, frà gli infiniti parti del suo insegno, hà dato alla luce la vita della Serenissima Principessa dell' universo, descritta con si alto stile, e con si elegante soave, e dotta facondia, che genera sentimenti di stupore ne più eminenti intelletti. Non mancano donne, c'hanno fatte gloriose le stampe con ogni sorte di perfette compositioni. Maddalena Salveti, Margherita Sarocchi, Isabella Andreini, Laura Teracina, Veronica Gambara, Vittoria Colonna, & altre infinite co' loro virtuosissimi scritti publicati han fatto conoscere al mondo tutto, di quai luminosi raggi di divinità risplenda coronata la mente feminile." Also, Zanette suggests Suor Arcangela "non ignorava l'opera della sue anticipatrici." The works of her predecessors were not unknown to her (212); Laura Benedetti, in her article "Arcangela Tarabotti e Lucrezia Marinella: appunti per un dialogo mancato," claims that surely the two knew each other and were familiar with each other's works, noting that Tarabotti refers to Marinella in her *Semplicita' ingannata* as an example of artistic and moral excellence. Marinella wrote one of the two encomiastic poems introducing *Paradiso monacale*; we might assume, at the least, Marinella was familiar with Tarabotti's work: Laura Benedetti, "Arcangela Tarabotti e Lucrezia Marinella: appunti per un dialogo mancato," *MLN* 129, no. 3 (2014): S87–S97. Project MUSE, doi:10.1353/mln.2014.0063.

[320] Biographical information from Doglioni: see note 314.

321 http://www.classicistranieri.com/liberliber/Moderata%20Fonte/il_mer_p.pdf/ complete text in Italian. *Il merito delle donne* was first published in Venice in 1600, eight years after the author's death in childbirth at age thirty-seven. No original manuscript exists. In the introduction by Nicolo Doglioni, her uncle and one-time guardian, we find a short biography of Moderata: *Il merito delle donne*, Autore: Moderata Fonte, curatore: Adriana Chemello. I defer to the lucid translation of Virginia Cox for the English version. *The Worth of Women*, ed. and trans. Virginia Cox (University of Chicago, 1997).

322 Cox, "First Day," *The Worth of Women*, 44–45.

323 Ibid., 259.

324 Moderata Fonte, *Il merito delle donne*, curatore: Adriana Chemello.

325 Cox, 62–3.

326 Zanette notes that Corinna speaks for the author, 212–213.

327 Cox, 237.

328 *The Nobility and Excellence of Women, and the Defects and Vices of Men*, ed. and trans. Anne Dunhill (University of Chicago Press, 1999).

329 In *Lettere*, Tarabotti mentions her mother only once, with a degree of tenderness. Her father is not mentioned specifically except for the reference to her limp that she inherited from him.

330 *Semplicità*, 19 "Con pretesti in apparenza santi; ma in realtà maluagi, chiudono con inganno forzatamente frà quattro mura d' un Monastero le semplici donne, facendole in perpetuo habitatrici d' una prigione, benché ree non d' altra colpa, che d' esser nate di sesso più delicato, e per questo anche più meritevoli d' esser compatite, servite, e sollevate, e non d' esser racchiuse in una carcere eterna."

331 *Semplicità*, 18–19.

332 http://www.e-text.it/ "Alla Serenissima Republica Veneta"; Arcangela Tarabotti, *L'inferno monacale*, curator: Francesca Medioli, 3: "Sul'ali della fama vola ad ogn'angolo più rimoto dell'universo che palesa come Voi, Serenissima Regina, concedete a qual si sia natione della vostra bella metropoli libertà non circonscritta, di modo che ne godono tutt'i crocifissori dell' Figliolo della vostra Santissima Protettrice."

333 "The dedication was preserved in the extant manuscript of *L'inferno monacale*": "Proporcionata è la mia dedicatione al vostro gran Senato, che, con incarcerar le figliole vergini, acciò si maccerino, salmeggino et orino in cambio loro, spera d'etternar voi, Vergine belissima, Regina dell'Adria."

334 *Paradiso monacale*, 1643; *Antisatira*, 1644; *Le lagrime di arcangela tarabotti*, 1650; *Lettere familiari e di complimento*, 1650; *Che le donne siano della spezie degli uomini*, 1651.

335 Zanette, 90. Footnotes refer to *L'inferno monacale*, 37–38, 41–43, and *Semplicita' inganatta*, 188. Also Francesca Medioli confirms it is her first written work in *L'inferno monacale di Arcangela Tarabotti*, ed. F. Medioli (Turin, 1990), 152–159. Tarabotti calls it her first work (see A. Tarabotti, *L'inferno monacale*, ed. F.

Medioli [Turin: 1990] 27). Published in Holland (1654), put on the Index of Forbidden Books in 1661 (Leiden: G. Sambix, 1654).

336 Tarabotti, *Paradiso monacale*, Libro Terzo, 156–7. Digital copy of 1,643 manuscript-reproduced Google Books.

337 Ibid., 41; "Libro Primo," *Paradiso monacale*, Arcangela Tarabotti, https://books.google.com/books?id=2jZAAAAcAAJ&pg=PR2&source=gbs_selected_pages&cad=2#v=onepage&q&f=false.

338 Quoted from *Semplicita' ingannata* in Zanette, 191.

339 Tarabotti, *Paradiso monacale*, 1.

340 Meredith K. Ray, *Writing Gender in Women's Letter Collection of the Italian Renaissance* (University of Toronto Press, 2009), 201.

341 The Sienese Buoninsegni was a member of Incogniti and friend of Loredan. He had originally read the treatise to an academic audience—men and women—in Siena in 1632.

342 Francesco Buoninsegni, *Suor Arcangela Tarabotti, Satira e antisatira*, curator: Weaver, Elissa, 17: "Altro non sono che illustre testimonianza della vostra schiavitudine e meritata pena dell'antico peccato. La colpa che spoglio i nostri primi parenti della veste dell'innocenza apri loro ancora gli occhi alla nudita delle membra… Quindi la vergogna della propria nudita e l'inclemenza del cielo indussero la necessita del vestire.Oggi il fasto femminile ha cangiata la necessita in superbia e la donna, gloriandosi nell'insegne del suo servaggio doppiamente colpevole, ha convertito in trionfo del suo lusso il gastigo del suo delitto."

343 *Satira e antisatira*, 16: "Ma e' vanita il credere di dissuadere alle donne la vanita del vestire, se prima non le spogliamo dell'ignoranza."

344 *Satira e antisatira*, 31–2.

345 Pompeo Molmenti, *Venice: The Decadence*, 207.

346 *Satira e antisatira*, 45: "La veste, dunque, nella donna e un argomento e una testimonianza della modestia sua e dell'odio con ch'ella deve e vuole aborrire la colpa e non del peccato di cui ella e innocentissima."

347 This work was published in 1650, two years before Arcangela's death.

348 Tarabotti's letter recipients, with few exceptions, are patricians and members of the upper classes.

349 Letter 113.

350 See Medioli for self-editing and Zanette, 376. Also, letters 157 and 231.

351 Letter 13 includes reference to Tarabotti's works; she shows motherly tenderness toward her first two *partori* (births).

352 Ray and Westwater, "The Tears of Arcangela Tarabotti," in *Letters familiar and formal* (Toronto: Iter Inc., 2012), 287–296.

353 Ibid.

354 Ibid.

355 Letter 112.

[356] Zanette suggests the recipient of this letter is Bertucci Valier. Zanette also believes that the letter volume, without the encomium, would have never been published (377).

[357] Letter 148.

[358] Ibid.

[359] Tarabotti responds to the Italian translation of the misogynist tract in Latin attributed to "Orazio Plata," published in 1647, "Che le donne non siano della spezie degli uomini," sardonically asserting "women are not members of the human species" (89); Theresa M. Kenney, *Women Are Not Human* (New York: Crossroad Publishing Company, 1998).

[360] Tarabotti also argues in Book 1 of *Tirannia paterna* that woman made man perfect and complete, citing Genesis 1:31, interpreting the words such as "man should not be alone."

[361] *Antisatira*; Zanette, 132.

[362] Letter 32

[363] Zanette believes the sisters addressed in these letters were Lucia and Angela, 19–21.

[364] Letter 106

[365] Letter 188; "Una lettera di Vostre Signorie, venuta a consolarmi quando meno l'aspettava, m'obliga alla Vostra cortesia." Genesis 4: Cain killed his brother Abel, Cain, firstborn, committing the first murder. Envy and anger are the assumed motives for the older brother's murder of his sibling.

[366] Letter 145, "La dimanda e' giustissima e propria, perch'egli e' maritato, con figliuoli, e non ha alcun suo congionto, ne' della moglie, al quale potesse raccomandar la sua casa."

[367] Letters to other females include those addressed to Betta Polani, Alba Porti, Anna di Gremonville, Countess S., Madame d'Amo, Elena Foscola, the Marchioness of Galeranda, Countess Giulia Bissari, and Marguerite de Giubet—aristocratic and/or well positioned women.

[368]

[369] Letter 22

[370] For more information about convents and lacework, see *Early Modern Women and Transnational Communities of Letters*, ed. Julie D. Campbell and Anne R. Larsen.

[371] Letter 12

[372] Jackson, Emily, 1861–. *A History of Hand-made Lace: Dealing With the Origin of Lace, the Growth of the Great Lace Centres, the Mode of Manufacture, the Methods of Distinguishing And the Care of Various Kinds of Lace.* London: L. Upcott Gill, 1900. pp. 153–157.

[373] Letter 46, Madame d'Amo (Madame des Hameaux), the wife of Ambassador Jean des Hameaux, in Venice from 1642 to 1645, note 69, note 380, in *Lettere*; Tarabotti Italianizes the name.

[374] For further information about the chronology of Tarabotti's published letters, see Francesca Medioli, "Self-Representation in Tarabotti," *Italianist* 23 (2003): 71.

[375] Nicolas Bretel de Gremonville (1608–48) was the French ambassador to Venice from July 1645 to October 1647; a Illustrissimo ed Eccellentissimo Signor Nicolo Bretel, Signor di Gremonvile e Ambasciatore di Francia Appresso la Serenissma Republica di Venezia N.70 in *Lettere*.

[376] Zanette, 263.

[377] Letter 243.

[378] Zanette, 309.

[379] Lettere, letter 35, 93. "Di proprio pugno, alle cinque ore in tempo, che'L Suo cuore gioviva per la traboccante allegrezza della nascita d'un bambino, sono accidenti che trapassano la mia intelligenza," Tarabotti thanks him for writing to her in his own hand at five in the morning when his heart was "thrilled with joy" at the birth of his son.

[380] Ibid. "Ho inquirito conforme al Suo commando da mamosella de Ravano come le piace la compagnia d'un fratello, e la trovo tanto gelosa dell'amore di Vostra Eccellenza, che s'ella fosse maschio dubitarei d'un successo simile a quello de' primi Fratelli che nacquero al mondo."

[381] Ibid. "Ella piange e s'affligge dell'allegrezza de' genitori, ma con prudenza tale che fa istupidire chiunque la pratica. La compatisca Ella, e prossegua in amarla…"

[382] The author of this sonnet is not known.

[383] This reference is to Hercules in Rome and the Western world.

[384] Letter 39, "Con quell'amore come se fossero nate dalle mie viscere e le servo con quell respeto e diligenza che s'acconviene alla loro nascita."

[385] Letter 129, "Mamosella di Ravan, avendo sotto questo clima nutrito in se stessa un poco, no so se debbo dire di gelosie o pure d'invidia, seminata nel suo cuore da un timor grande di cadere dalla grazia di Lei, pare che incominci ad odiare il fratello, benche incerto, el ventre di Vostra Eccellenza, alla quale unitamente s'inchiniamo."

[386] Letter 58.

[387] Laven, 49.

[388] For information about Venetian marriages, see Marin Sanudo, Patricia H. Labalme, Laura Sanguineti White, and Linda Carrol, "How to (and How Not to) Get Married in Sixteenth-Century Venice (Selections from the Diaries of Marin Sanudo)," *Renaissance Quarterly* 52, no. 1 (Spring 1999): 43–72. University of Chicago Press on behalf of the Renaissance Society of America, stable URL: http://www.jstor.org/stable/2902016/. Accessed: 06-11-2016 22:26 UTC.

[389] Francesco Sansovino, *Venetia citta' nobilissima, Venice, 1663* (Gregg International Publishers Limited, 1581), "Matrimonii"; also in Laven, 231, note 23.

[390] *Inferno*, 11: "Le sete ed i colori per contessere le vesti sono chiamati dalla Siria e da Melibeo, il veluto, la felpa che non e 'd'opera piu che humana e' stimato in degno di coprir quelle membra che pur sono uscite da quel medemo ventre di dove naque l'altra sfortunata…"

[391] Letters 26, 73; also mentioned in Giovanni Dandolo's introductory letter in *Lettere familiari*. The three books would have comprised a trilogy in the spirit of Dante to include *L'inferno monacale*, *Paradiso monacale*, and *Purgatorio*; the latter, if written, has since been lost.

[392] Letter 37, Giovanni Dandolo (1613–1661), a Venetian patrician, Incogniti member, with whom Tarabotti communicated often as a close friend.

[393] ASV, Avogadori di Comun, Indice di matrimoni patrizi per nome di donna, 86, ter. 1 [reg. V., 87] in *Lettere familiari*, 94, note 127.

[394] Alexander Cowan, *Marriage, Manners and Mobility in Early Modern Venice*, 1, 2; Ashgate e-book, 207; "prove di nobiità" was essential to secure male off-spring's legal right to sit on the Great Council.

[395] Letter 45.

[396] *Tirannia paterna*.

[397] Letter 45: "Mi favorisca di rimandarmele, perche, essendo quell'oppera mia figlia e vergine, non vorrei che, stando nelle Sue mani, la incontrasse di quelle disrazie c'hanno incontrato altre." Here Tarabotti compares the fate of her work, *Tirannia paterna* (*Semplicita' ingannata*) to the plight of other virgin daughters.

[398] Letter 68: "Coll'informare A. dell'eta', della professione, e delle pretendenze dello sposo. L'ho trovata dispostissima a pigliarlo, quand'egli non sormonti tant'alto e che si conteni di una dotte agiustata al suo stato. Mille ducati al presente sono difficili da trovarsi; ella ha molte sorelle, le fortune scarse, i tempi stretti, e le carestie grandi."

[399] Letter 212.

[400] Letter 123: "La novizza assolutamente non vuole il N. perche' (lasciando le burle) sua madre tiene informazione ch'egli abbia pochissima robba, ed ella dice che quarant'anni sono troppi per una giovanetta."

[401] In order for the nun to have her manuscripts circulate, she needed copyists, samizdat, who clandestinely copied her tomes.

[402] Letter 215.

[403] "Happy is the husband of a good wife," Vulgate (Latin): Sirach (Book of Ecclesiasticus), chapter 26.

[404] Letter 215: "Donna forte tanto ricercata da Salomone. Sara' attiva nel governo della casa e contemplativa nello speculare i desideri del consorte per incontrali sempre."

[405] Letter 90.

[406] During the fourth session of the Council of Trent, in 1546, the Council insisted on the censorship of books, proscribed by the Lateran Council, especially concerning religious content, *de rebus sacris*. See "On the Index of Books," chapter 21, 279; *The Council of Trent, the Twenty-Fifth Session: The Canons and Decrees*

of the Sacred and Oecumenical Council of Trent, ed. and trans. J. Waterworth (London: Dolman, 1848), 232–89. Hanover Historical Texts Project.

407 Letter 247.

408 Letter 247: "Un minimo cenno che di cio' mi fosse arrivato all orecchio m'avrebbe…fatto salire in Cieo per provederLa di sedie proprozionate al Suo merito."

409 Betta Polani, Tarabotti's *consorella*, was called out of the convent by her uncle who had arranged for Betta to marry.

410 Letter 8. In this letter, Tarabotti also sends thanks to Loredan who wrote an introduction letter to *Paradiso monacale*.

411 Letter 8.

412 Zanette, 289: "Ma la sua causa occasionale permanente era il parlatorio: era questo che le offriva la piu' ovvia e grequente possibilita' di raggiungere la propria soddisfazione cioe' quella di farsi vedere e di piacere."

413 Zanette, 300, note 3.

414 Letter 40.

415 Ferrante Pallavicino (March 23, 1615–March 5, 1644) wrote scandalous satires very much in demand. Born into a scion of Italian families, early on, he became an Augustinian monk housed in Venice. His writing included severe criticism of Italian rulers, including the pope. Imprisoned, and eventually freed, he continued his irreverent work, anti-Jesuit and heretical, *La Retorica delle puttane* (The Rhetoric of the Prostitutes).

416 Monica Miato, *Gli Incogniti*, 115, notes 316, 317.

417 Monica Miato, L'Accademia degli Incogniti, Accademia Toscana di Scienze e Lettere, "La Colombaria," 114.

418 This letter probably was from 1643, since it refers to the first printed text, *Paradiso monacale*, before it went to press.

419 Letter 87: "A guiso di scimia immitar I literati senza saper quello che mi dica."

420 Zanette, 303.

421 Letter 10.

422 Letter 250.

423 Pope from August 9, 1644, to January 7, 1655.

424 Zanette, 305. Upon their departure from Venice, the Republic presented the madam with a gold necklace worth one thousand scudi and one of silver worth another thousand in recognition of their merit, circa May 6, 1645.

425 Letter 121, note 385.

427 Letter 253. With this letter, Tarabotti sends her "Soliloquio a Dio" (to Regina Donà) and *Tirannia paterna* to Signor Paolo Donado. She also thanks him for a book he lent her.

428 Letter 120.

429 Letter 94.

430 Francesca Medioli, "Arcangela Tarabotti's Reliability about Herself: Publication and Self-Representation," *Italianist*, 80–81.

[431] Letter 17.

[432] Medioli, in "Arcangela Tarabotti's Reliability," *Italianist* 23 (2003): 1, has dated this letter April 8, 1645. Medioli found a copy of it in the Archivio di Stato di Firenze. Medioli has also found there another two letters to the grand duchess, not published in *Lettere* (73, 88–89).

[433] Medioli, in "Reliability," cites letters retrieved from the Archivi Statali di Firenze written to Tarabotti from the duchess suggesting that the noble lady's interest in Arcangela had to do with the prayers she offered (82–83).

[434] For further information, Adriana Chemello, ed., *Alla lettera: Teorie e pratiche epistolari dai Greci al Novecento* (Milan: Guerini Studio, 1998), and Maria Luisa Dogio, *L'arte delle lettere: Idea e pratica della scrittura epistolare tra Quattro e Seicento* (Bologna, Italy: Mulino, 2000). Also see Cherewatuk and Wiethaus, *Dear Sister* (University of Pennsylvania Press, 1993) for medieval women letter writers.

[435] For more information about Aristotle's theory of virtue, see Nancy Sherman, *Fabric of Character: Aristotle's Theory of Virtue* (Oxford: Clarendon Press, 1989); for more information about Nietzsche's theory, see D. I. Harris, "Nietzsche and Virtue," *Journal of Value Inquiry* 49, no. 3 (2015), 325–328, and Christine Swanton, *New Directions in Ethics: The Virtue Ethics of Hume and Nietzsche* (Somerset: Wiley, 2015).

[436] Letter 1; Francesco Erizzo was the doge of Venice from 1631 to 1646; this letter was written in 1643.

[437] Ibid.

[438] Note here the "Black ink" connotes inferiority and perhaps alludes to Tarabotti's black attire and situation.

[439] Letter 61.

[440] Ibid.

[441] Letter 31.

[442] For more information about "face wants," see, for example, Penelope Brown and Stephen C. Levinson, *Politeness: Some Universals in Language Usage* (Cambridge University Press, 1978).

[443] Letter 31.

[444] Ibid.

[445] Ibid.

[446] Letter 33.

[447] Letter 33.

[448] ASV Archivio di Stato di Venezia, sezione notarile, testamenti, 83.35 in *Letters*, Ray and Westwater, note 136; Enrico Cornaro editors suggest that the recipient is probably Enrico Cornaro, son of Paolo (c. 1600–1663), a Venetian lawyer; ASV, sezione notarile, testamenti, 83.35. Cornaro is the recipient of several letters, each one in a friendly, respectful tone to a firm supporter and patron of the nun.

[449] Letter 112: "Tears…" is a short encomiastic work that Arcangela wrote for her friend and one-time *consorella*, Regina Donà (Donati), who died on March 31, 1645.

[450] We can surmise that in the years between Arcangela's investiture and first attempts at circulating her manuscripts, the nun dedicated time to reading and writing—but these in-between years, before circa 1639, do not offer detailed documentation.

[451] Tarabotti made the acquaintance of the marchesa through her contacts with the French ambassador and the French diplomatic community residing in Venice.

[452] The marchioness and the French ambassadorial entourage left Venice sometime between 1647 and 1648. Zanette, 424.

[453] *Inferno*, 104.

[454] *Inferno*, 12.

[455] Letter 232.

[456] Letter 149: "Finalmente doppo aver scritto un'infinita' di lettere a Vostra Eccellenza, mi capitano poche righe di Lei, nelle quali sento ad dimandarmi se sono viva o morta. Grazie a Dio sono vivissima e in stato d'oppormi a chi volesse ingannarmi, anzi di far che rimanga ingannato l'ingannatore."

[457] Ibid.

[458] Ibid.

[459] Ibid.

[460] Ray and Westwater confirm at least ten letters in the collection, although addressed to anonymous "N," Latin for nobody, can easily be traced to Aprosio as is made obvious with details that could only attribute the recipient of the missives to Aprosio. Aprosio was an Augustinian eremitic friar who entered the monastery at fifteen years old. He is also called Father Ventimiglia in reference to where he was born. He was an itinerant monk traveling through Italy and in Venice and, through the Accademia degli Incogniti, came to know Tarabotti whom he praised and encouraged for her *Convent Paradise*. He turned against her after she published *Antisatira* and composed *La Maschera Scoperta* for a publication Tarabotti blocked from print, a document that claimed she was not the author of her works

[461] Letter 194.

[462] Letter 194.

[463] Letter 36; Zanette, p. 267, clarifies that PN refers to Padre Tommaso Stigliani and the many publications of Aprosio against him.

[464] Letter 36.

[465] Zanette, 279. The biographer accuses Brusoni of sabotaging Arcangela whom he had supported and encouraged her quest to publish.

[466] Brusoni, 1660, Sogni di Parnaso in *Letters*, Ray and Westwater, 108, note 169.

[467] Letter 53.

[468] Ibid. Arcangela often referred to herself as Angelica.

[469] Letter 141.

[470] Letter 231.

[471] Ibid.

[472] Ray and Westwater, *Lettere*, 278, note 6 informs us that Tarabotti was afraid that Brusoni's work would suggest that she was not the author of *Tirannia*, not yet published at this time.

[473] Emilia Biga, "The Mask Uncovered," *Una Polemica Antifemminista Del '600: La Maschera Scoperta Di Angelico Aprosio* (Ventimiglia: Civica Biblioteca Aprosiana, 1989).

[474] Letter 113: "Signor congnato, la Sua prudenza comprende ben meglio di me che non v'e' cosa che passando per tante bocche possi rimaner occulta…"

[475] Ibid.

[476] Ibid.: "Poiche' pazzo sarebbe chi si fondasse nelle lodi degli uomini che, s'ora essaltano, di la' a momenti biasmano e mal trattano."

[477] Ibid.

[478] Ibid.

[479] Letter 9.

[480] Letter 220.

[481] Letter 18. This censure relates to the publication of *Lettere*.

[482] Zanette, 1, my translation.

[483] Pray to Christ: beseeching Christ from the bottom of his heart; literally from the bowels of Jesus; from the letters of Saint Paul; the epistle of Saint Paul to the Philippians, chapter 1.

[484] *Che le donne siano della spezie degli uomini* in 1651.

[485] Zanette, 1.

[486] Letter 125.

[487] Letter 17, 71, note 65; Ray and Westwater, *Letters*: The duke was Odoardo Farnese (1612–56).

[488] Ray and Westwater suggest this book was about the life of Saint Elena, the namesake of Suor Arcangela, 270, note 704.

[489] Letter 239.

[490] Letter 69.

[491] Letter 92.

[492] Letter 127.

[493] Letter 116. Ray and Westwater note that the error Tarabotti made was to confuse two Roman emperors, 178, note 407.

[494] Zanette, 449.

[495] Ibid.

[496] Letter 97.

[497] The fifteenth verse of the seventh chapter of the gospel of Matthew in the New Testament warns about false prophets and is part of the Sermon on the Mount: "Beware of false prophets, which come to you in sheep's clothing, but inwardly they are ravening wolves."

[498] Letter 21. Ray and Westwater suggest that the manuscript most likely is *Che le donne*; Ray and Westwater, *Letters*, 78, note 82. The editors also suggest that the recipient could be Loredan, Aprosio, or Pighetti.

[499] Ibid.

[500] Ibid.

[501] Letter 32.

[502] Ibid.

[503] Letter 240.

[504] Ibid.

[505] Medioli, "Self-Representation," 162.

[506] Zanette, 90.

[507] Stephen R. Ell, "Three Days in October of 1630: Detailed Examination of Mortality during an Early Modern Plague Epidemic in Venice," in *Reviews of Infectious Diseases* 11, no. 1 (Jan.–Feb. 1989): 128–139. Published by Oxford University Press, 128; Zanette records the number of deaths at 46,000 (447); Chambers and Pullan estimate one-third of the population (113).

[508] Ell, 133.

[509] Joanne M. Ferraro, *Venice: History of the Floating City*, 145.

[510] Zanette, 447.

About the Author

 arsha Fazio is Senior Lecturer of Renaissance Literature and Linguistics at Arizona State University.